Phonics FOR DUMMIES®

by Susan M. Greve

BICENTENNIAL
1807
WILEY
2007
BICENTENNIAL

Wiley Publishing, Inc.

Phonics For Dummies®

Published by
Wiley Publishing, Inc.
111 River St.
Hoboken, NJ 07030-5774
www.wiley.com

Phonics

FOR

DUMMIES®

About the Author

Susan M. Greve has been a reading specialist for 23 years. She taught first and second grade for four years and has been a publisher, editor, and a reading and curriculum consultant for schools and home-schooling parents.

Susan's methods of teaching phonics are based on those of Sister Monica Foltzer, OSU (Order of Saint Ursula), who was a nationally known pioneer in the field of phonics. Prior to her death in 2001, Sister Monica was a teacher, guidance counselor, principal, and a reading and curriculum consultant. Susan was a student of Sister Monica's at the Institute in Intensive Phonics at Xavier University in Cincinnati, Ohio.

In 1997, Susan acquired Sister Monica's Professor Phonics Systems and has published and edited the Professor Phonics series ever since. Her day job includes her book business and tutoring. Susan developed a reading assessment test that has been very successful in analyzing reading problems and helping numerous children and adults. Susan hosts a website, www.professorphonics.com, and has done phonics workshops across the country. She was the project manager of the *Professor Phonics with Me and My Mouse* CD-ROM.

Susan attended Mercy School of Nursing, which at the time was affiliated with Miami University in Oxford, Ohio. She considers her nursing experience a great aid in helping her assess children with learning weaknesses.

Susan lives in Cincinnati, Ohio, with her husband. She teaches her grandchildren to read and enjoys spending time traveling, sewing, reading, and gardening.

Dedication

This book is dedicated to Sister Monica Foltzer, OSU.

Author's Acknowledgments

I am indebted to the following people for their assistance, encouragement, opinions, guidance, advice, and input throughout this project: Joanne and Eric Engel, Kathie Condit, Kathi Davis, Patrick Greve, Babina Bajracharya, Angie and Chas Eddingfield, Kendal Krouse, Kristine Bedel, Maribeth Lind, Jessica Faust, Assistant Professor D'Arcy Smith at Wright State University, Jerome Doerger, and Jenna Rockey.

Many thanks to the staff at Bridgetown Frisch's for not charging booth rental during those marathon proofing sessions.

Publisher's Acknowledgments

We're proud of this book; please send us your comments through our Dummies online registration form located at www.dummies.com/register/.

Some of the people who helped bring this book to market include the following:

Acquisitions, Editorial, and Media Development

Project Editor: Natalie Faye Harris

Acquisitions Editor: Michael Lewis

Copy Editor: Sarah Faulkner

Technical Editor: Alicia Sparks

Media Development Specialist: Laura Moss-Hollister

Editorial Manager: Christine Meloy Beck

CD Production: Recorded at Wright State University in co-operation with 2:27 AM Inc., Produced and Directed By: D'Arcy Smith, Sound Engineer: Matt Rosenfeld, Voice Over Talent: Jerome Doerger

Media Development Manager: Laura Carpenter

Editorial Assistants: Erin Calligan Mooney, Joe Niesen, Leeann Harney, David Lutton

Cover Photos: © Datacraft/Getty Images

Cartoons: Rich Tennant (www.the5thwave.com)

Composition Services

Project Coordinator: Heather Kolter

Layout and Graphics: Claudia Bell, Brooke Graczyk, Denny Hager, Joyce Haughey, Stephanie D. Jumper, Barbara Moore, Heather Ryan, Christine Williams

Anniversary Logo Design: Richard Pacifico

Proofreaders: Aptara, Susan Moritz, Jessica Kramer

Indexer: Aptara

Special Help: Victoria M. Adang, Stephen R. Clark, Traci Cumbay, Peter Weverka

---

Publishing and Editorial for Consumer Dummies

Diane Graves Steele, Vice President and Publisher, Consumer Dummies

Joyce Pepple, Acquisitions Director, Consumer Dummies

Kristin A. Cocks, Product Development Director, Consumer Dummies

Michael Spring, Vice President and Publisher, Travel

Kelly Regan, Editorial Director, Travel

Publishing for Technology Dummies

Andy Cummings, Vice President and Publisher, Dummies Technology/General User

Composition Services

Gerry Fahey, Vice President of Production Services

Debbie Stailey, Director of Composition Services

Activities at a Glance

Contents at a Glance

Table of Contents

Introduction

· ·

*W*hen the subject of phonics comes up at a PTA luncheon or a family gathering, I see many parents scratching their heads. My reputation as a phonics tutor ultimately brings them to approach me with comments like these:

> ✔ "I can read okay, but my spelling is atrocious. Is this because of the way I learned in grade school?"
>
> ✔ "I never learned from the phonics approach. Maybe that's why I hate to read so much."
>
> ✔ "I was always labeled as one of the slow kids because I had so much trouble reading. Do you think it was because we didn't have phonics training?"

Every one of these parents shares the same fear and desire. They want to protect their children from the kind of problems they had to endure. And I give every one of them the same answer: All the children I've helped could master any subject after they caught on to reading.

Most phonics books are written for teachers. This book is for anyone. If you want to know what phonics is, how to use it, and how important it is in learning to speak, read, write, and spell, you'll benefit from this book.

After you understand the value of phonics, you realize how far your — or your child's — reading skills can advance. I destroy the myth that phonics works only for some people and assert that phonics helps 100 percent of the time. And reading well is the first step to unlocking all the opportunities available to everyone. Many people think phonics is much more complicated than it actually is. To put it simply, phonics is merely about sliding sounds of letters together to make words. It's a science of application and is under the umbrella of linguistics. Its popularity has grown due to the fact that educators now acknowledge that learning phonics is of the utmost necessity in teaching children to read, write, spell, and speak.

The word *phonics* has become a household word (mostly due to a little voice on the radio that says "Hooked on Phonics works for me!"). The phonics revolution that began in the last ten years has made many products available, such as LeapFrog educational games, Reader Rabbit, and Hooked on Phonics, to name a few. Besides the games, companies develop plenty of TV programs, CDs, videos, and DVDs for phonics. Even though technology has definitely narrowed the gap between home and school, the requirements for a good reader haven't changed. A good reader is able to recognize words instantly, has superb word attack skills, comprehends what she's reading, and applies her skills on a daily basis. The use of a good phonics program helps to develop each of these skills to the highest degree.

Phonics For Dummies has attitude: I want to give to you my positive and confident attitude that you're up to the task of teaching your child to read through phonics. I show you that phonics is an essential tool that you can use to help your child speak, read, write, and spell. And the best part is that you don't need a master's degree to learn phonics or to teach it to someone else.

About This Book

Phonics For Dummies helps you discover that you're competent to learn or teach phonics. And better yet, you're able to teach or learn reading, spelling, writing, and language to the best of your ability. On first examination, this book may seem complicated, but never fear: It's a precise and thorough strategy for becoming an expert in applying phonics to the language arts.

I focus on certain techniques that are the building blocks to a better understanding of the English language. These techniques help you or your child conquer the difficulties in reading or writing. Say goodbye to

- Being a slave to a wild guessing game
- Reading with a lack of expression
- Poor word attack skills
- Slow-paced reading
- Weak comprehension
- Skipping words you can't read
- Relying on the context to "read" unknown words
- Guessing at words by using pictures

With the help of this book, you can

- Improve reading and spelling skills by going back to square one
- Learn about pronunciation and accent
- Increase your fluency in decoding multisyllable words
- Discover related subject matter and valuable resources
- Polish your skills with practice and application exercises

Whether you're a parent, teacher, or curious adult, you can get as much or as little out of this book as you want. You can start from the beginning and use the step-by-step approach, or refer to the Table of Contents or Index to focus on your own areas of interest. Or just use *Phonics For Dummies* as a handy reference guide. Each chapter of the book is like a plug-in unit — you don't have to rely on other chapters to understand it.

Conventions Used in This Book

This book defines phonics, which makes it necessary to use some jargon. Four-year-olds can dig the lingo, so I know that you can, too. It's stuff like, "Breve means short," "Macron's long," "Define a consonant," and, "Where does the accent belong?" As you read through this book, you use words like *diphthong* and *umlaut* as regularly as a linguistic professor. I believe that vocabulary grows in people who use it wisely from birth on. The same goes for using symbols, known as diacritical marks, when learning to read. You and your child can find great delight when looking up a word in the dictionary and exclaiming, "See the schwa! No accent on that syllable!" In the long run, this know-how puts kids ahead and helps in future dictionary work.

The other conventions that look bizarre are sentences or headings that start with lowercase letters. Some examples are: *ing, er, ed, sh, nk, i, wh, u,* and so on. These odd letter combinations are italicized so that you can spot them easily. Because they're the heart of the book, you see them everywhere.

Because this book may be used by a parent or teacher with a student or by someone improving his or her own reading skills, I use *he, she, you, child, learner, parent,* and *instructor* to cover all the possibilities. The chapters contain a mix of all these terms, wherever and whenever each noun or pronoun fits. I also arrange a dedicated space for exercises to reinforce the lessons.

What You're Not to Read

If you're short on time and just want to get down to the nitty-gritty of phonics, you can skip the stuff in the gray boxes, also known as *sidebars.* I include this sidebar information for those of you who want to know the *whys* of everything or who just want to dig deeper into the details of phonics.

Foolish Assumptions

While organizing this book I made some assumptions about you:

- ✔ You're interested in teaching someone to read.
- ✔ You have a curiosity about phonics and want a self-help book.
- ✔ You know that look/say reading doesn't work for everyone.
- ✔ You need help in choosing phonics-associated reading materials.
- ✔ You want a ready reference book on phonics.

If you identify with my foolish assumptions, you're ready to go! Take a little more time to read the following sections to get a real feel for how this book works.

How This Book Is Organized

Even though each lesson builds one on the other, you can still pick and choose the chapters that you want to examine. The following is a rundown of each part in *Phonics For Dummies*.

Part I: Getting Ready to Read with Phonics

I start with practical advice about teaching your child to read. You go over the first steps of learning and find out how easy and inexpensive it really is to teach someone. I show you instructional theory that's straightforward and understandable. In this Part, I explain phonics in general, the method I follow in this book, and simple formulas for success. This part offers information and quick tips that are kid and parent friendly.

Part II: Exploring the Fundamentals of Phonics

In this Part, you learn to read, spell, and write quite well. Before embarking on two-syllable words, you jump headfirst into blending consonants and vowels. You become familiar with the many faces of vowels; students of phonics may refer to this part often, because it wraps up the 16 basic vowel sounds.

Part III: Moving Beyond the Phonics Basics

Why do the British say *li' bree* for *li' brer' ee* or *gehr' uj* for *guh rozh*? Why do Aussies say, *guh dye'* and Americans say *good day*? This is the place where you learn about accents and getting to the root of words. You also explore unusual spellings and get to meet the softer side of *c* and *g*.

Part IV: Tackling the Trickier Side of Phonics

Did you know that most dictionaries use eight sounds of *a* and almost as many for the other vowels? What about those words like *cough, thought, sure,* and *chiffon*? This is the place where you find the quirks of phonics. The classification of these peculiarities is the crème de la crème of this part.

Part V: The Part of Tens

Most people love to hear the top ten songs of the year, the top ten recording artists, movies, golf pros, and so on. (Did this fixation start with the Ten Commandments?) This part gives you quick hits of information that enhance your phonics practice — grouped in tens, of course. It also contains appendixes with useful information, including what's on the CD.

Icons Used in This Book

For Dummies signature icons are those little round pictures you see in the margins of the book. I use them to laser your attention to key bits of information. Here's a list of the icons you find in this book and what they mean.

I highlight shortcuts and helpful hints for applying guidelines of phonics with this icon.

Some information bears repeating. I mark points that are worth going over again and again with this icon.

Certain practices may set your practice back instead of moving it forward. I use this icon to keep you on sure footing by alerting you to treacherous ground.

Sometimes, I go into more detail than you need, and I let you know with this icon that these passages are safe to skip. By all means read these sections if you're interested, but know that you can safely pass these paragraphs over and still become a phonics champ.

You find sample tests, stories, and other activities to assess what you learned in a chapter at paragraphs marked with this icon.

This icon tells you to listen to the accompanying CD for additional information.

Where to Go from Here

Now it's time to get your head in the game. Peruse the chapters and look at the lessons in them. If you want to begin at the beginning, dig right in at Chapter 1 and move forward in an orderly fashion. But you don't have to do it that way. Each chapter is modular, meaning that a particular lesson is self-contained. Use the Table of Contents to help you find your area of interest. Need help teaching a child to blend? Jump straight into Chapter 3. If you've already progressed in phonics and want to get to the more difficult levels, you can start in Part III.

Part I

Getting Ready to Read with Phonics

The 5th Wave   By Rich Tennant

"Phonics should be easy. We already know he likes to make noise."

In this part . . .

In the chapters in Part I, I tell you what phonics is and show you how to teach phonics concepts to your child. You also get the tools you need to help your child use her knowledge as she learns to read more difficult words and sentences. I also provide fun ways to reinforce the lessons, and explain how to tell when your child is ready to move ahead with her reading skills. By the end of this part, your child will be able to read her first words!

Chapter 1

Pondering the Power of Phonics

*Y*ou've already seen your child through walking, talking, eating with utensils, potty training, and countless other processes. Reading is just another part of growing and discovering. Reading is necessary for success in life, and phonics can help. Phonics is a method of word recognition. It helps children understand how to slide letter sounds together to form words. If you're curious and have some knowledge of phonics, you need to know from the get-go that this book presents a specific phonics approach to reading and spelling. This book, in itself, is very basic because I wrote it for a parent and a child. But no matter what age you are, this book can help you.

Several years ago I taught phonics to two middle-aged men. Both had suffered from look/say teaching in grade school, and had feeble decoding and spelling skills. I taught the same lessons that applied to any beginner: the sequential flashcards and the vowel chart. After they realized that they could decode unknown words, they were on their way. Because they were both intelligent and successful people, they applied their knowledge and greatly improved their skills.

In this chapter, I give you a brief introduction to phonics and the way this book approaches it to help you and your child master the art of reading. This chapter also outlines the concepts you see throughout this book and how I (as an experienced phonics tutor) approach the subject with children. With equal doses of patience and perseverance, and help from this book, your phonics routine will run as smoothly as a fine-tuned Cadillac.

Taking the First Steps toward Using Phonics

Getting your child reading at the earliest possible age and keeping him happy at the same time makes the whole process of learning to read easier. Learning to read isn't supposed to consume every moment. As your child enters this stage of discovery, he needs to be busy with other things — like playing outside, having a hobby or two, learning board games, experimenting with art supplies, and so on.

The phonics approach to reading proves itself to be the best. It isn't reading in itself; it's the best method for word recognition, far superior to the look/ say (see the word/say the word) approach. Phonics covers all the bases. Sliding sounds together to make words gives way to instant recognition of the words as you progress in your reading. Phonics training also makes for excellent spellers.

Phonics, quite simply, is a method of learning to read in which you connect sounds with letters or groups of letters. For example, *c, k,* and *ck* can all represent one sound: /k/.

The term *phonic* shouldn't be confused with the word *phonetic,* which simply describes the sound of human speech. I use *phonetic* occasionally in this book when describing sounds of letters or words, but the term doesn't apply to the letters or words themselves.

Some words are purely phonetic in that they don't have any sort of visual reference, such as the words *and* or *but.* Words that have a visual reference, such as nouns like *cat* or *rabbit,* are often referred to as *sight* words or *look/say* words throughout this book.

Whether you choose home-school or regular school for your child, your goal is to educate him to his unique capacity. You want to help him develop his inherent talents and abilities, which will serve him for his entire life. When you teach him to read, you're there with him at the beginning of his intellectual achievement.

Phonics For Dummies contains a program that you can use to instruct your child in how to read. There are many methods for teaching phonics, but the one used in this book involves teaching a child to read starting with the following:

A remarkable offshoot of phonics

When you take the phonics approach to teaching your child to read, your child learns to use his language skills in an organized way. The method starts with the most basic elements of language and then builds on them a little at a time. Your child is accumulating layers of skill and is able to hang on to them. (Saxon math books take a similar approach to mathematics.)

You've probably heard someone say something like, "My mind is like a sieve! I read or hear something, and it goes right on through!" Teaching your child with an organized method keeps him from ever having to utter these words. It's akin to painting a great piece of art by using the brush as a tool rather than splashing paint and allowing it to stick where it may. Learning to read with phonics (the brush) programs the brain to retain information. Children enjoy unlocking new words, and when the words are unlocked, the retention is easy. The end result enables them to quickly grasp unknown words, learn their definitions, bank the knowledge, and then move on to the next level.

- ✔ The most frequently used words
- ✔ The most often used letters that make up the words
- ✔ The easiest-to-sound letters that make up a word

This means that you aren't teaching the alphabet in alphabetical order, which may be a new concept to you, but it's a successful and tried-and-true method.

You can use this method to help your child pronounce the consonant and vowel sounds of the alphabet, decode words, and read. Your child will learn guidelines for interpreting different letter patterns. Along the way, he'll discover how to read in a logical and methodical manner. The phonics program breaks down learning into succinct, compact units so that your child can learn one skill at a time without getting frustrated. Phonics becomes fun and easy for your child.

There is a bit of a controversy regarding how to teach phonics. Educators disagree about how large a role phonics should play in learning to read and how often teachers should use phonics in teaching reading. But learning to read, spell, and write is only part of phonics.

The phonics approach I present in this book enables your child to think logically in terms of reading and spelling words. He'll develop techniques for processing and using the information. You'll see him progress quickly from lesson to lesson.

Getting Your Child (And You) into the Swing of Things

Before getting into the nitty-gritty of phonics, you first need to examine and warm up to the idea of instructing your child. To learn how to read, the student depends on an instructor. Who might that be? This book confers the title upon you! No parent has to be a PhD to teach his or her child to read, write, and spell. By following the instructions in this book, you can wear the crown of Master Teacher. You can discover all the techniques you need to teach your child how to read and spell.

Your self-confidence rubs off on your child. Realizing the importance of a positive attitude is half the battle. The rest is letting go of your doubts about success and trusting the teaching method that I present in this book to do the job.

Atmosphere and timing

Children learn best in a quiet, stress-free atmosphere where they know what to expect. Before diving into the first phonics lesson, accustom your child to the idea of "school time" — a part of the day devoted to learning phonics. Let him know that this time is special, not a time for play or watching TV. Eventually, your child will accept the guidelines and even begin to look forward to your time together.

Watch your own stress level as you conduct the lessons. You may grow frustrated when your child isn't grasping a lesson as quickly as you'd like, but don't let it show. Call the lesson short if you have to. Or go over a phonics concept that your child is already familiar with to get back on track.

For most children, keeping a schedule is important. Children learn better if their lessons come at a specific time each day because they know what to expect and can mentally prepare themselves for learning.

Applying the skills consistently

When your child is ready for some application, he'll start to apply his newfound skills at the local restaurant by grabbing crayons and printing feverishly on the kids' placemat, quizzing you, following mazes, and asking to play hangman. If that isn't enough, he'll be reading the road signs — or at least picking out the letters. He'll sound out words on the cereal box, sing along with a phonics song Grandma gave him, or actually pick out words in a Dr. Seuss book. Even better, he'll be reading by repetition and phonics in Mac and Tab. With your help, he can apply the skills he's learning every day.

Provide age-appropriate material for your child to read. He'll be reading quite well by the time he masters the material through the end of Part III, but you really don't want him reading a front-page crime report in the local newspaper. Even though he's able to decode multisyllable words, he won't necessarily comprehend them in an adult context. Early on, the challenge and need is to provide lots of material that he can easily read so that the previously acquired skills can be successfully practiced.

Helping you and your child look forward to your lessons

Most people remember kindergarten as a wonderful experience. They liked kindergarten so much because it wasn't a traditional class, but a class that involved hands-on learning and experimentation with different kinds of materials, as well as a class that engaged all the senses — not just the eyes and ears. The techniques I introduce in this book can help you turn "school time" into something your child will look forward to and remember fondly, like kindergarten.

Singing

You absolutely have to start with singing the ABC's. As kids learn their ABC's and the sounds that go with them, their innate creativity and talent comes to the fore and they groove on the fun of learning. Put anything to song — vowel guidelines, syllabification guidelines — even if you have to invent a melody. Children are natural learners when material is presented in song. They'll repeat your songs and remember the guidelines they refer to.

Playing games

This book is filled with activities that make learning fun. You don't necessarily have to follow the directions to a T. Mix it up a little. For example, instead of telling your child to point out the short *a* in one of the reading lessons, give him an ice cream cone and allow him to take a lick every time he sees a short *a*.

Glory and praise

Your child will beam with pride when he reads his first word, sentence, and paragraph. He'll brag to Grandma, the other kids, and anyone who will listen. Lay the praise on thick and give him the attention he deserves for a job well done.

Livening it up with flashcards and other teaching aids

Throughout this book, I give detailed explanations about how to use various teaching aids. Here's a short list of the teaching aids that you need in order for your child to get the most out of his learning time:

- ✔ **Flashcards and charts:** These visual aids can help a great deal in reading instruction, and they make the learning experience more lively and cheerful.

- ✔ **Craft and writing materials:** You need paper, pencil, crayons, markers, and a pair of scissors.

Sight words (those that kids learn to know on sight without decoding by sound) make great flashcards. When you flash sight words to a bunch of kids, you find out which ones are visual learners (those whose strength lies in seeing the word as a whole better than another) and which little angels are auditory learners, whose listening skills are stronger. Using the phonics method to teach reading and spelling enhances all the learning processes.

You can write anything you want on a flashcard. It's a great device for combining work with fun. Your child can work through the flashcards by himself or ask someone else to go through them with him. While you're getting your lesson ready for the day, hand the flashcards to your child and he can quietly flip them himself until you're ready. For more info on using flashcards, see Chapter 2.

Getting an Overview of the Phonics Fundamentals

In teaching children to read with the phonics method in this book, each lesson builds upon the next, and one skill leads to another. This way, as children accumulate knowledge about phonics, they learn with confidence. The following pages explain how different phonics concepts are introduced and how they build on one another. You get a solid idea of what's in this book by reading these pages.

In every chapter in this book, I present a specific approach to phonics. The chapter lessons go something like this:

1. **Your child warms up by reading flashcards with sounds and words.**

   This activity engages speech, sound, and sight.

2. **Your child listens attentively as you read a story, and then you ask questions to assess your child's listening comprehension skills.**

3. **You and your child read the phonics tables and assimilate the lesson.**

   You ask the child to spell words from the lesson, and he responds to the spoken directions by spelling the words orally (thereby engaging yet another sense).

4. **You dictate words and sentences to your child for your child to write.**

5. **Your child reads aloud for his pleasure (and yours) so that you can determine how well he's progressing.**

Starting with the basics

Starting in Part II of this book, your child discovers that letters make sounds, sounds make words, and words make sentences. From there, you teach the four most commonly used and easily understood letters — *m, s, t,* and *a.* By using these letters, you can spell many words and even write simple sentences. Spend as much time as you need on these letters. You want your child to feel confident using them before he gets into blending letters to make sounds. You also teach the child two sight words, *a* and *the.* As your child progresses, you add more sight words to the list of words he should memorize.

Be sure to distinguish between small words that can be sounded and true sight words. For example, *do* and *of* and *done* are true sight words. However, *cat* and *dog* and *three* aren't sight words because they can be sounded.

In Chapter 3, I ask you to introduce the letters *m, s, t,* and *a* in your very first phonics lesson. These letters are easy to print. When you introduce these letters and sounds to your child, he sees, says, sounds, and blends them. In this first lesson, he reads several words formed by combining those letters. You also teach him the sight words *and, the,* and *a.* With these look/say words — or sight words — your child can read short sentences from the first lesson. He may also be able to print them as you dictate the sounds to him.

Blending basics

After your child knows the sounds of letters, you work on blending them together to make words, as shown in Chapter 3. Blending may be the biggest hurdle your child faces. Don't lose patience. Some children pick up blending right away; others need time and practice. Most children can fly through their phonics lessons after they understand blending.

Vowel sounds and digraphs

Your child explores more consonants, and then he discovers the rest of the vowels and their short sounds. About this time, your child will be able to read simple sentences. Chapters 4 and 5 prepare your child for bigger words and words that are harder to spell. He's introduced to *digraphs* (two consonant letters blended together to make a completely new sound, like *ch*) and plural words.

Vowels and diphthongs

In Part II of this book, your child passes from the beginning to the intermediate stage as he learns how to read and decode words with various kinds of long vowels. I also introduce the elusive *y* and *w,* the two consonants that can also serve as vowels, and *diphthongs* (two letters joined to create a completely new sound).

Plunging into advanced phonics

Part III of this book deals with words with two or more syllables, their structure, and their pronunciation. By now, your child has a large vocabulary and is reading smoothly. I explain what diacritical marks are (they're the marks and symbols that appear in dictionaries to tell you how to pronounce and accent words), and I tell you how to read these marks to find out how to pronounce words, as well as how to find out where to put the accent in a word.

Word endings and tenses

Next, your child moves ahead to the *ed, ing,* and *er* suffixes. Your child's reading level expands at this point, as he discovers the difference between the present and past tense. He also learns to double the consonant and drop the *e* when spelling words with the *ed, ing,* or *er* ending.

Some new sounds and unusual spellings

Your child explores the soft sounds of *c* and *g,* and although I introduce a few guidelines to make it easier to handle these sounds, your child has to memorize most of the *c* and *g* words for spelling purposes. Your child has now reached the point where memorizing becomes more necessary, and he's introduced to words that need memorizing, such as *eight, though,* and *cough.*

Prefixes and suffixes

Your child will have reached the advanced phonics level by now. He tackles suffixes and prefixes, explores roots, and begins to understand how prefixes and suffixes can change the meaning of a root.

The minor players

Part IV of this book looks into exceptions to the guidelines of phonics. It looks at the odds and ends of phonics, including these items:

- ✔ **The schwa:** The schwa sound takes the place of most vowels, and exists as a concession to pronunciation. It makes the quick *uh* sound.

- ✔ **New digraphs and sounds:** In this new digraph, one of the letters makes its normal sound, and the other is silent (as in *knife* and *write*). You also look at words borrowed from foreign languages that don't conform to English guidelines.

- ✔ **Vowel criminals:** Some vowels follow absolutely no pattern (as in the words *carry* and *mirror*). Your child looks at these vowels, as well as some long vowels (as in *old* and *find*) and the letter pairs *gh* and *ou.*

- ✔ **The letter *x* and the *zh* sound:** The letter *x* makes three sounds — you explore all three and look into the *zh* sound, which is in more words than you probably realize.

At this point, your child is officially an expert. Compliment him, brag to your relatives, and show some pride. Your child has earned it. But most of all, rest easy knowing that his academic career will be much easier because of this phonics training. And give yourself a pat on the back for being a great teacher.

Ramping Up to Exciting Books and Readers

After your child is reading, you can cultivate a love for reading! When you and your child are well into Part II of *Phonics For Dummies,* you've passed the point of no return. Sounds ominous, but I want to assure you that your child is well on his way to being a fluent reader. After he knows how to blend sounds to make words, there's no end in sight to what he can read. You get to decide what kind of books to choose. If you want to supplement his reading, this section prepares you for making great choices in reading material. What your child likes to read really matters!

Phonics storybooks

A typical phonics storybook is one that emphasizes word families; that is, the book contains very few sight words in the stories but places heavy emphasis on phonetic words. However, providing your child with the right books can be a challenge. You can recognize appropriate books by their use of a lot of repetitive and phonetic words. Most school libraries contain some, but many local libraries don't. Your best bet is to try the bookstore. If you're willing to pay a few bucks, you can find *Bob* books and maybe some *Mac and Tab* books. Ask the salesperson to do a search for you; she may come up with some goodies. Another possibility is a school supply store. Your last option is surfing the Internet for used books.

Including look/say readers

A typical look/say reader not only uses sight words but also makes use of repetition. Look/say readers are a lot easier to find than phonics readers. Almost every old reader book dating back to the 1930s is a look/say book. If you can find them, using them as supplements is fine as long as your main method of teaching is phonics. I use the word *supplement* in a serious way.

Don't let your child guess at a word. Telling him is better than letting him guess. After all, he's supposed to be reading for fun.

Because the sight words are so repetitive, your child is practically memorizing the stories. You can often find old look/say readers at book sales. You may also find them in school libraries.

Keep in mind that most children's books that you find in the library or book-stores are look/say or whole language books. Whole language and look/say books are similar because neither emphasizes phonics.

Fun with Dick and Jane

Kids often fly through the classic, adorable *Dick and Jane Readers* that you can still purchase at your local retail outlets and toy stores. When your child reads a book that has a lot of repetition (like the *Dick and Jane* books do), the cadence may fool you into thinking that his reading skills are superb. But keep in mind that he may not yet be a phonetic reader. These books are okay to use, because they exercise the visual aspect of reading and are great prac-tice for fluency and expression. Another fact is that many of the words are phonetic, and through repetition, your child learns. Kids start to see entire sentences instead of reading just one word at a time.

At the risk of sounding inconsistent, I want to tell you why I like *Dick and Jane* for reading for pleasure:

 ✔ They use pictures that are heartwarming and inspire children to put themselves into the story.

 ✔ They activate the Dolch list (see Chapter 2), which is 85 percent pho-netic, and use the words in repetition.

 ✔ They enhance fluency, expression, and comprehension.

I hope I don't offend my *phonetics only* buddies, but I believe these books can have a limited role in teaching. I don't advise using the teacher's manuals, but let the kids enjoy the stories.

Boosting Skills with Fun Activities

If kids are good at just one thing, it's having fun. And the more fun they have learning, the more fun you'll have teaching them. Keep your teaching on the lighter side and your reading sessions will never become a chore. Instead of having your child hunker down with gobs of worksheets, give him a variety of activities that lighten the load of homework. Give him a small number of activities and make each one count. Ask for only ten minutes of work five times per week. These activities make good practice, and practice, you know, makes perfect.

In this book you encounter a variety of activities. They're designed for your child to print either directly in the book or on a separate piece of paper. All the activities that you find in the chapters are streamlined for the lesson at hand. In fact, the activities in this book can be used as models to enable you to create your own activities. Look for the Activity icon throughout this book as a guide to fun activities for you and your child. Chapter 18 also includes a list of activities to enjoy.

I advise you to make copies of the exercises, which allows you to preserve your book if you so desire.

Chapter 2

Setting Up Your Teaching Aids and Techniques

*T*he saying "practice makes perfect" makes perfect sense. That is, if all that practice is helping you get better! The hard, cold fact about practice is that you have to do it, no matter what skill you're seeking to gain or enhance. Natural born talent is only the beginning. The rest is practicing with an eye on improving. The same is true with phonics.

Athletes have drills that help them improve their skills, and so does phonics. But phonics drills (or activities) can be lots of fun — almost like hosting your own little game show. With a little creativity and some cutting and printing, you're on your way to phonics success!

In this chapter, I show you great teaching aids, techniques, tools, activities, and more; all are aimed at helping your child get phonics in a flash. And that's aid number one!

Getting Phonics in a Flash with Flashcards

Because kids hunger for attention and activity, flashcards are a great way to liven up lessons. Using flashcards is more than just showing the card quickly and giving the answer. It's also a way for you and your child to have fun together. Most parents enjoy seeing their children light up with excitement and animation during a flashcard exercise.

Okay, flashing a card isn't the be-all and end-all of education. But if you play your cards right by using flashcards and organizing them well, you have a first-rate technique.

In the days of the bare-bones classroom, the teacher and student were often at the chalkboard. Columns of phonetic and sight words were written, pointed out, and drilled. Teachers sent flashcards home for math practice. Perhaps for thrifty purposes, reading cards didn't come home. Teachers did allow the students to bring home their *Dick and Jane* readers to practice with Mom and Dad. To this day, teachers send math flashcards home because it's an old custom that's tried-and-true. I say that what's good for the goose is good for the gander, or in this case, what works for math works for phonics. Gather your supplies and get ready to roll!

Starting off with the Dolch list

This book provides tons of words throughout the chapters in Parts II, III, and IV, but a good starting point for picking words for your flashcards is the Dolch word list. In the 1940s, Edward W. Dolch, PhD, surveyed many children's books. From this survey, he came up with a hand-tallied list of words, including pronouns, adjectives, adverbs, prepositions, conjunctions, verbs, and nouns repeatedly found in children's books of that time. In 1948, he formulated these words as the most frequently encountered in reading. The Dolch word list, which is still in use today, is made up of 315 words. Dolch didn't list his words by word difficulty, but rather by the frequency with which these words appear in print.

Following are the first 100 words of the Dolch word list, which include about half of all words in material written in the English language. Children who are learning to read typically use these words in their speaking and listening vocabularies:

the	you	are	this
of	that	as	have
and	it	with	from
a	he	his	part
to	was	they	or
in	for	at	one
is	on	be	had

by	do	make	first
word	how	like	water
but	their	him	been
not	may	into	call
what	if	time	who
all	will	has	oil
were	up	look	its
we	other	two	now
when	about	more	find
your	out	go	long
can	many	see	down
said	then	number	day
there	them	know	did
use	these	way	get
an	so	could	come
each	some	people	made
which	her	my	may
she	would	than	part

Educators refer to Dolch words as *sight* words because these words need to be recognized on *sight*. Even though the words on the Dolch list are considered sight words, the list breaks apart and overlaps with phonic words.

Making your own flashcards

Before you go out and spend money on materials for flashcard construction (or premade flashcards), see whether you can find the basic items you need at home. Despite best efforts, nearly every home has a junk drawer. And take a look at the samples in Appendix C. Here are some tips for creating flashcards:

   ✔ **Using the best markers:** Sharpie markers don't bleed through the paper as easily as other markers. I like the chisel-tip Sharpies for clearly printing the letters. No bleed-through means you can use both sides. Use blue or black markers for visual ease.

✔ **Selecting suitable paper:** Make your own flashcards with 3-x-5-inch index cards or *oaktag* (a thin but stiff card or cardboard that's used to make typical Manila folders). If you can't find oaktag, you can cut Manila folders into 2-x-3-inch cards (minimum size). Oaktag is the best, because it holds up and works well with Sharpies.

✔ **Finding the right cutting tools:** A paper cutter comes in handy, but you can use a ruler and scissors.

✔ **Printing correctly and legibly:** Always make sure that you print the letters correctly when making the flashcards. Copy the alphabet from Figure 2-1. You can go to a school store and buy a printing tablet, which shows you how to print the letters.

✔ **Considering the computer:** You can have a grand old time making flashcards on the computer. I recommend comic sans font for the exactness of the printing letters.

✔ **Creating multiple sets:** You can make more than one set of flashcards. For example, post one set of cards on the wall so that your child can look at the cards daily. Another set may be personalized 2-x-3-inch cards that your child can transport in her pocket or your purse.

The Alphabet

Figure 2-1: Presenting the uppercase (first) and lowercase (second) versions of each letter of the alphabet.

Now you decide what to put on the flashcards. Your cards can be set up like any of the following:

✔ **Individual sound cards** that have the individual letters on the front of the card. Include uppercase and lowercase letters. For example, *M m.*

✔ **Picture keywords** that have the picture, the keyword, and the sound on the front of the card.

- ✔ **Phonics flashcards** that have the beginning of a word on the front of the card and the complete word on the back of the card. For example, you can have *ma* on the front of the card and *mat* on the back.

- ✔ **Sight word cards** that have a word from the Dolch list, like *the*, on the front of the card and nothing on the back of the card. (Check out the earlier pages of this chapter for more info on the Dolch list.)

- ✔ **Segments of words** for decoding on the front of the card and the whole words on the back of the card. For example, *shŏ p, thră sh,* and *bŭt ter* are on the front of the card, and *shop, thrash,* and *butter* are on the back.

- ✔ **Vowel guidelines** on the front of the card and the pattern on the back of the card. For example:
  - Front: When a word or syllable has only vowel and it comes between two consonants, the vowel is usually short.
  - Back: Cvc (consonant-vowel-consonant)

- ✔ **Symbols** (diacritical marks) on the front of the card and the definitions on the back of the card. For example:
  - Front: -ə
  - Back: Quick *uh* sound, called a *schwa*

- ✔ **Vocabulary words** on the front of the card and the definitions on the back of the card.

Keep your card materials and ideas handy throughout your phonics lessons. As you progress through your lessons with your child, you can keep adding more cards while discarding the ones your child already knows well.

Putting your flashcards to use

Start flipping the flashcards fairly slowly and then go faster and faster as the exercise goes on (or as your child gets the hang of it). Flop the cards down on the table with great drama, putting them in one stack for right and another stack for wrong. Get buttons or pennies and plop them down on the winning cards.

Your child may be flustered and lively at the same time. She may beg you to go slower, but she'll get in the game and join in the fun. (Back off just a little if she gets too stressed.) Make her challenge herself to do better and go faster. As you speed up, your voices get louder. You can make a progress chart, have prizes each time you go through the flashcards, or give privileges as a reward. Sit down to work on flashcards for about 10 to 15 minutes at a time, and you and your child will be thrilled with the results.

The Leitner system

In the 1970s, German science popularizer Sebastian Leitner proposed using flashcards to support memorization by way of spaced repetition. His method, known as the Leitner system, sorts flashcards into groups according to how well you know each card. To use this method, you try to recall the solution written on a flashcard. If you succeed, you send the card to the next group. But if you fail, you send it back to the first group. An obvious advantage of the Leitner method is that you can focus on the most difficult flashcards, because they remain in the first group. The result is, ideally, a reduction in the amount of study time you need.

 Most of the Dolch words can indeed be sounded because they're phonetically regular words. Thus, when a child makes an error or can't recall a word quickly, she should be encouraged to sound out the word.

 The biggest mistake you can make is to tackle too many cards at one sitting. Try not to bite off more than you can chew. Knowing 5 words well is better than trying to learn 20 words and forgetting most of them by tomorrow. If you work with too many words, your child will forget them. Spread your flashcards sessions out over two to three days, and repeat them often. Some kids are speed demons who pick up on words quickly, and others take longer.

If you play your cards right, you'll make quizzing easy. In addition, your child will receive, understand, and retain the information because of the following reasons:

- You compacted the information.
- Looking at the card ensures that your child is seeing what she has learned.
- Distributing the sessions over a few very brief intervals during the day imbeds the information through repetition.

 Carry the flashcards with you so that your child can look at them in the car, in the doctor's office, and so on. I'm not trying to make you obsessive, but I am suggesting that you make the most of very small windows of time when you can fit in two to three minutes of card flashing.

Posting the cards on the wall is another good way to use them. You can use a yardstick or laser to point to the word as your child reads it.

Managing your flashcards

Whether you're a messy Bessie or a neat freak, keeping your cards straight is a good idea. It helps keep your kid's brain tidy and saves you time — if the cards are in order, you don't have to go through the old stuff she already knows. In the first few weeks, you're dealing with a small stack that you can keep in a plastic, zippered sandwich bag. You can even spring for three sandwich bags: one for the cards your child already knows, one for the work-in-progress cards, and one for the cards that are waiting to explode upon the scene. While these bags are keeping your flashcards in order, you may develop organizing solutions tailored to you and your child's lifestyle. If you're not finding the time or desire to do this, check with the organization geeks and explore some of their modes. This list gets you started:

- Use a small box and make four dividers for it — one for cards you review every day, one for cards you bring out every three days, one for the once-a-week cards, and one for the cards you break out only once a month. New cards go in the front compartment because you want to review them every day. When your child knows a card, you move it back gradually. If she gets one wrong, that card goes back to the first compartment.

- If you're really industrious, you may purchase a pocket chart to hold your flashcards. The chart and its contents (flashcards) are for you and your child to see at all times.

- Go to a box store and look for little boxes that fit the size of your flashcards.

Charting for Phonics Success

Charts allow you easy access to volumes of information. Your child gets an overview of learning to read in mere seconds of viewing. All you have to do is point and explain the material, or point and ask her to read it to you. Charts are portable and time saving.

Teachers love charts. Nothing gives character to a schoolroom like colored charts. When you walk into a first-grade room, the boards and walls are lined with charts indicating the days of the week, the months of the year, sight words, phonics charts, and so on. The colorful décor almost blinds your senses.

The teacher who decorated that room has a purpose for every item there. That doesn't mean you should use charts like wallpaper for your kitchen or family room. No one wants his house to look like the classroom in a public school. Unless you have a special space for your child's whatchamacallits, the refrigerator is probably the limit. Finding a place for charts can be as simple as putting them between the pages of this book.

Making charts

Every once in a while, you may feel emboldened to make charts to help you with your instruction. After all, a parent teaching a child is all about personalization, and charts tend to be very personalized.

You decide how to craft your charts, but your information must be golden. Because you're teaching one-on-one, you can:

- **Copy your charts to whatever paper size is best for you and your child.** If you're making a wall chart, for example, it should be fairly large (poster size). Young children require large lettering, so make the chart's contents big enough to read.

- **Determine the size of smaller charts by the print in children's books.** Slip these charts between the pages of this book, stack them on the kitchen counter, or lay them on the table.

- **Place the vowel chart on a wall or fridge if you have space.** You can make a copy of the vowel chart in Figure 2-2. The vowel chart is the core of the vowel system, so you want your child to know it well. If you have any wall or fridge space, put the vowel chart there for the next few months.

- **Make copies of your charts, and give your child her own copy.** Lamination is a great way to keep your charts neat and readable — even if you end up spilling coffee on them.

- **Move the charts close enough to the child so that she can read them.** If you need to, you can enlarge the charts with a copier.

Because you're teaching a child, your charts should be plain and understandable. Lucky you — I bequeath to you my best charts. The work is done. The pedagogy (instructional theory) is terrific. All you have to do is use them. The charts in this chapter specifically target the information that your child should know. The most generally accepted reasons for using charts are that they:

- Summarize information
- Make great visual aids

✓ Make large chunks of information easier to understand

✓ Ease reviewing

✓ Make great reference sheets

Using charts

Your child comes out way ahead by using my charts. I designed them specifically to give the most information possible to beginning readers. You can add to the charts as you go along. Try to keep the information as organized as you can so that the child doesn't feel chaotic as she absorbs the information.

Charts are meaningless unless you put them into operation. Here are some tips on how to use them:

✓ Start the session with an overview of material on the chart.

✓ Explain the information by pointing to the chart.

✓ Point to the material on the chart and drill with your child.

✓ Refer often to the chart.

Key Words for the Basic Vowel Sounds

First sound or Short sound	Second sound or Long sound	Third sound	Diphthongs
ăpple	āte	all = a³	owl = ou / ow
ĕlephant	ēat		
Ĭndia	īce		oil = oi / oy
ŏstrich	ōld	to = o³	
ŭmbrella	ūse	put = u³	urn = er / ir / ur

Figure 2-2: Refer to this vowel chart often when reading through the other chapters of *Phonics For Dummies*.

Beginning with the Roman alphabet

What better place to begin than to do as the Romans do? Make cards for each letter of the alphabet, and include upper and lower cases of the alphabet.

After you and your child look at the alphabet, see whether she enjoys this little ditty. See whether she can pick out the *a*'s and *b*'s, or give her a lesson on the uppercase and lowercase *a*.

Nursery Rhyme

Great A, little a,

Bouncing B!

The cat's in the cupboard,

And can't see me.

—Mother Goose

Keywords: Matching pictures and sounds

Keywords are tools to unlock the sounds. The word lists and tables in Chapters 3 through 9 contain keywords. You can make copies of them or use them when you come to the lesson. This section presents the keywords in their entirety. When you teach this with this tool, look at the keyword card, see the picture, say the name of the picture, and say the sound. Memorize them well. Then think about the keyword and start the sound, as shown in Figure 2-3. See Appendix C for keyword card examples you can use.

Vowel chart

Figure 2-2, earlier in the chapter, shows the basic vowel sounds that come from the five vowels, *a, e, i, o* and *u* (*y* is a special case and is treated mostly as a consonant in this book). Reviewing this chart on a daily basis while learning phonics is a good idea because, later on, when your child knows the vowel chart well, she'll be comfortable with using all the vowel sounds in her phonics lessons. This chart can also become part of the progress log (see the later section "Keeping a progress log" for more info).

Keywords

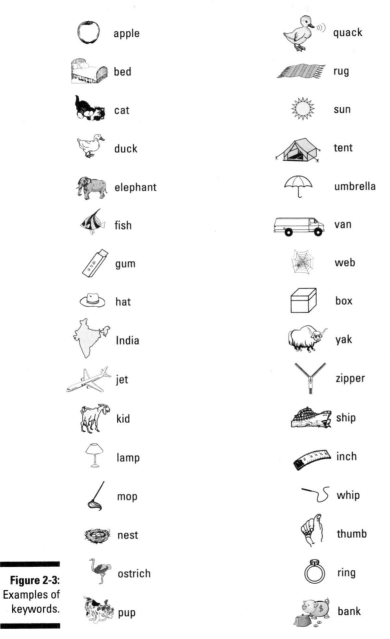

Figure 2-3:
Examples of
keywords.

Consonant sounds

The consonants sounds shown in the following list go a bit beyond the basics by including some extra combinations and odd sounds. Look through the list and notice, for example, that there are two sounds of *th*. More consonant sounds are explored throughout this book, but for now, this list is an excellent reference for the main consonant sounds:

✔ /b/	bed	✔ /t/ tent
✔ /d/	duck	✔ /v/ van
✔ /f/	fish	✔ /w/ web
✔ /g/	gum	✔ /y/ yak
✔ /h/	hat	✔ /z/ zipper
✔ /j/	jet	✔ /ch/ chess
✔ /k/	kid	✔ /sh/ shark
✔ /l/	lamp	✔ /zh/ measure
✔ /m/	mop	✔ /th/ thumb
✔ /n/	nest	✔ /th/ this
✔ /p/	pup	✔ /hw/ wheel
✔ /r/	rug	✔ /ng/ sing
✔ /s/	sun	

Picking Up Phonics with Word Strips

You can turn word families into an awesome method for spelling and reading by using word strips. Cutting oaktag paper into narrow strips that look like bookmarks and printing rhyming word families on them is a dynamic phonics tool. *Word families* are groups of words that have a common pattern. For example, a cvc (consonant-vowel-consonant) pattern contains words like *tan, ran, pan, man, can, ban, fan,* and so on.

Most people don't know that average first graders are capable of spelling at least 1,200 words by learning word families. You make that happen by using the word strips in Chapters 3 through 9. Print them on paper and work the strips with your child. Word strip practice enables her to spell and read oodles of words in just a few short months.

Forget all the gizmos and fancy features of the school stores and catalogs. To make word strips, you need only oaktag paper, scissors or a paper cutter, and a marker.

In the beginning lessons, your *bookmarker* (also known as a *word strip*) doesn't need to be more than 3 inches wide and 6 inches in length. At this point, you don't have very many rhyming words to print. Picking out words is a snap — you can grab them right from the word lists in Parts II and III. If you happen to have a really great run like the *-ay* word family, you may want to cut your strip a little longer. If it's too long and hangs out of the bottom of the book, it's no big deal.

Here's an example of a typical word strip. Your child will read about 15 words from this one alone: *bay, say, cay, day, Fay, gay, hay, jay, lay, may, nay, pay, way,* and *Ray*. If she's into the harder stuff, you can add *stay, bray, flay, fray, de-lay, cray-on, slay, gray, pray, stray,* and so on. This family adds up to some great learning!

Activity: Using Word Strips

Preparation: You need paper and a fine-tip marker. You can prepare the word strips on the job. It takes only a minute or two if you follow the instructions in the preceding section.

To play:

1. **Hand the child a word strip, and ask her to place it on the table.**
2. **Place her finger under each word and ask her to read that word.**
3. **Articulating the words, she reads the list twice, hearing the rhymes.**
4. **Ask your child to spell each word on the strip out loud.**
5. **Ask your child to write each word on the strip.**

After using any or all of these steps, you and your child can decorate the strip on the flip side with dates and stars for work well done.

Engaging the Senses with Phonics

In this section, I provide techniques for learning to read. Novelties in teaching methods are ongoing, but educators generally go back to the methods that have been used for centuries — namely dictation, drill, and memorization. When you put in a little time learning the methods and applying them, your child's skills may grow beyond your expectations. Any way you want to personalize your methods is great. Need some ideas? Read on.

Spelling out loud

A spelling bee is a great exercise; the learner first hears the spelling word from the instructor. The child then speaks the answer by saying the word and spelling it out loud. Hear the word. Say the word. As she does this, she needs to picture the spelling of the word in her brain. As you progress, you no longer need to make pictures as often, because spelling becomes involuntary. If you drive down the road often enough, you get to know the way like the back of your hand.

You may want to introduce the finger spelling technique here. To do so, your child says the word out loud and says each sound in the word, as she holds up a finger for each sound. Then she says the letter(s) for each of the sounds.

Writing from listening

To discover whether your child understands a phonics lesson, from time to time dictate one syllable (mat), short vowel words (back), and simple sentences to her. In a typical lesson, she's at a table with a pencil and a printing tablet. At first, the words you dictate should be those that follow a regular phonetic pattern — examples include *dog, had,* and *sit,* as opposed to *do, was,* and *one.* And so begins her first writing lesson. Kids' fine motor skills develop at different rates, so be prepared for some primitive printing. Along with learning how to print, your child learns about punctuation, capitals, and so on.

My printing expert taught me a cardinal rule about printing: Start at the top of the head and move down to the tummy. Here are some additional tips for proper printing (see Figure 2-4):

- ✔ Always print from the top of the letter downward.
- ✔ Don't stroke upwards.
- ✔ In general, work from left to right.

For children who need extra help making pathways to the brain, a tactile surface may aid their printing. A rough surface like sandpaper creates more stimulation for remembering the letters. I often use a rough surface in my teaching, and I ask the learner to use her index finger to write. She can write on a variety of surfaces that offer tactile stimulation, including air, a table, a wall, a sofa, cement, a car seat, sand on a beach, a breadboard, or someone's back. As she writes, have fun guessing what she's writing. All kids can profit from this exercise.

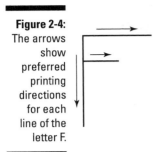

Figure 2-4:
The arrows show preferred printing directions for each line of the letter F.

Memorizing with mnemonics

"A rat in Tom's house might eat Tom's ice cream." What in the world does that have to do with phonics? It's a mnemonic phrase that can help you remember how to spell a-r-i-t-h-m-e-t-i-c! Get it? The first letter of each word in the sentence makes up the word *arithmetic*. It's just like a secret code!

Most people learn by using mnemonics without ever hearing the word. *Mnemonics* refers to a memory device. The device can be verbal, such as a poem or a special word that jogs the memory, or it can be a word that you write down to jog your memory. People often use mnemonics for making lists. This remembering tool bases itself on the fact that your mind can remember things better if you attach a mnemonic to information you think you'll forget.

For example, say you need to remember a license plate number: CNN10XP. You can remember it mnemonically by assigning the following information to it:

- ✔ CNN is a cable news station.
- ✔ Ten is the age of a neighbor's son.
- ✔ XP is the operating system of your computer.

Using mnemonics, you can come up with some pretty nutty stuff, but it works!

Managing Phonics Progress

Keeping a record of your child's progress is very important — you want to make sure you're covering all the bases. Keeping a log helps you remember where you've been and see where you're headed. And you end up creating a tangible piece of memory. You don't need anything complicated. The upcoming sections show you that simple is better.

Keeping a progress log

A progress log gives you and your child the tools you need to keep track of her development. Think of this log as a report card that you and your child view with great interest. This log contains reading, phonics, spelling, and much more. Get started right away so that she can chart her course. Table 2-1 shows you a sample progress log.

Table 2-1	Sample Progress Log		
	Knows It	*Improving*	*Needs Help*
Comportment			
Hands on table			
Feet on floor			
Eyes straight on material			
Holding book properly			
Correct pencil grip			
Word Knowledge			
Flashcards			
Sight words			
Phonetic words			
Word strips			
Skill boosters			
Dictation			
Oral spelling			
Chart Review			
Reading Tasks			
Smooth reading			
Fluency			
Expression			
Words per minute			
Comprehension			

	Knows It	*Improving*	*Needs Help*
Who, what, when, where, why, how			
Sequence of events			
Predicting outcomes			

Is the child getting it?

How do you know whether your kids are getting it? First of all, most children can learn to read, write, and spell. Every classroom in America has the challenged and the Einstein of the class. Some children learn faster than others, but that isn't the whole picture. Some of the brightest children can have weaknesses in the language arts.

Have confidence that your child learns well. She may fly through the phonics lessons, or she may plod through them at a slower pace. It doesn't matter as long as she moves forward.

She's getting it if:

✔ She responds to the flashcards with relative ease.

✔ She reads the tables with relative ease.

✔ She spells one-syllable words by ear and on paper.

✔ She responds to comprehension questions.

✔ She understands the worksheets when you explain them.

Smoothing disruptions to the routine

From time to time, parents are unable to continue the daily routine. Sooner or later, circumstances get in the way — it happens to everyone. So how do you keep the ball rolling and maintain effectiveness? Here are tips for keeping phonics skills sharp when the daily routine wanes:

✔ Do word strips in small increments when you can.

✔ While you're planting your flower garden, doing routine work on the computer, lying on the couch with a headache, and so on, ask your child to sit near you and read from a very easy reader or a table from one of the chapters.

- ✔ Keep the flashcards handy and whip out a few and flash for five minutes.

- ✔ If you and your child are in the car, think of some simple one-syllable words and ask her to spell them.

- ✔ Hand her a very simple worksheet and a pencil and tell her to work the exercise while you're under the hairdryer at the salon.

- ✔ Go to Chapter 18, find some activities for independent work, and prepare ahead for those long trips in the car.

- ✔ Go to Chapter 19 and discover more awesome phonics resources for kids.

Rewarding successful learning

One sure way to unlock your child's brilliance is through positive reinforcement. All you have to do is say the word *treat* and your child's face probably creases into a wide smile. Treats vary from a small piece of candy to a Disney World Cruise. I'm sure you can come up with something in between or whatever is most appropriate for your child. I want you to realize the value of rewarding your child. Rewards are intrinsic to human nature; all people love treats and look forward to them. Children are no exception. Your child works harder if she can look forward to a treat. So put your thinking cap on and come up with your own personalized choice of delights.

Part II
Exploring the Fundamentals of Phonics

The 5th Wave   By Rich Tennant

"We do phonics drills every day here in the kitchen. David is only up to 2 letter combinations, but the parrot is blending consonants and vowels."

In this part . . .

In this part, you and your child move into the foundations of phonics — those basics you must know to begin reading. You start with consonants and explore blending sounds. Then you move on to short-vowel sounds and begin reading very short stories. You and your child also discover things like the diphthong, where you make new sounds out of old vowels, and contractions. As the chapters move along, I pick up the learning pace, and you and your child begin to enjoy reading even more!

Chapter 3

Starting with Simple Consonants and a Vowel

In This Chapter

▶ Getting into blending

▶ Using scripts and other techniques

▶ Looking at consonants and keywords

▶ Examining the letter *a*

*B*ecause *m, s, t,* and *a* are frequently used letters, they form a logical starting place for phonics. This chapter explores these consonants first, because they have only one sound each. Then I show you the short vowel *a.* After discovering step-by-step techniques for blending and more, you meet and blend the letters and the short sounds of all the consonants. It's time to dig in!

Knowing how to dig in makes less work for you and your child. If someone asks you which letters in the English language are used the most, you may say, "Definitely not the *x* or *z.*" A safe answer!

As I also mention in Chapter 1, a safe — and logical — answer to teaching a child to read is to start with the following:

✔ The most frequently used words

✔ The most often used letters that make up the words

✔ The easiest-to-sound letters that make up a word

The method in *Phonics For Dummies* follows this directive. Remember that you aren't teaching the alphabet in alphabetical order. This chapter gives you the simplified instructions that you need to apply in the rest of this book's chapters. If you can plow carefully through to the end of this chapter, the rest of the journey presented in this book will be smooth sailing.

For the sake of unity, all the consonant keywords (such as *mop, tent, apple,* and *sun*) are included in this chapter, although not all are basic consonant sounds.

Digging Into Blending

This book uses blending tables (see Table 3-1) to present a template of techniques for teaching blending. Keep in mind that the study of blending sounds together to make words can be called *decoding, word study, word analysis,* or *word attack.* Many experts use this lingo. These techniques include

- ✔ Scripts
- ✔ Blending tables
- ✔ Vowel sounding

The section wraps up with flashcard activities to perfect blending skills and some fun games to boost blending skills. You'll apply all the techniques and tips in this section as you dig in further with consonants (see the later section, "Going Deeper With Consonants and Keywords," in this chapter).

Now is a good time to make flashcards of *a, and,* and *the.*

Using scripts

Going step by step calmly moves you and your child forward, which is why some instructors write their lessons into scripts. Scripts are just like the scripts you imagine for plays or movies, and they can be tough at first. They help your child move from a single unit of thought to the broader picture. In following the steps of a script, everything lines up neatly. If you end up having to practice it a couple of times, that's okay.

Here's an example of how to set up a script: The instructor (that's probably you) prints the following sentence on a piece of paper or white board: *Sam went to sleep.* Follow the script to introduce a sentence, which is a related group of words that has a subject and a predicate, and expresses a complete thought. In this exercise, you're going from the sentence (the whole) to a single word, and then to the sounds that make up the word. Follow scripts to introduce the sentence and get your child started spelling and reading:

Instructor: "Today you're going to start to read by learning all about the letter *m*."

Point to the letter *m* in the alphabet and then show the learner a flash-card with a small *m* printed on it.

Instructor: "The name of this letter is 'em'; the sound of this letter is *m-m-m*. What is its name? What is its sound?"

The learner answers these questions. Don't stress the name of the letter. Learning word recognition requires you to emphasize the sound. Point to the picture of the *mop,* and say *mop,* slowly exaggerating the *m* sound.

Instructor: "This keyword helps you to remember the letter *m.* Every time you see this letter, I want you to see the picture of a *mop* in your mind, and I want you to hear the sound of the first letter. This picture will unlock the sound of this letter just as a key unlocks the door."

Let your child or learner draw a mop, use a mop, or pantomime the word. Do anything you can to teach the keyword so dramatically that he can't forget it.

Your child now prints *m* in the air, on the white board, or on lined paper, which already has an *m* on it to copy. While lettering, he needs to train himself to sound the sound quietly each time he prints it.

Instructor: "Say its sound, not its name."

Pass out a skill booster to reinforce the letters. He again quietly sounds out the letters.

Continue the script method with *s* and with *t.* Soften the ending on *t* so that it doesn't sound like *tuh* (*t* with a short sound of *u*). The last *t* in *tent* gives you an excellent sound.

If you're unfamiliar with any sounds in this book, be sure to listen to the appropriate tracks on the CD.

You can also condense the script down into a miniscript, if you like, similar to the following:

Instructor (pointing to the sentence): "This is a sentence."

Give the child a moment to look at the sentence.

Instructor: "What is it?"

Learner: "It is a sentence."

Instructor: "Fine, now this sentence has four words. (Point to them.) I will erase three of these words. (Erase everything but *Sam.*) The word *Sam* is left. The letters of the alphabet make up the word *Sam.* Here's an *S* (pointing to it). Here's an *a,* and here's an *m.*"(Again pointing.)

The learner then sees how letters make up words.

Using blending tables

Climb into the driver's seat — you're ready to rev up for the first of many blending tables. *Blending* is merely sliding sounds together to make words. Knowing how to blend sounds to make words is a vital key to reading success.

You may be tempted to add *uh* to the beginning consonant sound, *muh-ah-t.* No, no, no! Don't do it! Listening to the tracks on the CD that accompanies this book will clear that problem fast.

Table 3-1 shows you how to blend four of the most often used letters: *m, s, t,* and *a.* To walk your child through a blending table, start at the top of the first column and read down the column, blending the sounds of the letters. Do this with each of the top set of columns in order. Then move to the bottom set of columns and do the same thing.

After taking your child through both sets of columns, read the sentences and do the keywords.

Table 3-1		Example of a Blending Table		
m	S	t	s	m
ma	Sa	ta	sa	ma
ma t	Sa m	ta t	sa t	ma ss
mat	Sam	tat	sat	mass

Have your child read the following short, simple sentences for practice. The goal is for him to be able to read as he speaks, so you want him to read each sentence to himself and then say the sentence out loud with expression, naturally speaking the words in the sentence.

Matt sat.

Sam sat.

Sam sat at a mat.

You can adapt keywords for your child's flashcard collection. As your child gets used to the cards and you're flashing them, prompt him by asking "Letter, sound, keyword?" You can mix up those directives, or just say "Sound?"

Suggested keyword cards include the following:

Mm: mop

Ss: sun

Tt: tent

Aa: apple

For the corresponding sounds on the CD, please listen to Track 1 for *m,* Track 2 for *s,* Track 3 for *t,* and Track 4 for short *a.*

Sounding all the vowel sounds

Learning the letter *a* is a harder procedure because the phonics method in this book covers all three sounds of *a* in one lesson, instead of starting with just the short *a*. Although teaching the three sounds together may seem confusing, the technique works well. You can memorize three sounds almost as easily as one. The benefit of the overall view proves itself in later lessons. Take a look at the vowel chart in Chapter 2 for reference.

Here are some tips to help you uncover the three sounds of *a*:

✔ When introducing *a,* use the terminology "first, second, and third sounds of *a*." Later shift to saying "short, long, and third sound of *a*." The first way may be easier in the beginning, or you can use the terms interchangeably if you want to. The reference words for the sound become familiar and form a correct foundation for future dictionary work.

✔ Even though you use only the short sound of *a* in Chapters 3 through 6, knowing the other sounds is a tremendous help in unlocking words in later chapters.

✔ If your child encounters a word that has one of the other two sounds of *a* in it, such as *lake* or *saw,* he can decode it just from using the overall view presented in the vowel chart.

When you know all three sounds, you're also able to experiment. Any *a* that you meet in a word makes either the first, the second, or the third sound. Try all three — in that order — and get the right word by using the context. It's tied up neatly in one package for you.

Phonics For Dummies is written so that you can teach either the short sound alone or all three sounds of *a*. However, if you do the latter, refer to the vowel chart in Chapter 2 for the keywords for these three sounds. Then try the following script:

> **Instructor:** "The name of this letter is 'ay,' but I have a surprise for you! *A* has three sounds! Say *apple* after me slowly. (Exaggerate the *a* and say the rest at a normal rate.) This is the first sound and the first keyword.
>
> "Now say *ate.* (Exaggerate the *a*.) This is the second sound and the second keyword.
>
> "Now say *all.* (Exaggerate the *a*.) This is the third sound and the third keyword. Always remember the sounds and the keywords in the same order. At first, we'll be working only on the first sound (the short one)."

You can easily retain keywords if you use a memory device called an *associative sentence,* which is a sentence designed to help you remember specific letters or sounds. You can make up your own, or use my cornball suggestion. For example, for the three sounds of *a,* you can use "I ate all the apple." Association is a great aid in phonics.

When your child is learning the correct printing of *a,* review the three key-words, the three sounds, and the associative sentence. When he prints the letter *a,* have him sound it quietly each time. He can sound either the short *a* or all three sounds of *a,* depending on how the letter is introduced. This practice is the standard procedure for all the vowels. The vowels *e* and *i* have only two sounds. The vowels *a, o,* and *u* have three sounds each. See the Cheat Sheet in the front of this book for the keywords. Don't forget to look at the Chapter 2 vowel chart.

Perfecting the blending

Even a powerful vowel like *a* does not a language make. Combining it with other letters is a challenge you introduce with a few easy steps.

As you work through the following steps, repeat any or all of them until you're confident that your child gets the idea. Blending the initial consonant and vowel is the most important step on your journey to reading smoothly.

You need patience and perseverance when you're first working on blending. Blend *ma*, and then *sa*, and then *ta* together — don't sound the letters in isolation. By this I mean, don't say *m*, pause and say *a*. Put these sounds together in a nanosecond of time. Your homemade cards for these directives are *t, s, m, a, ma, sa,* and *ta*. The first three cards are consonants that blend with the fourth card, which is a vowel. The blending cards are *ma, sa,* and *ta*. Although you're using the *ma, sa,* and *ta* cards first, proceed to create the *ma t, sa t,* and *ta t* cards also. You may want to have your picture keyword cards in the mix or refer to them before you start the instruction.

Follow these steps to help your child become a master blender:

1. **Hold up the flashcard with *ma* printed on it.**

2. **Read the word to your child.**

   As you say *ma*, make sure you slide both sounds together as you slide your finger underneath the word.

3. **Ask your child to say *ma*.**

4. **Repeat steps 1 through 3 with *sa*.**

5. **Repeat steps 1 through 3 with *ta*.**

   This combination is a little harder because you can't say these two letters slowly together. If you try, it sounds like *tuh-ah*. To clip off the sound, imagine the end of the word *tat*. Do you hear the end *t*? That's the clipped off *t* you need.

6. **Show your child a flashcard with *ma t* printed on it with a definite space between *a* and *t*.**

7. **Ask your child to say *ma t*.**

8. **Present the entire word *mat* with no breaks between any letters.**

9. **Ask your child to say *mat*.**

   When your child can say this word correctly and smoothly, he has decoded his first word all by himself — a tremendous accomplishment.

The process in this section is the logical method for decoding all the words in Table 3-1, and for any further independent word analysis. Good word analysis (decoding) is just a matter of knowing sounds and blending them together.

Recipe for smooth reading

After reading the first sentences following Table 3-1 and learning super blending instructions within this chapter, you and your child are ready to learn a simple technique for smooth reading. From the get-go, your child becomes a smooth and fluent reader. If you do as I say, you prevent him from becoming a *word reader*. I define this as a slow, choppy, flat-toned reader. This habit is hard to unlearn.

Here's how to become the best reader in the class:

✔ From the first moment the child begins to read, tell him to read every word of the sentence silently. (Remember that with proper word study, he should know every word in the sentence.)

✔ After the silent reading, tell him to say the sentence as if he's talking. Proceed to the next sentences in the same manner.

✔ Illustrate the procedure first by reading several sentences this way. Read the sentences with accent and fluency, and ask the child to repeat the sentence to you.

In a comparatively short time, the silent reading step falls by the wayside and smoothness in oral reading becomes automatic.

After your child gets the hang of sounding out words, it becomes as engrossing as a puzzle. The danger is that sounding out words will become an end in itself. So, from the very first sentence, you must make reading meaningful by asking a few questions: "Who sat? What did Matt do?" These questions bring the child back to the ground and help him remember that the words have meanings. He can easily answer the questions in the short sentences after Table 3-1. But as his reading skills advance, asking the who, what, when, where, why, and how questions will help his comprehension advance as well. Also, this practice assists him in learning how to construct and diagram sentences.

For best results, learn a new phonics lesson every day early in the morning when you and your child are fresh. Make frequent use of flashcards to focus attention on new material and as a means of rapid review. Even if your schedule prevents you from this routine, you should review the flashcards every day and then go on to something new. No matter how short the lesson, keep moving forward.

To recap: Your child has three sight words: *a, the,* and *and* in his flashcard box. Along with those he has the *m, s, t, a* keyword cards, the *m, s, t, a* phonetic flashcards, and some *ma, sa, ta* phonetic blending cards. You can add a few whole word blending cards such as *mat, sass,* and *at.*

Check out Figure 3-1 to see samples of your first pile of flashcards. In this chapter, I give you more keywords that you can use for flashcards. Refer to Chapter 2 for details on handling your flashcards. Appendix C contains keyword card examples you can photocopy and use for this chapter's lessons.

As you proceed in the lessons and when your child reads the tables, be ready with keyword cards, homemade letter cards, and blending cards.

Figure 3-1:
Sample flashcards for *m, s, t,* and *a.*

A a

apple

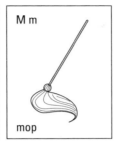

M m

mop

S s

sun

T t

tent

Activity: Marking with the Breve (˘)

Preparation: Copy these sentences, or rewrite them for your child. He needs a pencil.

To play: Place a breve over the *a* in each word.

Example: Săm săt.

1. Matt sat.
2. Sam sat.
3. Sam sat at a mat.

Answer Key: 1. Mătt săt. 2. Săm săt. 3. Săm săt ăt a măt.

Activity: Fill in the Blanks

Preparation: Copy these sentences, or rewrite them for your child. He needs a pencil.

To play: Fill in the blanks with one of these words: sat, mat, am.

1. Matt sat at a _____.
2. Sam _____.
3. I _____ Sam.

Answer Key: 1. mat 2. sat 3. am

Going Deeper with Consonants and Keywords

Grab the beginning instructions for scripts from the beginning of this chapter, and the table and the tips, and apply them to the rest of the chapter. You may wonder why I present this particular sequence of letters. When I first learned the phonics method, I had no idea that you don't teach the ABC's in alphabetical order. You have to trust me on this. Each grouping of letters is in its place for a reason . . . the reason being that it works better!

Dam and gas

Phonics teaches the *d* and *g* next because of their ease in lettering. After the child can print the letter *a,* he can easily learn to print *d* and *g.*

When sounding these letters, use the same care that you use in sounding the *t.* Avoid the *duh* and *guh* sounds. In fact, don't spend much time on the single consonants. Concentrate on the keywords and blend with the vowels as quickly as possible.

Add the *da* and *ga* flashcards to your collection. With the flashcards *ma, sa, ta, da,* and *ga,* you can rapidly review the three sounds of *a.* If you choose to teach all three sounds, first flash the short *a* sound, and then the second sound of *a,* and then the third sound.

As your child adds new consonants and vowels to his knowledge, he continues to review every day. The main emphasis stays on the short sounds that I present up to and including Chapter 6. Table 3-2 shows how to blend some consonants sounds with *a.* Follow each column from top to bottom to blend the sounds and form the keyword.

Table 3-2		Blending Table for D and G			
d	g	d	g	t	s
da	ga	da	ga	ta	sa
da d	ga g	da m	ga s	ta g	sa d
dad	gag	dam	gas	tag	sad

Dam isn't a bad word

Most of the time when I teach Table 3-2, the subject of *dam* and *damn* comes up. The kids are reluctant to sound this word because they think that they're saying a bad word. I always stop and draw a picture of a dam. We discuss beavers that build dams, and the kids are reassured that this word is okay. Obviously, the curse word damn may have crossed their paths at some time, but this gives you the opportunity to teach a little science lesson. You can often include a science, history, or vocabulary lesson along with the phonics lesson.

After your child masters the words in Table 3-2, have him read the following sentences for practice. The goal is for him to be able to read the way he speaks.

Mag sat a dam.

Dad sat at a mat.

Sam sat at a dam.

Use the following keywords to help your child learn the *d* and *g*:

Dd: duck

Gg: gum

For the corresponding sounds on the CD, please listen to Track 6 for *d* and Track 7 for hard *g*.

Fad and hat

Table 3-3 requires the same blending and reading that Table 3-1 requires. *F*'s and *h*'s are easy to blend. Hey, you want to test your child's hearing? Ask him to close his eyes and hear you sound *f*. Ask him what he hears. He should say *f*. Now ask him to close his eyes while you sound the *th* sound — as in *thud*. He should repeat *th*. You're testing his *auditory discrimination,* which is the ability to hear similarities and differences in sounds. Be sure to do this exercise frequently to make sure he hears the sounds correctly. Lots of times, kids with chronic earaches don't hear the sounds properly.

Fish in hats: Grammar versus imagination

When your child is reading sentences, inject a little grammar. Have you and your child ever seen a fish wear a hat? Probably not, but you can have a grammatically correct sentence that's total nonsense. Now is a good time to explain this to your child, because he has not only started to read sentences, but is also at the age of discerning what's real and unreal. When you teach grammar you teach sentences and composition.

Table 3-3		Blending Table for F and H		
f	h	f	h	h
fa	ha	fa	ha	ha
fa t	ha d	fa d	ha m	ha g
fat	had	fad	ham	hag

After your child masters the words in Table 3-3, have him read the following sentences for practice.

> Matt had a ham.
>
> Tad had a sad hat.
>
> A hag had a fat ham.

Suggested keywords for this section include the following:

> Hh: hat
>
> Ff: fad

Start your lesson with a review of names, keywords, and sounds of previously taught letters. It's okay to overstress the new sounds in the words at the beginning of the table. Make sure, however, that your child doesn't read all words stretched out like that. Try not to get involved in sloooow sounding of the sounds in words.

For the corresponding sounds on the CD, please listen to Track 8 for *f* and Track 9 for *h*.

Pad and rat

If you have a sharp sense of hearing, you may realize that some of the basic consonant sounds are voiceless. *Voiceless* means that you can make the sound with no vibration of the vocal chords. Earlier in this chapter, I spend some time on the *t* so that you know not to add the dreaded *uh* to it. Be just as careful with the puffy *p*. Say *p-!* (a popping noise) instead of saying *puh*.

In this section, I also introduce you to the *r*, an easy sound to pick up at the beginning of a word, but a killer at the end of a word. Kids commonly can't say *rrr*. Adding a layer of confusion is the difference in pronunciation throughout the United States and also in Great Britain and Australia. Have you ever been to Puth — I mean Perth? The British dictionary solves your problem if you can't say *rrr* — the word *doctor*, for example, is pronounced *dok' tuh*. Instead of affecting a British accent, I encourage you and your child to do your best with the American *r* sound.

Check out Table 3-4 to blend the letters *p* and *r*.

Table 3-4		Blending Table for P and R			
r	p	r	p	r	P
ra	pa	ra	pa	ra	Pa
ra t	pa d	ra g	pa t	ra p	Pa m
rat	pad	rag	pat	rap	Pam

After your child masters the words in Table 3-4, have him read the following sentences for practice. The goal is for him to be able to read as he speaks, so you want him to read each sentence to himself and then say it out loud with expression, naturally speaking the words in the sentence.

Pam had a map.

Dad had a fat ram.

A rat had a pad.

Use the following keywords to help your child learn the *p* and the *r*:

Pp: pad

Rr: rat

For smooth reading, follow these steps:

1. **Think the keyword:** *rat*

2. **Articulate just that sound needed:** *r*

3. **Blend the consonant with the vowel and continue to the next sound:** *ra t*

4. **Read the sentences silently first and then orally as you would say them in conversation.**

For the corresponding sounds on the CD, please listen to Track 10 for *p* and Track 11 for *r*.

Nap and bat

I want you to teach the *b* far after the *d* (see earlier in the chapter for more on teaching the *d*). Many kids have a hard time seeing the difference between these two letters. This type of error really hurts when your child is saying the wrong sound because he confuses *b* and *d*. When you're ready for this phonics lesson, you want to make a big deal only out of the structure of the *b*. In other words, don't say the *d* goes this way and the *b* goes the other way. Also, don't tell him about the problem before he actually makes the mistake . . . you may just put ideas in his head. Some children don't encounter this problem, so you may get lucky.

Here's a technique to help your child keep *b* and *d* straight:

1. **Draw a picture of a baseball bat and a baseball and say, "The bat comes before the ball when it's a *b*."**

2. **Trace over the picture from left to right and say, "The bat comes before the ball."**

3. **Trace the *b* in the air and on the table, saying "*b. b. b. b. b.*"**

The *n* sound and its keyword, *nest,* present very little trouble. Sometimes kids with weak auditory skills may confuse the sound with *m*, but it's not terribly common. Have your child read the blending table for *n* and *b* (Table 3-5) by using his freshly learned skill.

Table 3-5			Blending Table for N and B		
n	b	n	b	n	b
na	ba	na	ba	na	ba
na p	ba t	na g	ba n	na b	ba d
nap	bat	nag	ban	nab	bad

When your child masters the words in Table 3-5, have him read the following sentences for practice.

Dan and Ann ran.

Mag and Pam nab Nat.

Tad and Dad nab Nat.

Use these keywords when you're teaching the *n* and the *b*:

Nn: nap

Bb: bat

For the corresponding sounds on the CD, listen to Track 12 for *n* and Track 13 for *b*.

Van, jab, wag, and quack

These four letters (*v, j, w,* and *q*) have few practice words, because so few one-syllable words that start with these letters have the short sound of *a* in them.

Q is a special case because it is always written in English followed by *u*. This *u* isn't sounded as a vowel. To show that the letters *q* and *u* belong together, they're underlined (qu). Be sure to teach the easy sound of *w* and make sure your child is familiar with the sound of *k* before teaching *q* (*qu*), because its sound is *kw*.

The letter *j* is easy, and so is *v*. Both are a snap for the kids. Table 3-6 helps you blend the sounds.

Table 3-6			Blending Table for V, J, W, and Q			
v	j	w	qu	v	j	qu
va	ja	wa	qua	va	ja	qua
va n	ja b	wa g	qua ck	va t	ja m	qua ff
van	jab	wag	quack	vat	jam	quaff

After your child masters the words in Table 3-6, have him read these sentences for practice. You want him to be able to read the way he speaks, so ask him to read each sentence to himself and then say it out loud with expression.

Jack had jam and ham.

Van can wag a rag.

Kat can quack at a pal.

Use the following keywords when you're teaching these letters:

Jj: jab

Qq: quack

Vv: van

Ww: web

For corresponding sounds on the CD, listen to Track 14 for *j,* Track 15 for *v,* Track 16 for *k,* and Track 17 for *w.*

Yakkety yak with tax and zap

X has three sounds, and the most common is *ks,* which is the one I'm sticking to for now. Help your child master the *k* and *s* sounds first, and then mastering *x* should be easier. The letter *y* is a stinker. For some weird reason, most kids have a rough time learning it, perhaps because unlike most (but not all) other consonants, when you say the name of the consonant, you're not saying its sound. That is, when you say the name of the letter *b,* you're saying its sound. However, when you say the name of the letter *y,* you're saying the /w/ sound. I sing the "Yakkety Yak Don't Talk Back" ditty, which helps. Thanks to words like *zipper* and *zoo,* kids usually get *z*! Table 3-7 helps you blend these letters.

Table 3-7		Blending Table for X, Y, and Z			
y	z	y	l	y	t
ya	za	ya	la	ya	ta
ya p	za g	ya m	la x	ya k	ta x
yap	zag	yam	lax	yak	tax

After your child masters the words in Table 3-7, have him read the following sentences for practice. Ask him to read each sentence to himself and then say it out loud with expression, naturally speaking the words in the sentence.

> Max had a map and an ax.
>
> A yak can ram Jack.
>
> Van can razz Ann and Dad.

Keywords to help you teach these letters include the following:

> Yy: yak
>
> Xx: tax (x)
>
> Zz: zap

For the corresponding sounds on the CD, listen to Track 3 for *s*, Track 16 for *k*, Track 18 for *y*, and Track 19 for *z*.

The secret of successful learning is to link as much as you can with other subjects. When your child has the basic consonants and short vowel *a* down pat, he's reading lots of words, so you can zero in on some sentence structuring with him. Soon, through this step-by-step process, he'll be able to write and read his own creative sentences. Try the following tips to give his beginning attempts the greatest impact:

- ✔ Practice capital letters, periods, and the meaning of sentences by copying the practice sentences after each table in this chapter.

- ✔ After giving instruction on capitals and punctuation, and after lots of copying practice, have your child apply these skills when writing simple sentences from your dictation.

- ✔ Finally, ask your child to try it on his own by writing simple and correct sentences.

Pulling it all together

This review gives your child great satisfaction as he realizes that he has the power to unlock every one of the words in the following list, showcasing the short sound of *a* as in *apple*. Play "up and down the ladder" by going up and down the list, pointing to words as he reads them:

bad	gag	man	sag
ban	gab	nap	sad
bag	gap	nab	Sam
bat	had	nag	tag
back	hag	Nan	tam
cap	ham	pat	tan
can	hat	pad	tab
cab	jab	pan	tax
cad	Jack	pal	van
dam	jam	quack	vat
Dan	lad	rap	wag
dab	lap	rag	wax
fan	lag	rack	yap
fad	lack	ram	yam
fat	mat	ran	yak
gas	mad	sat	

Have your child read these sentences for practice after he masters the words in the previous list:

Dan can jab at a yak.

Jack had a cap.

A lad ran at a tan van.

Now you can begin a new phase of association: auditory awareness. That's just a fancy way of saying ordinary dictated spelling. If you arrange the words into rhyming lists (word strips — check out Chapter 2), this task will be easier for your child, and he'll have almost instant success as long as the first word is correct. Word strips are introduced here, because now you have all these consonants to use with the short vowel. In this example, the word strip is used as a dictation tool for spelling on a printing tablet. Some examples are:

bad, cad, dad, fad, had, lad, mad, pad, sad, add, ad

bag, hag, gag, jag, lag, nag, rag, sag, tag, wag

back, hack, lack, jack, pack, quack, rack, sack, tack

Make sure that you stress the correct left-to-right initial blending in dictation, such as *ba d, ca d*. Be careful not to teach the -ad family, because your child will focus on the end of the word, which teaches regressive eye movement, meaning that the child reads the end of the word first and then goes to the beginning — a recipe for disaster. Can you imagine reading smoothly with that maneuver?

When you dictate spelling words, say the word, use it in a sentence, and then repeat the word. Because your child's printing is in the early stage, don't burden him with too many words. I suggest five words at this point in time. However, his reading prowess allows him to read tons of words.

At this point of your teaching, with the addition of a few common sight words — verbs (were, was), prepositions (of, to), pronouns (I, you), and the articles (a, the) — the possibilities for creative sentence writing widen considerably. Here are some key strategies for making sentence writing a success:

- ✔ Don't use too many sentences at any one time.
- ✔ Don't introduce too many new words at one time.
- ✔ In general, use about five words, maximum, in one sentence.
- ✔ The idea is to do just a few, but do them correctly, demanding sentences with the correct punctuation. Unlearning bad habits is difficult. Of course, you also don't want to be so strict that you hurt your child's feelings. Sometimes, you need to give a little. If he's writing a letter to Daddy, ease off.
- ✔ Use some nonphonetic words like *of, to,* and *was.* Your child needs to know that not all English words are phonetic. He must cope with words that don't sound like they're spelled or don't follow the guidelines of phonics.

As nonphonetic words like *of* begin to show up, find a box and call it *jail*. Put *of* in the box, because it doesn't follow the guidelines. I get dramatic here, and the kids learn *of* by sight, because it's a bad guy! Your child will love throwing a word in jail and letting it out when you need to flash the word to him.

When teaching *the* and *a,* don't allow the kids to say *thee* and *ay.* These are correct pronunciations only when employing emphasis. Most of the time, both of these words have a short-short *uh* sound.

Learning punctuation, declarative, interrogative, and exclamatory sentences comes naturally as you progress. Keep it simple and your child can learn by reading sentences and little stories. Some examples are:

> Dan and Jim were at the dam.
>
> Were Dan and Jim at the dam?
>
> Mom, Dan, and Jim were at the dam!

Next Stop: c, k, ck, and l

You're clicking along with *click* and *clack* — an exciting time to be adding the *ck.* The *k* sound shows itself as *c, k,* and *ck.* It makes it easy to sound but hard to spell.

The *l,* on the other hand, has a sound all its own. Say the *l* sound and notice your tongue's position. Different, eh? With a keyword, *lamp,* it's not a problem for sounding and blending, but at times the kids get it visually confused with the number 1, or they say "I".

The quantity of your word bank is growing by leaps and bounds. On some oaktag paper, print the letters *m, s, t, a, d, g, f, h, p, r, n, b, c, k, l,* and *ck* — all in lowercase. Cut them apart so that each letter is on its own card, and place them in a box. Throw lots of *a*'s in the mix. Your child can scatter them out on the table and make words from them. You can guide him toward making up sentences, also. Bear in mind that he's just a beginner. If he makes five words with the letters, that's awesome. This practice reinforces correct reading and spelling.

Reinforce this lesson by asking your child to copy the letters and words in Table 3-8 on a printing tablet. As you go along, your child can do so many little things to advance his skills. He should sound quietly to himself every time he's doing these miniactivities.

Table 3-8			Blending Table for CK		
c	l	c	l	k	ck
ca	la	ca	la	ka	ack
ca n	la p	ca t	la d	ka zoo	la ck
can	lap	cat	lad	kazoo	lack

When your child masters the words in Table 3-8, ask him to read the following sentences for practice.

Kat can pack a bat.

A man had a pan and a rack.

A lad ran back at a cab.

Keywords that help you teach the letters in this section include the following:

Kk: kid

ck: clock

Cc: cat

Ll: lamp

Although I show you four keywords, Table 3-8 presents just two sounds. Hard *c* has the sound of *k,* and it's the only sound of *c* that you teach your child for some time. The consonant digraph *ck* also has the sound of *k.* It's used at the end of most short-vowel words for which the *k* sound immediately follows a short-vowel sound. A *consonant digraph* comes about when two letters join together to make a new sound.

The *ck* is easy to sound, but spelling it can be tricky. Don't expect your child to use *ck* correctly for a little while. This is where the *visual sense* sets in, and he begins to see these two letters together. Try not to get involved with the soft *c* (as in *ice*) for a long time. If you read a word like *nice,* tell him it's a soft *c,* but teach it as a sight word for now. The sound will undoubtedly come up before you get to the lesson in Chapter 13.

Here are two recommended sight words to add to your flashcards: *were* and *was*. By this time, your child is getting the hang of look/say words along with oodles of phonetic words. Ask him to count the words in the tables he's read so far, and find out many words he knows.

For the corresponding sounds on the CD, listen to Track 16 for the hard *k* sound, and Track 20 for *l*.

Chapter 4

Finishing Short Vowels and Seeing Patterns

*I*n this chapter, you switch gears and go from exploring the sound of short *a* to exploring the short sounds of these four vowels: *i, u, o,* and *e.* Learning how to read words with these four vowels (and the letter *a*) is the first step in reading. It amazes me how well most kids handle it. Early in the study of phonics, sound patterns begin to emerge, and it always delights me to see children beginning to recognize these patterns as they discover how to read.

Becoming acquainted with vowels and consonants is the beginning of reading success. Besides explaining four new vowels, this chapter explains how to introduce the structural pattern of consonants and vowels. Being able to read and spell a lot of words is within your child's grasp when she masters the concepts in this chapter. I include lots of short-vowel ministories for practice.

Exploring the Short i Sound

Here's an effective way to teach your child the short *i* sound: Show her a short *i* flashcard — make one for "India," for example — and say, "ĭ, *India.* Repeat after me: *i* (letter name), /i/ (letter sound), India (keyword)." *India* makes a very a precise, short-vowel letter *i* sound.

Moving from short *i* to short *a* may startle your child, and explaining the difference between vowels and consonants may be difficult. I ease into it by trying to talk without vowels and showing how speech sounds without vowels. I introduce myself to the children by using only the consonants in my name, *Ssn Grv*. Then I talk without vowel sounds, asking them to do it as well. After a few minutes of this, everyone is laughing. By explaining to children how vowels give the language cadence and flow, you're really on your way.

Consider the correct blending of the consonants with short *i* as your child recites the words in the following list. The list illustrates how different consonants blend with the short *i* sound. Although the blending is relatively easy, remember that your child is just learning a different vowel sound, so take it slowly. Read down from the top, savoring the way these *i* words sound. You can copy the words from this and any of other lists or tables in this book.

bib	fix	kit	quiz
big	fizz	lid	rib
bill	gig	lit	rig
bin	gill	mid	rim
bit	hid	mill	sill
did	hill	miss	sip
dill	him	mitt	sit
dim	hip	mix	tin
din	jig	nick	tip
dip	Jill	nip	wick
fib	Jim	pill	wig
fill	kid	pin	will
fin	kill	quick	win
fit	kiss	quill	zip

Follow the list with a reading lesson using the following sentences, making sure that your child reads these silently first, and then says them out loud. This will be the constant procedure for the vowels as you move along:

Dick and Sis will mix jam.

Jim can sit and hit a tin lid.

Bill and Rick did a quick jig.

If your child has trouble understanding what sound the short *i* makes, tell her to say the word *it*. Tell her to notice the position of her mouth and tongue as she says the word *it*. Tell her that the *i* sound in *it* is the short *i* sound.

Activity: Short Stories

To play: Here are some short stories that your child can read to reinforce the short *i* sound:

- **The Big Bib:** Liz had a big bib. The big bib was for Nick. Sis will fix the big bib for Nick. Did the big bib fit him?

- **A Quick Jig:** Tim and Sis were at the rim of the hill. Sis ran to Rick. Sis did a quick jig for Rick and said, "It is a quick jig."

- **The Big Wig:** Jill had a wig. The wig was big for Jim. The big wig was for Sam. Jim and Jill will miss the big wig.

Activity: Word Strips: Short i

Preparation: You need paper and pencil.

To play: Sit next to your child, and read the following word strip (Chapter 2 explains how to teach with and create word strips):

big, rig, wig, dig, fig, pig, gig, jig

bit, fit, hit, lit, kit, mitt, pit, quit, sit, wit, zit

dip, hip, jip, lip, nip, pip, quip, rip, sip, tip, zip

For the corresponding sound on the CD, listen to Track 21 for the short *i*.

Understanding the Difference between *a* and *i*

I introduce vowel sounds in Chapter 3, where your child discovers the sounds made by the letter *a*. At this point, as you introduce the letter *i*, you want your child to understand the differences between *a* and *i*. She needs to clearly understand that different vowels make different sounds.

One way to teach her the difference between the vowels is by reciting the words in the following list to review the sounds of *a* and *i* with your child; then have your child read the words. As your child reads them together, she'll get used to differentiating the two sounds:

bid	lass	pat	razz
cat	Liz	pick	rid
cad	map	pig	sis
cam	mass	pip	tack
gal	miff	pass	tick
hat	Nan	quip	tiff
jazz	nick	quit	Tim
kick	Pam	rat	zip
kin	pack		

For practice, after your child recites the words in the list, have her read the following sentences. Have her read them silently first, and then say them out loud.

Jill had a big fat pig.

A man did fill a vat.

Rick had him pick a kit and a wig.

Making the Acquaintance of Short u

The short *u* sound is fun and easy to teach. Many people automatically want to add the *uh* sound when making the sound of most consonants. For example, to pronounce the word *bite*, you say *buh-ite*. Words that make the short *u* sound include *cub*, *gut*, and *tug*. Have your child practice reading the short *u* words in the following list:

buck	bum	cub
bud	bus	cud
buff	but	cuff
bug	buzz	cup

cut	hut	pup
duck	jug	putt
dud	jut	rub
dug	lick	rug
dull	lull	rum
fun	lug	run
fuss	muck	sub
fuzz	mud	suck
gull	muff	sum
gum	mug	sun
gun	mum	sup
gut	muss	tub
hub	null	tuck
huff	nun	tug
hug	nut	tut
hull	puff	tux
hum	pug	yum

For practice, after your child recites the words in the previous list, have her read these sentences silently first, and then say them out loud.

Gus will run and hug Sis.

Liz had a bug, a duck, and a pup.

Tim can fix a jug and a cup.

Activity: Jokes

Preparation: You need paper and pencil.

To play: Rewrite this joke on a piece of paper. Then read the joke out loud to your child. Tell her to listen carefully for words that have the short *u* sound. After she identifies them, write them on a printing tablet for her to copy.

Slugs in a Huff

Q. What did the unlucky slug say to the other slug, who had cuffed him and run off?

A. You bum! I'll get you the next slime!

Answer Key: slug, cuff, run, bum

Activity: Stories

To play: Here are some very short stories that your child can read to reinforce the short *u* sound.

A Big Bug

Bud had a big bug. The big bug was a tick. The bug will buzz at the pug.

The Tan Rug

Gus had a cup of fuzz. The fuzz was from a tan rug. Gus will lug the rug to the sun.

Fun in the Mud

Bud had a mutt. The mutt was a pug. The bug and the pug dug the mud and hid a bug.

As your child progresses in reading, you can refer to the Dolch list in Chapter 2 and add a few sight words to her flashcard collection. The word knowledge enables your child to advance in sentence reading a bit faster. Sight words here include *from, I,* and *you.*

Here are some suggested word strips for short U:

> cut, but, gut, hut, jut, mutt, nut, put, rut, tut
>
> rug, bug, dug, hug, lug, jug, mug, pug, tug
>
> bum, gum, hum, mum, sum, yum

For the corresponding sound on the CD, listen to Track 22 for the short *u* sound.

Summing Up Short a, i, and u

Quite soon, your child will progress to the short *o* sound, but first, she should clearly understand which sounds the short *u, i,* and *a* make. Make sure your child can read these three short-vowel sounds before proceeding to the next letter. If your child makes an error while reading these words, gently correct her. Remind her that with a short-vowel sound, the vowel doesn't say its letter's name. For example, short *a* says *aahhh* (what doctors ask you to say when they look at your throat), not *A* (like the letter grade).

Use the following list as a guide:

bud	jag	quiz
bun	jam	rip
but	Jud	rum
cuff	kid	sack
cull	kill	sass
cuss	lack	sap
dam	lick	sick
dub	luck	sip
dug	mud	tap
dun	mull	tat
fat	mutt	tax
fill	muss	tub
fizz	nap	wax
gap	nib	will
Gus	pit	yap
hub	pun	zip
huff		

For practice, have your child read these sentences. Have her read the sentences silently and then aloud.

A man had a sick duck and pup.

Bud and Jill had mud in a tub.

Russ will sit and hug his tin bus.

Activity: Stories

To play: Here are some very short stories to reinforce short-vowel sounds. Ask your child to read the stories smoothly and with expression.

Fun for Rick

Rick dug the mud. The mud and the muck was fun for Rick to dig. Sam said Rick was a nut to dig at the mud.

Sam and Jill

Sam and Jill sat at the mud hut. Jill had a sub for Sam. Sam had a nut for Jill. The sub and the nut were big.

Fun at the Tub

Dick and the duck had fun at the tub. The duck hid the tub and a cup at the mud hut. Dick will look for the tub and the cup.

Getting Acquainted with Short o

I'm inclined to burst into song when I teach the short *o* sound. I like to sing, "I am an ŏpera singer! I sing ŏ!" Then I sing the scales. The bolder children usually sing along with me, and if the children don't get the message of what the short *o* sounds like, I get out the tongue depressor and tell the kids to open their mouths and say, "Ŏ." My keyword card for the short *o* has an *ostrich* on it. This word has a great short *o* sound and gives you the opportunity to teach your child about the ostrich burying its head in the sand.

The short sound of *o* is the most difficult vowel sound to say exactly the same way in all words that have the sound. When you make the short *o* sound, the throat muscles tend to constrict, so encourage your child to relax her throat when making the *o* sound. The best way to get a child to make the short *o* sound properly is to have her practice saying the word *ostrich*.

The short sound of *o* is the most difficult vowel sound to say exactly the same in all words. When you sound it alone, your throat is in a very relaxed position. As soon as a consonant precedes the *o* or follows it, the throat muscles slightly tense and modify the sound. The best advice to give is to get as close as you can to the *ostrich* keyword and let it go at that. Now it's time to recite the short *o* within words. Check out the following list:

bob	doll	hot
bog	don	job
box	dot	jog
cob	fob	joss
cod	fog	jot
cog	fox	lob
cop	gob	lock
cot	got	log
dock	hock	loll
doff	hog	lot
dog	hop	mob

mock	pot	sod
mom	pox	sop
mop	rob	tock
nod	rock	Tom
not	rod	top
pock	rot	toss
pod	sob	tot
pop	sock	yon

For practice, have your child read the following sentences. Have her read them silently first and then say them out loud.

Mom and Rob had pop.

Bob got a rock in a sock.

Don and Tom will hop on a box.

Activity: Joke

To play: Have your child shout the short *o* sound "ŏ" when she hears the short *o* vowel sounds in the following joke.

Tom Popp's Alphabet

Little Tom Popp's first grade teacher, Mrs. Hopkins, is quizzing the kids on the alphabet.

"Tom," she says, "what comes after *o*?"

Tom ponders the question and says, "Yeah!"

Answer Key: Tom, Popp, Hopkins, on, ponders

Activity: Stories

To play: Here are some short stories your child can read to reinforce the short *o* sound.

Bob and the Hot Dog

Sal was a fat cat. Bob was a lad. Bob had a hot dog in his van. Sal hid in the back of the van. Bob ran and ran. Sal got the hot dog.

The Job

The boss had a job for Tom but the lad was six. Tom ran to his dad. Rob did the job for Tom. The boss was not mad at Tom.

The Box for Dad

Jim and Jack had a box at the top of the hill. The box was not for Dad. Mom said Dad was mad at Jim and Jack. Jim and Jack got a box for Dad.

Activity: Word Strips: Short o

Preparation: You need paper and pencil.

To play: Sit next to your child and read the following word strips (Chapter 2 explains how to teach with and create word strips):

bob, cob, fob, gob, job, lob, mob, rob, sob

cot, dot, got, hot, jot, lot, mot, pot, rot, sot

bop, fop, hop, lop, mop, pop, sop, top

For the corresponding sound on the CD, listen to Track 23 for the short *o*.

Introducing Short e

Here I introduce your child to the short *e* as heard in the word *elephant.* This sound can be tricky, because it's spoken differently depending on which region you live in. Do you say *pinny* or *penny*? Do you say *cint* or *cent*? Listen carefully as your child says the first syllable, *eh,* in *elephant.* If she has a hard time pronouncing the short *e* sound or making the distinction between *e* and *i,* have her say the word *echo* or *etch.*

The *e* and *i* have something in common: Neither has a third sound, which is good news because that's two fewer sounds for your child to know. For additional reference, please review the vowel chart in Chapter 2.

Have your child read the short *e* words in the following list:

beck	bell	bet	den
bed	Ben	deck	fed
beg	Bess	dell	fell

fen	met	Ted
fez	neck	tell
get	Ned	ten
hen	Nell	vex
jell	net	web
jet	peck	wed
keg	peg	well
led	pen	wet
leg	pet	yell
less	red	yen
let	Rex	yes
Meg	sell	yet
men	set	zed
mess		

After your child recites the words in the list, have her practice by reading the following sentences, first silently and then out loud.

> Bess met Ben and hid him.
>
> Peg will wed Jim yet.
>
> Nell will get less gum.

Activity: Joke

Preparation: You need paper and pencil.

To play: Have your child identify the words that make the short *e* sound in this joke. Then have your child print the words with one syllable as you dictate them. Also, ask her whether she understands the joke.

Ben's Elephant

Ben: Hey Rex! My elephant has no trunk!

Rex: What a mess! How does it smell?

Ben: Terrible!

Answer Key (short *e* words): Ben, Rex, mess, smell, terrible

Activity: Stories

To play: Here are some very short stories that your child can read to reinforce her understanding of the short *e* sound.

A Wet Pet

Bess met a wet pet. The pet was a red rock. The rock fell and hit a net web.

A Keg to Sell

Ben had a jug of jam. Can Ben sell Ted a pot of jam? Ted did not have a keg for his jam. Bill will sell a keg to Ted.

A Red Bell for Rex

Rex led ten men to the van. The van had less gas. Rex let Ned have a red bell for his van.

Jen and the Pig

Jen had a pet pig. The pet pig had a big pen. The pigpen had mud in it. The pig did not sit in the pen. The pig did not run in the pen. The pig is a pal and a pet.

Activity: Can You Hear Me?

To play: Can You Hear Me? is a game that can be played with one to ten people. This game helps teach the short *e* sound and gives practice in auditory perception.

1. **Assign your child a name that starts with a short *e*.**

   Some names to choose from: Edward, Emmett, Eldon, Ezra, Elmer, Elliot, Edgar, Eric, Emily, Esther, Effie, Ellen, Eleanor, Etta, Esmeralda, or Emma.

2. **Have her hide and instruct her not to come out until she hears her name being called.**

3. **Call out all the *e* names I list in Step 1.**

4. **When you call her name, have her come out and say her name.**

   You can keep playing the game, giving her a different name each time. The parent can switch roles with the child. The idea is to hammer home the sound made by the short *e*.

Activity: Word Strips: Short e

Preparation: You need paper and pencil.

To play: Sit next to your child and read the following word strips (Chapter 2 explains how to teach with and create word strips):

> bed, fed, Jed, led, Ned, red, Ted, wed, Zed
>
> bell, dell, fell, hell, jell, quell, sell, tell, Nell, well
>
> bet, get, jet, let, met, net, pet, set, wet, yet

For the corresponding sound on the CD, listen to Track 24 for the short *e*.

Recognizing Consonant-Vowel-Consonant (CVC) Patterns

After you and your child finish with the short vowels, as covered earlier in this chapter and in Chapter 3, your child may begin to notice that when a vowel appears in a word, it often appears between two consonants. Has she asked you for help in figuring out this pattern? Most one-syllable, short-vowel words (such as *hop* and *dig*) present a consonant-vowel-consonant (cvc) pattern. Because 62 percent of words in English have short vowels, your child would do well to recognize the cvc pattern. This way, she can quickly decode many different words.

I like to wait to introduce the consonant-vowel-consonant pattern until the short vowels have been covered, because I'd rather have children find it on their own. If you give your child some hints, she may find the cvc pattern in words such as *cat* and *dog*. When kids find patterns on their own, they usually don't tell you. It merely becomes an unconscious part of their reading progress.

Learning vowel patterns is phonics in action. Decoding words is like solving a puzzle. When first presented with pieces to a picture puzzle, your child works hard to fit them together and derives great satisfaction upon completing the puzzle.

At first, simply say, "When an *a* comes between two consonants, it's usually a short *a*." Use the same approach with all the short-vowel sounds. The idea is to let her notice the pattern before trying to explain what a vowel is. Then she's able to accept the definition of the word called *vowel*.

Teaching patterns

In order for your child to read well she needs to be able to recognize vowel patterns, such as *cvc*. In the previous chapters, she read four-letter, one-syllable words. The *cvc* blueprint presents itself in all the phonics words she has learned thus far. But now I introduce it as a pattern that she'll see, not only as a whole word, but also in parts of words.

Vowel patterns are the building blocks for word constructions. Each time your child figures out how the pieces go together, the words that follow that pattern get easier and easier to read. At some point, she finishes that one and wants a new puzzle to solve.

Eventually, reading's no longer a puzzle, and becomes something she does automatically. Kids stop getting satisfaction from decoding, and begin reading for enjoyment. Some kids get to this stage very quickly; others take longer. But the benefits of recognizing vowel patterns help all kids get to that stage.

Discovering the cvc guidelines

Usually, when a word or syllable has only one vowel and the vowel comes between two consonants, the vowel is short. This cvc (consonant-vowel-consonant) guideline is also sometimes called *the sandwich pattern*. Think of the cvc pattern looking something like a sandwich, with the consonants forming the bread slices and the vowel serving as the peanut butter.

Your child needs to memorize this guideline. Sorry, there's no getting around it. I prefer to call memorization a "repeat after me" experience. Add a flashcard covering this guideline to her collection so that she can hold it in her memory bank. Even if a child forgets the guideline, she can see the pattern and apply it.

Have your child point out the consonant-vowel-consonant patterns in the words in the following list:

back	did	fell
bad	dill	fig
bin	dip	fog
cup	dud	gun
cut	fed	hem

jell	pep	vex
lad	rob	web
less	rot	wed
mat	set	well
nick	sock	yak
null	tip	yell
peg	Tom	

After your child decodes the words in the previous list, have her read the following sentences for practice. Have her read them silently first and then say them out loud.

Tom did well at his job.

Jed set a rock on the moss.

A lad fell in a bin.

Chapter 5

Joining Consonants Together to Make More Sounds

*T*his chapter plunges into discovering letters that join together to make totally new sounds from what I cover in the earlier chapters, as well as blocks of letters that keep their own sounds when they join together. For beginning readers, sounds such as those made by *wh, th,* and *ng* can be difficult. This chapter offers many fun techniques to help a child explore these and other sounds in reading. Your child can discover how to blend consonants at the start and end of words (beginning and ending consonant blends), how to pronounce vowels at the beginning of words, and how to sound out the *tch* sound, among other things.

To keep your child on the straight and narrow as he learns to read, this chapter describes concepts, but at the same time provides hands-on learning techniques. I add a few more sight words and some fun stuff with tongue twisters, ditties, and other skill boosters. Everything has been bumped up a notch in this chapter. Therefore, your child may need to slow down a bit in order to absorb all the material in this chapter.

Delving into Digraphs (Two Letters, One Sound)

A *consonant digraph* is a two-letter combination that produces a single speech sound in which the sound isn't represented by either letter alone (*ch, sh, th,* and *wh,* for example). *Ch* is a common consonant digraph; examples include *inch* and *chill.* It makes its own sound — a sound that has nothing in common with the sound made by *c* or the sound made by *h. Sh* is another common consonant digraph; examples include *ship* and *cash.* Again, *sh* makes a sound completely different from the sound made by *s* or *h.* If you have trouble remembering what a digraph is, consider the etymology of the word: In Greek, *di* means "two" and *graph* means "letter."

Your child can learn to sound consonant digraphs easily by isolating them in the keywords, and making keyword cards. Keyword cards are incredibly useful for learning digraphs because they allow your child to make an instant connection to different sounds. Make sure your child makes use of the following keywords before reading Table 5-1: *inch, chip, ship, whip, this, thumb, ring,* and *bank.* These words contain all the consonant digraphs that are introduced in this chapter. Accordingly, make flashcards of these individual digraphs: *ch, sh, wh, ~~th~~, th, ng, nk* (the *~~th~~* is for the sound in *the* and *then*). Teach and review them until your child understands that these particular combinations of letters are "two-in-one" jobs.

Discovering consonant digraphs

Now that you've been introduced to digraphs, you can make the leap to actually sounding out some of the words. For this lesson, look at the consonant digraphs that are embedded in the short-vowel words found in Table 5-1. Work through the table as usual. Ask your child to go from the top down in the columns.

Because this lesson involves a different and more difficult concept of blending, it should be undertaken at a slow, even pace. At this point, your child has the short vowels down; now he can concentrate on learning consonant digraphs.

Table 5-1		Consonant Digraphs		
ch	*sh*	*wh*	*~~th~~*	*th*
chap	shell	when	this	thud
chill	ship	which	them	think

ch	sh	wh	~~th~~	th
chum	shut	wham	that	math
chin	shot	whiz	then	thank
chess	sham	whiff	than	thrill
chop	shed	whip	with	thrash
rich	shun	whim	thus	path
inch	mash	whet		cloth
pinch	cash	whit		moth

Have your child read these sentences silently first and then say them out loud, for practice:

> Will Chuck shun his chum?

> Which shell did his dad mash with a ring?

For the corresponding sounds on the CD, listen to Track 25 for *sh*, Track 26 for *ch*, Track 27 for *wh*, Track 28 for *th*, and Track 29 for *~~th~~*.

Sounding seven digraphs

I call the seven consonant digraphs the basic ones. I'm hinting that more may come, but in this chapter I concentrate on the basics. Observe in the following instructions on sounding these digraphs that letters your child already knows as individual sounds change into new sounds when joined.

Chugging along with ch and sh

The *ch* and *sh* sounds are the easiest of the bunch. With *ch*, you can take advantage of the ruler and use it to show your child what an in*ch* is and how to mark off an in*ch*. You can also try the "chug-a-chug-choo-choo" method of reinforcing what a digraph is. Take your hands and rotate them like turning wheels, saying, *ch, ch, ch* as you make the train sound. You can even sing the "Little Red Caboose" song.

Older children may know some exceptions to the basic *ch* sound that I present here and point them out to you. "What about *chute, ache,* and *Christmas*?" they may ask. These words contain the letters *ch,* but they don't follow the basic *ch* sound. Explain that the English language is complicated, and point out to the children how smart they are for noticing the different ways that *ch* is used.

A word about line markers

In the phonological process of sounding out words, a child can get offline, lose his place, and have to double back. This can break his concentration and tear his fluency to shreds. If the child's finger isn't helping him locate words on the page, I recommend temporarily using a line marker such as a ruler or strip of cardboard. A line marker can really help him to stay on track and concentrate on developing smooth reading skills. It also discourages young readers from looking around the page for contextual clues such as pictures — a very bad habit that can slow down advances in reading skill. I suggest using a line marker that has no designs on it, that covers the width of the page, and is a pleasant color. You can make one or buy one. In time, as your child learns to read, you can discard the line marker.

The *sh* sound is also simple. Beside the keyword *ship*, you can put your finger on your lips and say *shhh!*

Whipping through wh

The diagraph *wh* is correctly said in a "blowy" manner. Don't be confused by the fact that the *wh* digraph comes off as a *hw* sound. Tell your child to make the sound for the consonant digraph *wh* as if he were blowing on a pinwheel. You can also tear off a piece of tissue and tell him to put it on the top of his hand and blow it off to make the *hw* sound. Say, "That's the sound for *wh*" as the tissue falls to the floor. (Some common *wh* words are nonphonetic. These words include *who, whom,* and *whose,* which have a silent *w.* I get to those miscreants later.)

Twice the fun with th and th

Th has two distinct basic sounds — voiced and voiceless. To make both sounds, you start by placing the lips and tongue in the same position. However, the sounds originate in different places:

- ✔ **Voiced th sound:** The voiced *th* sound originates in the throat. You can hear it in *that* and *there.* If your child says these words correctly, he can feel their vibration by placing his fingers lightly on his throat. Show your child the line through the *th* in the flashcard that indicates a voiced *th* sound and tell your child to think of this line as his tongue. When he makes the *th* sound, say, "Tickle your tongue." This is a kinesthetic tool to distinguish between the two sounds of *th.* A ask him to do the exercise because it actually does tickle his tongue.

✔ **Voiceless *th* sound:** The voiceless *th* sound originates in the tongue and teeth, as in the words *thud* and *think*. If your child is typical and has lazy throat muscles and lazy lips, he may need to practice the voiced *th* until he feels a very slight vibration. Children accustomed to speaking English say these sounds by ear and seldom have difficulty. However, people who are new to speaking English may have trouble making the voiceless *th* sound.

Reinforcing consonant digraph sounds

Are you ready for a round of skill-boosting activities? Your first encounter is with word strips. If you need to learn what they are and how to organize them, you can refer to Chapter 2. Is your child up to unscrambling words, marking with the breve, and filling in the blanks? Make way for the tongue twister and poetry readings. Skills are seriously sharpened with these reinforcement tools.

Activity: Markings with the Breve

Preparation: You need paper, pencil, and the following word list. You may copy these words or rewrite the exercise for your child.

To play: Have your child place the breve (˘) over the short vowels in the following words. Write the marked vowel on the line next to the word.

Example: thĭs ĭ

    1. chill _____

    2. rich _____

    3. with _____

    4. thin _____

    5. song _____

Answer Key: 1. chĭll ĭ 2. rĭch ĭ 3. wĭth ĭ 4. thĭn ă 5. sŏng ŏ

Activity: Tongue Twisters Poems, and Ditties

To play: Following are some ditties to help your child master the consonant sounds he has just learned. Ask your child to read these and point out the consonant digraphs.

Blue

One blue shoe

One blue hat.

I like blue,

But not on a cat.

Answer Key: <u>bl</u>ue

When you ask your child to read the previous poem, please note that the word *blue* is a common word in books for beginning readers. He needs to know it as a sight word at this juncture.

Sing Sing

Sing, Sing, what shall I sing?

Cat's run away with the pudding-string!

Do, do, what shall I do?

The cat has bitten it quite in two.

Answer Key: <u>sh</u>all

Blending Endings

An *end blend* is a blend of two consonants at the end of a word. *Last, band,* and *task* are examples of end blends. In an end blend, the basic sounds of the consonants involved don't change. Even though the consonants are placed together, the sound made by each consonant can be distinctly heard. For example, in the word *last,* you can hear both the *s* and the *t* sounds. Your child merely blends the familiar consonant sounds as one, and slides them together with the vowel. Reading end blends seems easy, but it still requires practice.

Understanding the difference between end blends and digraphs

As I explain earlier in this chapter (see "Delving into Digraphs"), two consonants joined together to make one sound is called a digraph. Examples of digraphs include *ch, sh, th,* and *wh.* A consonant digraph makes a completely new sound from two consonants. An end blend, by contrast, doesn't create a single new sound because the letters maintain their individual sounds.

A word alert is in order here: The end blends *fact, bulk,* and *jinx* are difficult words for many children to pronounce. Pay close attention to how your child pronounces his words, especially if he has articulation weaknesses. Those weaknesses need to be corrected.

Lots of words are often difficult to pronounce. Take, for example, the word *ask.* Some kids will say *ax* rather than *ask.* It's also common to hear people say *sall* or *sor* for *saw.*

Discovering end blends

So many words, so little time! Do you know how many short-vowel consonant-blend words there are? Hundreds and hundreds! And your child will be able to spell and read all of them after completing these blending lessons.

To start, have your child practice the consonant blends by reading the words from the following list:

act	bank	cent	fast
adz	bask	damp	felt
ant	belt	dent	fend
apt	bend	desk	hand
ask	bent	elf	held
asp	best	elm	helm
band	camp	end	help
bang	can't	fact	hemp

honk	mink	rant	send
hung	nest	rapt	sing
jest	next	rasp	sink
kept	pact	rend	song
lamp	pant	rent	sunk
land	past	rest	tank
last	pelt	ring	thing
left	pest	rink	vamp
lent	pink	tact	vast
mask	quest	task	wing
mast	ramp	sand	zing
melt	rang	self	
mend	rank		

For practice, have your child read these sentences silently first and then say them out loud:

Will a man send him a desk and a lamp?

Don left and kept his red belt.

Bess sent him a gift at camp.

Practicing what you've learned is always a good idea. The more you apply your newly found knowledge, the more adept you become. Making bookmark-style word strips pays off when your child reads columns of rhyming words fluently.

Activity: Finding the End Blend

Preparation: You need paper, pencil, and the following exercise. You may copy these sentences or rewrite the exercise for your child.

To play: Read each of the following sentences. Choose the two end blends in the sentence, and write the words on the lines.

Example: Brant began to look for his mask. <u>Brant</u> and <u>mask</u>

1. Jim went to check on his plot of land. _____ and _____

2. The lad did his best on his task. _____ and _____

3. Kent was at the helm when the ship sunk. _____
   and _____

4. I can't see past the bus. _____ and _____

5. An ant is such a pest at a picnic. _____ and _____

Answer Key: 1. went, land 2. best, task 3. Kent, helm 4. can't, past 5. ant, pest

Activity: Word Strips: End Blends

Preparation: Write the following words on strips of precut cardstock paper (they may be used for bookmarks). Each set of words in this activity gets its own strip. Remember that you can cut your word strips to any length you want. Chapter 2 explains how to teach with and create word strips.

To play: Sit next to your child and read the following word strips. Some of the word strips may contain words that haven't been introduced yet. That's okay because word strips are rhyming adventures.

dust, crust, bust, just, lust, must, rust, gust

bent, dent, vent, lent, Kent, tent, sent, went, rent

band, sand, hand, land

Beginning Blendings

After a child catches on to the end blends, he can look to the beginning of words for *initial blends*. Most children find initial blends more difficult than end blends. The *r* blends are particularly hard because you have to sound them smoothly as well as rapidly.

Here are a couple of techniques for introducing initial blends:

✔ Write *dra, dre, dri, dro,* and *dru* in a column on a whiteboard or piece of paper. Using the short-vowel sounds, connect the sounds you wrote to different letters and have your child follow along as you pronounce the new sounds. For example, write the letters *fra* and have your child pronounce these words as you alter the final letter: *fre, fri, fro,* and *fru*.

✔ Go from the known to the unknown. Write *ra,* and under it, *dra*. Write *re,* and under it, *dre*. Write *ri,* and under it, *dri*. Write *ro,* and under it, *dro*. And finally, write *ru,* and under it, *dru*. You pronounce the top combination and then the lower one as your child repeats what you say.

✔ Use flashcards. Displaying the flashcards as rapidly as your child can read the "words" makes for a great workout. Make a list of as many combinations as you can think of and put them on flashcards. Each card gets an individual blend. For example, some good blends are *scra, scri, scro, scru; spla, splu, spli, splo, sple;* and *stra, stri, stro, stru, stre.* These blends are really challenging. Be careful not to make blends of nonexistent combinations.

Uncovering beginning blends

Have your child practice beginning blends by reading the words in the following list. Make sure that he blends the consonant sounds smoothly:

brag	drag	grand	prop
bran	dram	grid	scrap
brass	dress	grill	scrub
brat	drill	grim	scruff
bred	drip	grin	sprig
brig	drop	grip	stress
brim	Fred	grit	strip
crab	fret	gruff	struck
crack	frill	pram	strut
crag	frock	press	track
crib	frog	prick	trap
crock	from	prig	trim
crop	frost	prim	trod
drab	grab	prod	truck

Have your child read these sentences for practice:

Will mom trim and press a dress?

A truck struck a fat frog.

Will Rick grab it from its nest?

Most initial blends contain the letter *r, l,* or *s,* as in *pra, fla,* and *sma.* Coach your child to say the blend and the vowel so smoothly that there's no break between the letters. For example, correct your child if he says *buh-rim* or *buh-red* rather than *brim* or *bred.* After your child develops the correct technique, he'll slide the sounds together without any difficulty.

Mastering initial blends

Practicing the initial blends is a good idea because they're harder to read than the others. Finding them within several words enhances the development of composition skills. Word strips are excellent for rhyming and reading.

Activity: Finding Initial Blends

Preparation: You need paper, pencil, and this exercise. You may copy these sentences or rewrite the exercise for your child.

To play: Read the following sentences. Choose the correct initial blend word from the three words on the right. Circle the word and then print it in the line.

1. The _____ sat on a pad in the pond. (fend, frog, log)

2. The little lass took a nap in the _____. (cat, lull, crib)

3. Pam had a rip in her blue _____. (dress, dog, red)

4. Do not _____ the pop, Jack. (spin, spill, fix)

5. Pat had a big _____ on his leg. (bump, gap, bond)

Answer Key: 1. frog 2. crib 3. dress 4. spill 5. bump

Activity: Word Strips: Initial Blends

Preparation: Turn the following lists into word strips. Chapter 2 explains how to teach with and create word strips.

To play: Sit next to your child and read the following word strips:

> drip, grip, jip, quip, lip, slip, trip, whip, snip, flip, blip, nip, pip, rip, tip, yip, zip, dip
>
> bog, fog, cog, dog, frog, grog, hog, jog, log, smog
>
> scrap, trap, strap, flap, gap, yap, lap, slap, clap, wrap, pap

Using word strips puts rhyming words into action by injecting word families into the context of exercises in spelling and reading. If a child has a weakness in sliding sounds together to make words, it's a wonderful means for improvement.

Activity: A Bag of Bran

To play: Read this story to practice beginning blends. See whether your child can pick out all the words that have beginning blends.

> Fred and Sam went to the bin to get some bran. The bag of bran had grit on it. Sam was mad as it was for Mom and Dad. Fred was grim and had to slap the grub and grit from the bag. Sam got a scrub rag and got the dust off. The task did end and the lads felt well.

Answer Key: Fred, bran, grit, grim, slap, grub, from, scrub

Activity: Word Strips: All sorts of consonant blends

Preparation: Turn the following lists into word strips (Chapter 2 explains how to teach with and create word strips).

To play: Sit next to your child and read the following word strips:

> shut, but, rut, cut, gut, hut, jut, mutt, nut, putt
>
> chum, bum, rum, hum, drum, plum, sum, mum, slum, yum
>
> wham, bam, cam, dam, dram, cram, glam, gram, ham, sham, jam, slam, lam, Pam, mam, pram, ram, tam, swam, yam, tram
>
> thump, bump, clump, dump, frump, grump, lump, mump, pump, plump, rump, trump, slump, jump
>
> bing, cling, fling, ding, king, sling, sting, ping, ring, sing, wing, ting, zing, string, swing
>
> stank, bank, crank, dank, Frank, drank, Hank, lank, plank, prank, swank, tank, rank, yank
>
> cash, rash, bash, dash, gash, mash, lash, splash, stash, smash, hash
>
> inch, cinch, finch, clinch, winch
>
> bang, fang, gang, hang, pang, rang, tang

Examining Some Blending Quirks

As always, the English language has some quirks. I examine two in this section that warrant some special attention.

I first introduce the *ck* in Chapter 4, with the keyword *clock*. Its quirkiness consists of the fact that the *k* sound has three different spellings — *k, c,* and *ck*. The *tch* is another real curve ball, and you read all about it in this section.

Checking on the ck

The consonant digraph *ck* shows up at the end of most short-vowel words ending in the *k* sound. Amid all this talk about consonant digraphs, I'll let you in on a little secret: Your child learned the *ck* digraph when he learned the sound of hard *c*. I didn't call the hard *c* a digraph at the time, but *ck* fits the bill for a digraph; it comprises two letters that have one sound.

Decoding *ck* words is a cinch, but use the following list for practice anyway. By now you will have determined how strong or weak your child's decoding ability is. The list presents a way to sharpen your child's ears for hearing the sounds in a word and writing those sounds on paper. After short vowels, make sure that your child writes *ck* for the sound of *k*.

back	duck	peck	snack
beck	flock	pick	sock
black	frock	pluck	stack
block	hack	prick	stick
brick	jack	quack	struck
check	kick	quick	suck
chick	lack	rack	tack
chuck	lick	rock	thick
click	lock	sack	track
clock	luck	sick	trick
cock	mock	slack	truck
crack	muck	smack	tuck
deck	neck	smock	wick
dock	pack		

Have your child read these sentences for practice:

Can Fred pick up the snack from his truck?

Has the man struck his duck with a stick?

Can the hen peck and prick at his neck?

Activity: Filling in the Blanks

Preparation: You need paper, pencil, and the following activity. You may copy these sentences or rewrite the exercise for your child.

To play: Read the following sentences. Choose words from the word bank to correctly complete the sentences.

Word bank: back, clock, deck, rock, stack, truck

1. The rags are in a _____.
2. The kids went to sun on the _____.
3. Frank set the _____ for six.
4. Jan and Ron hid the _____ in the grass.
5. The yellow _____ has a bed in the _____.

Answer Key: 1. stack 2. deck 3. clock 4. rock 5. truck, back

Activity: Poems and Stories to Reinforce the ck Sound

To play: As you read the following, ask your child to shout when he hears a *ck (k)* sound at the end of a word. Be sure to let him try reading these items, too!

Jack Be Nimble

Jack be nimble

Jack be quick

Jack jump over

The candlestick.

Answer Key: Ja<u>ck</u>, qui<u>ck</u>, candlesti<u>ck</u>

The Ant and the Frog

Once an ant fell into a pond.

"Help me! I am lost in the pond," she said.

Next to the bank of the pond was a big branch that hung into the pond. There was a frog on this branch and he wanted to help the ant.

"Hang in there," he said. "I will send one of my pads that I sit on. Get on it and it will help you."

The black ant sat on the pad and she did land on the bank of the pond. She said, "Thank you for this, my chum!"

After that the frog was by the pond. He wanted to be in the sun.

There was a man that wanted to nab the frog with his yellow net and get him in a sack. But the ant was on a stick next to the pond and ran fast to help the frog.

The ant bit the man in the leg, and he did yell, "You got me! You bit me!"

Then the frog took one look at the man and said, "Oh my! I must scram!" He left fast and was glad that the man did not nab him.

The frog went back to thank the black ant for her help. She said, "This is what a pal is for."

Answer Key: bla<u>ck</u>, sa<u>ck</u>, sti<u>ck</u>, ba<u>ck</u>

To enhance the previous lesson, you can ask your child the following questions to find out how well he comprehended the story, "The Ant and the Frog." Comprehension always involves asking who, what, when, where, why, and how.

1. Who are the three characters in the story?
2. Where does this story take place?
3. What time of day do you think it was?
4. What does a pond look like?
5. What color did you picture the pad?
6. How did the pad get from the frog to the ant?
7. Why did the ant need the pad?
8. Why did the frog want to bask in the sun?
9. Danger appeared in the form of . . . ?
10. Was there anyone to help the frog?
11. What did the black ant do?
12. A lesson from the story is . . . ?

Now is a good time to make flashcards of the following sight words: *me, be, by,* and *after.*

Introducing tch

Another quirky tidbit in the exploration of blends and digraphs is this: Immediately after short vowels, the *ch* digraph is spelled *tch*. Examples of words following the *tch* pattern include *batch, stretch,* and *hatch*. The sound is really a trigraph, not a digraph, because *tch* is three letters, not two. But who's counting?

Some words in the English language don't follow the *tch* pattern. Those words include *much, such, rich,* and *which*. In these words, the *ch* digraph follows a short vowel, but the digraph is spelled *ch*, not *tch*.

Read the words in the following list to practice words ending in *tch*:

batch	ditch	match	stitch
blotch	Dutch	pitch	stretch
botch	fetch	retch	switch
catch	hatch	scotch	thatch
clutch	hutch	sketch	twitch
crutch	ketch	splotch	

Have your child read these sentences silently and then say them out loud for practice.

Glenn fell in a ditch.

Frank can notch his belt.

Alf will sketch dogs.

Activity: A Sad Lad

Preparation: You need paper and pencil.

To play: Read the following story and then copy or rewrite it onto another piece of paper. Circle the words that contain a consonant digraph. Rewrite those words below the story.

My pal, Scott, was the lad with the brown crutch. Did you see him at the back of the class with some kids? He fell in a ditch last month and the front of his leg has a twist to it. The Doc got a look, set it, and Scott is still in shock. My mom said that if he has a good stretch he will get well fast. Scott said to her that he wants to pitch his crutch and not be sick. He will be sad until he can.

Answer Key: with, crutch, back, ditch, month, shock, stretch, pitch, crutch, sick

Activity: Tongue Twister

To play: Read the following to your child and ask him to pick out the *tch* and *ch* end sounds. Let him try to say the tongue twister, too.

Which watch did which witch wear and which witch wore which watch?

Answer Key: whi<u>ch</u>, wa<u>tch</u>, wi<u>tch</u>

Dealing With Vowels at the Start of Words

Chapter 4 introduces the consonant-vowel-consonant pattern. When a word or syllable has only one vowel, and that vowel comes at the beginning of the word, the vowel is usually short. It's the vowel-consonant pattern. Examples of this guidelines include the words *add, egg,* and *ill.*

To boil down these two patterns as they apply to short-vowel words or syllables:

- ✔ The short sound of *a, e, i, o,* and *u* shows itself by coming between two consonants in a syllable or a word.
- ✔ The short sound of *a, e, i, o,* and *u* shows itself by coming at the beginning of a word.

Use the following list to practice making the sounds that vowels make when they appear at the beginning of words:

add	ebb	if	on
am	Ed	ill	ox
an	egg	in	undid
and	elf	it	up
apt	elm	odd	upset
at	end	off	us

Have your child read the following sentences silently first and then say them out loud for practice:

If Al is ill, Mom will help.

Ed undid the thick string.

It is odd at the end.

Word associations trigger the memory and their usage comes in handy quite often. Picturing an elf is a cute little gimmick for remembering a short-vowel guideline, for example.

A word search is a clever tracking device. Tell your child that he's a word detective and he's going after short-vowel words that are hiding.

Activity: A Story to Reinforce the Vowel-Consonant Pattern

To play: Ask your child to read the following story and find the words with the vowel-consonant pattern.

Ann and Ed went into the shop to see Dad. He asked them to add up the cans of ham.

He said, "In my shop you can look at the odds and ends of cans and tell me if the ham in the cans is still fresh."

The two of them will see if Dad's stock is still fresh. They can do it as they can add. Ed can look on the end of the can to see it. He will tell Ann and she will get a pen and print it on the pad.

Ed said to Dad, "The cans are still fresh to sell, Dad."

He said, "Thanks, kids, you are a help to me."

It is fun to go to Dad's shop.

Answer Key: Ann, Ed, into, asked, add, up, in, at, odds, and, ends, of, if, is, if, it, as, on

Chapter 6

Pursuing Plurals and Compound Words

*I*n this chapter, you and your child embark on a very important adventure — how to make one into many. This chapter covers plurals, and it shows how you can form plural words by adding an *s* or *es* to short-vowel words. Because adding *es* to a short-vowel word adds an additional syllable to a word, this chapter also lightly touches on multisyllable words and the challenges that children face when they read these longer words. Finally, this chapter examines a special kind of multisyllable word, the compound word.

Exploring Plurals in Speech and Spelling

The word *plural* means more than one. Plurals can range anywhere from two cats to one million pennies. Of course, you already understand that plurals can be a low number or a very high number, but you may need to explain this idea to young children. By the time a child reaches age 5 or 6, she knows what "more than one" means, and that adding an *s* or *z* sound to a word is one way to make it plural.

How you pronounce the plural of a word depends on whether the word ends in a voiced or voiceless consonant.

- ✔ **Voiced consonants:** The vocal cords vibrate when you sound out a consonant at the end of the word, like *rag, dog, ham,* and *can.* You can determine this by placing your fingers on your throat as you speak the voiced sound. When you make these words plural, the *s* sounds like a *z.* For example, *rags, dogs, hams,* and *cans.*

- ✔ **Voiceless consonants:** The vocal cords are relaxed (they don't vibrate) when you sound out a consonant at the end of the word, like *bat, top, kick,* and *staff.* The sound is made by the tongue and lips, and when you make these words plural, the *s* sounds like an *s.* For example, *bats, tops, kicks,* and *staffs.* Examples of voiceless consonants are *t, p, k,* and *f.*

You can figure out whether a consonant is voiced or not by making a word plural with an *s* and listening to the sound that it makes. If you want to, you can place your fingers on your throat to feel the absence or presence of a vibration that indicates the sound.

Have your child practice saying the singular and plural words in the preceding bullets out loud, listening for the voiced and voiceless consonants and the difference in the *s* and *z* sounds.

After your child hears and understands the different sounds — *s* or *z* — that indicate a plural, you can introduce her to the mechanics of spelling plurals. You want your child to understand that the presence of the *s* or *z* sound indicates a plural noun, of course, but for spelling purposes, you also want her to know that she has to add *s* or *es* to a word to make it plural.

Pronouncing the *z* sound when necessary comes naturally, but you need to make sure your child doesn't spell plural words and singular, present-tense verbs with a *z.* For example, some kids tend to replace the *s* with a *z* in plurals when they're spelling. For example, for a word such as *dogs,* they may write *dogz* because that's how it sounds. Your focus as a parent must stay on the sounding factor as it relates to spelling and reading. Point out that some plurals make the *z* sound when you speak them aloud, but that the *z* is never used when spelling plurals.

The singular *s* in action words

Besides adding an *s* to a noun to form a plural, you also add an *s* to form a present-tense, third-person singular verb. For example, in the sentence "He wins," the *s* is added to the word *win.* Here's some excellent news for placing the *s* at the end of present-tense, third-person singular verbs: Verbs follow the same phonics guidelines as their noun buddies. For example, in forming the simple present-tense, third-person form of the verb *jump,* you have to add only an *s.* For the purpose of keeping it simple for a beginning reader, you can point out this guideline to your child: Add an *s* to form plurals and some present-tense verbs.

The Letter s Counts for a Lot

The letter *s* is one of the top four commonly used letters of the alphabet. That's why your first decoding lesson includes the letter *s*. It's such an easy sound when you first learn it. The other part of *s* that you have to learn is that it has another sound — the *z* sound.

Making plurals with *s* and *z* when you're talking is inherent in the English language. No dialectical nuances here! You always think about *s* as an *s* sound when you write it, because you said *s* when you first learned to talk. This is the chapter where you draw the distinction between the *s* and *z* sound of the letter *s*. It comes early in the game of phonics, but you get just a taste and deal with some short-vowel nouns and verbs that you're going to turn into plurals or present tense verbs. Chapter 17 refers to the *z* sound as well.

In the following list, every word has an *s* on the end. This list contains a mixture of nouns and verbs that follow the voiced and voiceless guideline (see the "Exploring Plurals in Speech and Spelling" section). Read the words in the list and tell your child that, although some words sound like they end in *z,* most words end in *s* when she starts spelling them:

banks	drills	logs	suns
bats	drips	nests	swims
bluffs	fits	nods	taps
bugs	gifts	pills	tents
cabs	grins	rags	tots
cans	grips	scraps	traps
chests	guns	sets	trucks
clicks	hams	skips	tubs
cots	jets	sleds	twins
crams	kills	sniffs	wigs
cups	kings	specks	wins
cuts	kits	spells	yells
dogs	legs	stabs	
drags	lips	strips	

Your child may need a hands-on demonstration in *s* and *z* before plunging into the previous list. If so, walk around the house with a pencil and paper and point to different objects, saying, for example: "five can*s*," "three pencil*s*," "two broom*s*," "four rug*s*," and so on. Write down the plurals, and show your child how you added an *s* to each noun. Ask your child which plurals end with the *s* sound and which end with the *z* sound.

After your child masters the words in the previous list, have her read the following sentences for practice. The goal is for her to be able to read the way she speaks, so you want her to read each sentence to herself and then say it out loud with expression, naturally speaking the words in the sentence.

> Glenn crams scraps in his sacks.
>
> Will dogs gulp at bugs?
>
> Meg strips the tents of gifts.

No word should ever be read in a sentence unless your child has learned it before. (That doesn't refer to any tandem reading or pleasure reading that you do with your child.) Even though this is a phonics lesson, some sight words are added to get the child reading. These sight words definitely need to be learned before meeting them in a sentence. Speaking from a phonics viewpoint, the words your child meets in sentences are composed primarily with words that your child can decode. Refer to Chapter 3 for more information. Reading smoothly and correctly is the goal.

Activity: Plural Poem

Preparation: Make a copy of the following poem or write it on a piece of paper. Your child also needs a pencil.

Sight words: come, they, their, little

To play: Help your child read the poem. Then have her circle the plural words.

> One green frog swims in the pond;
>
> Two little frogs grab a pad to get on.
>
> In the nest sit three little chicks;
>
> Chicks and big dogs do not mix.
>
> Four little lads look and then;
>
> See five eggs with a big fat hen.

Six wet asps slink on the grass;

Will they catch their bugs at last?

Seven dogs will jump and run;

When eight cats come and have some fun.

Nine little pups sit on the mat;

Ten fat rats will come to chat.

Answer Key: swims, frogs, chicks, Chicks, dogs, lads, eggs, asps, bugs, dogs, cats, pups, rats

Activity: Hot Cross Buns

To play: Read the following poem out loud with your child. Ask her to tell you which words that end with *s* make the *z* sound.

Hot cross buns!

Hot cross buns!

One a penny, two a penny,

Hot cross buns!

If ye have no daughters,

Give them to your sons.

One a penny, two a penny,

Hot cross buns!

Answer Key: buns, daughters, sons

Activity: Making a Plural Word Strip

Preparation: You need a strip of paper at least 6 inches long and 3 inches wide, a pencil, a list of words, and a sheet of paper.

To play:

1. **Using the 6-x-3-inch strip of paper, create a word strip with one of the following lists of words.**

   Chapter 2 explains how to create and teach with word strips.

2. **Sit next to your child and listen to her read the word strip to you.**

3. After she's comfortable reading the words, ask her to spell them out loud.

4. Finally, ask her to write each word on a sheet of paper.

Word strips:

> sits, hits, pits, flits, bits, grits, mitts, spits, fits, skits, slits, quits, sprits, scripts, wits

> rags, drags, snags, gags, hags, lags, brags, flags, nags, stags, tags, wags, swags

Activity: Making Plural Words

Preparation: Copy or rewrite the following list of words. Your child also needs a pencil.

To play: Have your child read the word aloud and print the *s* ending on the line. Then ask her whether the word ends in the *s* sound or the *z* sound.

> let__
>
> nut__
>
> fib__
>
> top__
>
> tan__
>
> hen__
>
> tat__
>
> bum__
>
> rat__
>
> bet__

Answer Key: Ends in the *s* sound: lets, nuts, tops, tats, rats, bets; Ends in the *z* sound: fibs, tans, hens, bums

Adding *es* Is an Easy Thing to Do

When you add *es* to make a word plural, you add another syllable to the word. For example, *inch* is a one-syllable word, but the word is two syllables long when it's plural: *inches*. Similarly, when the letters *es* are added to a present-tense verb such as *catch,* the verb gets another syllable: *catches.*

 Luckily, adding *es* to a noun or verb follows the same phonetic guideline: Words (nouns and verbs) ending in *s, x, z, ch,* and *sh* form the plural or singular third-person present tense by adding *es* rather than *s.* When the *es* is added, these words acquire another syllable.

 Looking at plural words can be tricky when the singular word ends in *e,* and you add an *s* to make it plural (*home* and *homes,* for example). Kids can be confused by this (thinking *es* has been added) when they start reading. This is addressed in Chapter 7, where I talk about the silent *e.*

In the following list, every word has an *es* on the end. This list contains a mixture of nouns and verbs. Have your child read the table for practice. Tell your child to notice that each of these words is two syllables long — the extra syllable was added with the letters *es:*

axes	fizzes	inches	splotches
blesses	flashes	jazzes	stresses
buzzes	flexes	Joshes	taxes
cashes	flushes	misses	threshes
catches	foxes	mixes	tosses
clutches	frizzes	munches	twitches
crosses	fusses	musses	vexes
crunches	glasses	razzes	waxes
drenches	gushes	sketches	whizzes
fezzes	hexes	smashes	wishes
fixes	hisses	splashes	

 Remind your child that words that end in *s, x, z, ch,* and *sh* use *es* on the end to make them plural. Ask her to point out these letters in the previous list.

After your child has mastered the words in the previous list, have her read the following sentences for practice. Ask her to read them silently to herself first, and then read them out loud with expression to you, naturally speaking the words in the sentence. The goal is for her to be able to read as she speaks.

Fred tosses and smashes six eggs.

Pat clutches and munches a crab.

Jim splashes and drenches his lamps.

Activity: Little Tommy Tittle Mouse

To play: Read the poem together and ask your child to pick out the *es* words. You can also show her what happens with *mouse* and *house* if you make these words plural.

Little Tommy Tittle Mouse

Lived in a little house;

He caught fishes

In other men's ditches.

Answer Key: fishes, ditches

Activity: Making Plurals With es

Preparation: Copy or rewrite the following list of words. Your child also needs a pencil.

To play: Ask your child to say these words out loud and then write the plurals by adding *es*.

fax____

lass____

ash____

batch____

bench____

boss____

box____

toss____

mess____

snitch____

pass____

stitch____

kiss____

rich____

punch____

pitch____

lunch____

latch____

mass____

match____

moss____

dish____

Activity: Joke

To play: Read the joke and discuss it with your child. Ask comprehension questions (who, what, where, when, why, how) and ask her to predict a possible outcome. Then have her find the plural words formed by adding *es*.

The children line up for lunch at Sunday school. On the table is a basket of apples. The pastor had made a note and put it in with the apples: "Take only one. God watches you."

At the other end of the table were big bunches of chocolate chip cookies on dishes. A child had written a note, "Take all you want. God is watching the apples."

Answer Key: watches, bunches, dishes

Decoding Multisyllable Words

The word *syllable* sounds kind of academic. Most adults know what a syllable is but find it difficult to explain syllables to children. Tell your child that syllables are the building blocks of words. Just as different blocks make a building when they are stacked together, different syllables make a word when they are put together. If you want to get more precise, here are two ways to describe a syllable:

✔ A syllable is a word or part of a word pronounced with a single, uninterrupted sounding of the voice. For example, the word *fantastic* has three syllables: fan-tas-tic.

✔ A syllable is a word or part of a word with one vowel sound. For example, the word *dig* has one vowel sound, the *i*, so it's a one-syllable word.

I can't emphasize enough how earthshakingly important it is for your child to understand what syllables are when it comes to decoding words. Being able to understand syllables separates the top-notch readers and spellers from the so-so readers and spellers. Following are some activities to help your child decode multisyllable words.

Compiling Compound Words

I want to introduce you to some short-vowel compound words. It's appropriate to place them at this juncture, because it enables your child to take a peek into a phonics lesson that seems hard, but in reality is quite simple. Because syllables have had their *merest introduction* in this chapter, it's easy for her to see the two short-vowel words become one new word. The formal definition is: A compound word is made when two words are joined to form a new word.

For beginners, compound words can be problematic. When a child meets her first compound word, she realizes right away that it's longer. You can explain to your child that two short words can become one long word so that she better understands what compound words are.

Most first-grade students can learn simple, two-syllable compound words in the first semester of reading. Their self-confidence gets a huge boost when they can decode these "big" words. And kids love to tell everyone that they know about compound words!

How did compound words such as *cannot, hilltop,* and *cobweb* originate? The words began as single words said together, and over time, they were hyphenated to form compound words. As these words came into common use, the hyphen was dropped, and they became compound words. For example, the two individual words *zig* and *zag* became the hyphenated *zig-zag,* and then finally the single word *zigzag.*

Compound words are always being added to the English language. For example, recent years have seen the addition of *online, download,* and *upload.*

Practicing with compound words

The following is a kid-friendly list of compound words. Notice all the short vowels. Some of these words may be a little old fashioned, but no matter. The idea is to get kids used to reading compound words.

backstop	clamshell	kickoff	pumpkin
bandstand	cobweb	kidnap	setup
blacktop	desktop	letup	shellfish
bobcat	dragnet	madman	sundeck
brushoff	gunshot	matchstick	tinsmith
cannot	handgrip	midship	tiptop
catnip	hilltop	offhand	within
chestnut	himself	padlock	zigzag
chopstick	itself	pigskin	

After your child masters the words in the previous list, have her read these sentences for practice. The goal is for her to be able to read as she speaks, so you want her to read each sentence to herself and then say it out loud with expression.

His desktop pad had a zigzag blotch on it.

Fred has the pigskin for the kickoff.

Will Nan padlock the dog within a box?

Introducing short-vowel compound words is the first incursion into two-syllable single words. Some words are so compounded that it can blow you away. An example is *antidisestablishmentarianism*. After you decode the longest word in the English language word, write it in your notebook and quiz your friends with your newfound trivia.

Activity: The Donkey and the Grasshopper

Preparation: Make flashcards of the sight words and drill with them lightly before your child reads the story. Have a tablet and pencil handy.

Sight words: could, some, beautiful, always, good

To play: Ask your child to read the story. After she's finished, help her pick out the compound words. Dictate the compound words to your child as she spells them on a printing tablet. (You may need to break down the grasshopper word for her.) Because this is an adapted fable, the parent may want to explain and discuss the moral of the story.

At sunset, the donkey could hear some grasshoppers chirp. He said, "I want to make beautiful music like that." He asked the grasshoppers what kind of food they eat to give them their beautiful voices.

"We live only on the dew that falls on the grasslands," the grasshoppers said.

"I have always munched on hay," the donkey said, "but I will go uphill and try the dew."

By the next sunset, the donkey said, "I must be a nitwit! My voice is nothing next to the grasshoppers'. No matter how much dew I take, I am still not good. What helps them to sing does not a thing for me. I will go back to munch some bunches of hay."

Answer Key: sunset, grasshoppers, grasslands, uphill, nitwit

Looking at advanced compound words

The compound words in the following list are especially challenging. None are from previous lessons, and some may be out of your child's vocabulary range. But see whether she can read them, and be helpful when she gets stuck. If your child succeeds in decoding these words, she deserves a reward!

backdrop	crackup	fatback	handcuff
backtrack	crankshaft	flagship	handpick
backup	crosscut	flagstaff	handspring
bedrock	cutback	flatfish	hangdog
bellhop	cutoff	flintlock	hangman
buckshot	cutup	grassland	hemstitch
catfish	dogfish	halfback	henpeck
checkup	dogtrot	hamstring	hopscotch
claptrap	duckpin	handbag	hotbed
crabgrass	eggnog	handbill	hotshot
crackpot	eggplant	handclasp	humpback

hunchback	nitwit	sendoff	sunset
inkblot	nutmeg	setback	thickset
instep	nutshell	sickbed	thumbtack
invest	onset	slapstick	tomcat
jackpot	pickax	slingshot	tossup
kickback	pickup	slipshod	uphill
kingpin	popgun	snapshot	upset
kinship	quicksand	spendthrift	upswing
liftoff	ragtag	standstill	withstand
lipstick	redcap	standup	
logjam	sackcloth	stopgap	
muskrat	sandbox	sunfish	

Have your child read these sentences for practice. Ask her to point out each set of the two words that joined together:

Jack got into the pickup truck.

Clem was upset with his chum.

The jet began its liftoff.

Chapter 7

Making Long-Vowel Sounds

Long vowels play a major role in the words in the English language. This chapter discusses long and short vowels and shows you words that change from a short-vowel sound to a long-vowel sound with the simple addition of an *e*. Also, you see that when a word or syllable has more than one vowel, some vowels remain silent. And further, while *a, e, i, o,* and *u* are vowels, you discover that *y* and *w* can behave as vowels.

As always, this chapter has practical activities to help further develop your child's smooth reading and precise spelling skills.

Understanding the Long, the Short, and the Silent

In this chapter, I tell you about long-vowel sounds, which are the easiest to teach by far, because the vowel letter (*a, e, i, o,* or *u*) says its name. In *note*, for example, you can literally hear the letter *o.* In the word *mate*, you can hear the sound of a long *a.* And again in the word *site*, you can hear the letter say its name. This pattern repeats itself over and over again in the English language.

Now, stop a minute and think about the three words I just gave to show examples of long vowels: *note, mate,* and *site.* Imagine those words with no *e* at the end. Hey! It's like that *e* is magic or something! Add that silent *e* to the end of *not, mat,* and *sit,* and that one little letter changes both the sound and the meaning of the words. How cool is that?

Presenting the amazing magic e

You may not know it, but you've already seen plenty of "magic" *e* words in this book. It's also referred to as the silent *e*, and some even refer to it as Mrs. E (for reasons I don't understand). I like to call it the magic *e* because, well, it works like magic! Place the magic *e* at the end of a short-vowel word, and *abracadabra*, you get a long-vowel word.

For example, by placing the magic *e* at the end of *spit*, you turn that word into *spite*. And that's pretty powerful magic, too, because that one little letter completely changes both the sound and meaning of the word it's attached to.

When a word or syllable has only one vowel, in most instances you can expect it to be a short sound; but if the word or syllable has two vowels, you can usually count on the first vowel being long and the second one being silent. And that makes the magic *e* the strong, silent type!

As always with the English language, this guideline has exceptions. For example, the words *have, love,* and *give* all end with a silent *e,* but the first vowels are short.

Discovering the magic e at work

Now you get to see the magic *e* do its thing. In the following list, more words are transformed in meaning and short vowels change to long vowels. Notice the patterns in the words. Isn't it amazing that adding an *e* can change so much? Your vowel goes from short to long and the meaning changes.

Study the words in the following list with your child and see for yourselves how the addition of the *e* changes the meaning and sound of the words. Have your child practice by reading the words from the table.

bath, bathe	mop, mope	snip, snipe
cloth, clothe	quit, quite	thin, thine
cub, cube	scrap, scrape	tub, tube
cut, cute	sham, shame	twin, twine
grim, grime	shin, shine	us, use
grip, gripe	sit, site	whit, white

Have your child read these sentences silently first and then read them out loud. Point out the pattern of the short-vowel word (cvc, ccvc) and the long-vowel word (cvcv, vcv, ccvcv):

The twin will use the white twine for the gift.

Jane wants to shine her bike with the cloth.

Steve has a grim plan to bathe his dog.

Ask your child to recite the words in the following list. Make sure he sees and hears the cvcv (consonant-vowel-consonant-vowel) pattern as well. Focus on making sure that your child understands that the first vowel is long and the second vowel silent so that he can apply this guideline later:

bone	fine	nape	sore
care	fire	note	stove
code	fume	pare	take
cone	hire	pole	tale
cope	hole	poke	tone
cube	home	pore	tore
cure	hope	pure	tube
cute	joke	quote	tune
Dave	lake	rake	vine
dole	lame	robe	vote
dome	lobe	rode	woke
dote	Luke	rose	wore
doze	lure	rove	wove
dude	mole	sale	yoke
duke	mule	site	zone
dune	mute	sole	

Have your child read these sentences for practice:

Pete woke up in his own home.

Jane likes red and white roses.

Will Kate like the shape of the cape?

Activity: Waving the Magic e Wand

Preparation: You need paper and pencil.

To play: Write the following words in a column on a printing tablet or white-board: *fat, mat, rat, cap, pan, grip, hid, at,* and *us.* Ask your child to wave his magic wand, add an *e* with his pencil, and see the new words he makes as he adds the magic *e.*

Activity: Sentence Completion

Preparation: You need paper and pencil.

To play: Read each sentence and the word bank to the right of each sentence. Circle the proper word to complete the sentence, and then write the word on the line.

1. Jake, do you like to ride a _____? (kite, bike, like)

2. Jane can tell you a funny _____. (joke, poke, woke)

3. Gene and Pam will fix the box with _____. (cape, tape, came)

4. The dog, Mike, began to look for a _____. (tone, rode, bone)

5. There was a fire in our _____. (home, dome, lone)

Answer Key: 1. bike 2. joke 3. tape 4. bone 5. home

For the corresponding sounds on the CD, listen to Track 30 for long *a,* Track 31 for long *e,* Track 32 for long *i,* Track 33 for long *o,* and Track 34 for long *u.*

Using the macron to mark long vowels

Lexicographers (word experts who write dictionaries) use diacritical marks (sometimes called accent marks) to distinguish between the long and short sounds that vowels make. These marks are called the *macron* and the *breve:*

- ✔ A *macron* (‾) is a straight line. When it appears over a vowel, the vowel makes a long sound.

- ✔ A *breve* (˘) is a segment of circle. When it appears over a vowel, the vowel makes a short sound.

Some people sometimes call these accent marks the bar and the rocker. Many newer dictionaries don't use the breve to spell words phonetically on the idea that any vowel without a mark over it always makes the short sound. In all dictionaries, long vowels are marked with macrons.

After your child understands what the breve and macron are, he can mark vowels appropriately as short or long. When he's marking the second vowel in a long vowel word, he can cross out the second vowel to indicate that it's silent (for example, hōpe). Doing this is a good foundation for his later dictionary work. He can pretend that he's a secret agent using a secret code to mark the vowels.

The breve is the mark for the short vowel (˘). The macron is the mark for the long vowel (¯). (Refer to the pronunciation key in Chapter 10.) The patterns for the vowels are generally *cvc, vc,* or *cvcv.*

Activity: Marking Vowels

Preparation: You need paper and pencil. Make a copy of the following exercise or rewrite it on a piece of paper.

To play: Place a breve or macron over the vowels in each word and cross out any silent vowels. Rewrite the word on the line next to it.

Example: make māke

1. hope _____
2. an _____
3. like _____
4. chest _____
5. up _____
6. home _____
7. shine _____
8. made _____
9. on _____
10. blend _____

Answer Key: 1. hōpe 2. ăn 3. līke 4. chĕst 5. ŭp 6. hōme 7. shīne 8. māde 9. ŏn 10. blĕnd

Activity: Crab Snack

Preparation: You need paper and pencil.

To play: Have your child read this poem. Have him circle the long-vowel words and write them on his printing tablet.

> On crab Sam and Pat did dine,
>
> After catching in a trap made of pine.
>
> It made a fine snack
>
> And they both tried to stack,
>
> On their plates just as much as they can.
>
> —Marilyn Johnson

Answer Key: dine, pine, fine, tried, plates

Looking at Vowel Digraphs

A vowel digraph contains two vowels that make one sound. For example, the *ai* in *sail* and the *oa* in *loaf* are vowel digraphs. Some people call them vowel pairs. In these vowel digraphs, the first vowel is long and the second vowel is silent. To help your child remember how to pronounce vowel digraphs, he can remember this: When two vowels go a-walking, the first vowel does the talking, and the second vowel is quiet.

With vowels, as with consonants, "di" means two and "graph" means letter.

Notice that in the following word list, the two vowels are always next to each other. You end up with a vvc, cvvc, or a cvv situation as in *aim, bail,* or *bee.* You don't have the vcv of *ate,* like you do in the first word list in this chapter.

Use the following word list to explore vowel digraphs with your child. See whether he can discover the "walking, talking" guideline for himself. Simply correct him in the way he sounds the words, and wait for him to pick up the guideline on his own:

aim	coal	doe	float
bail	coat	door	floor
bee	coax	fair	foam
boat	deep	feed	gain

goal	keep	oak	seek
goes	lain	pain	soak
groat	loaf	quail	stain
hail	loam	queer	tail
hoed	maid	raid	toes
jail	moan	road	vain
jeer	nail	roe	wait
Joe	need	sail	week

Activity: Reading and Writing Sentences

Preparation: You need paper and pencil.

To play: This parent-child activity may be a little difficult, so put your heads together when you read the following paragraphs. Fill in the blanks with the keywords provided.

Keywords: bait, boat, day, gale, line, rain, sail

Jake liked to _____ his boat on the green sea. He took his pal, Wade, with him to get the _____ in shape to sail.

They went to the _____ shop to get some tadpoles. Shane ran the shop and asked them to wait in _____. There were lots of pals in there, too.

It began to _____ that day. It came in drops and then it began to come in fast and on its side. The wind was strong, too.

If they went to sea that day, Shane said there will be a _____. It was not a good _____ to sail.

Answer Key: sail, boat, bait, line, rain, gale, day

Activity: Poems

Preparation: You need paper and pencil.

To play: Ask your child to read these two short poems and write down the long-vowel words in each one.

Rain I

Rain, rain, go to Spain,

And never come back again.

Rain II

Rain, rain, go away,

Come again another day;

Little Johnny wants to play

Rain, rain, go away.

Answer Key: rain, Spain, again, away, day, play

Taking On More Challenging Vowel Digraphs

Using some of the vowel digraphs for auditory (ear) training can be confusing because words containing vowel digraphs can sound the same but be spelled differently. For example, *meat* and *meet* are spelled differently but sound the same. Two words that sound the same but have different meanings are called *homonyms* (see the second word list in this section for several examples). Your child may need to memorize these vowel digraphs in order to spell them correctly.

In *r*-controlled words such as *care,* exaggerate the long sounds of the vowels when saying them for the first time. When your child repeats the words rapidly, the long *a* in *care* sounds very close to the short sound of *e.* What part of the country you live in influences the way you say certain words.

Ask your child to read the words in the following list, and ask him to apply the correct sounds to the vowels whether they're short or long. He should have no trouble at all.

clue	hear	smear	suit
cue	hue	Sue	year
dear	near	sued	
fear	shear		

Have your child read the sentences and take care that he reads fluently with good expression.

Sue, the flute is in a case near the door.

The black dog began to fear the big mare.

The salesman will show us his wares.

WARNING!

The next word list is for reading practice only. Don't use it for a spelling lesson. Being able to decode these words gives your child a sense of accomplishment and introduces him to the strange world of homonyms (words that are spelled differently but pronounced the same):

be, bee	meet, meat	soul, sole
beach, beech	pain, pane	stare, stair
beet, beat	pair, pare	sweet, suite
close, clothes	pale, pail	tale, tail
dear, deer	peek, peak	teem, team
fare, fair	plane, plain	throne, thrown
feet, feat	pore, poor	tide, tied
flee, flea	read, reed	toe, tow
flu, flue	reel, real	too, two, to
hale, hail	road, rode	waist, waste
hare, hair	roll, role	week, weak
heal, heel	row, roe	whale, wail
leek, leak	sale, sail	whole, hole
lone, loan	see, sea	wine, whine
made, maid	seem, seam	woe, whoa
male, mail	sees, seas	you, ewe
mane, main	soar, sore	

Turning w and y into Vowels

Most people learn in school that the vowels are *a, e, i, o, u,* and sometimes *y* and *w.* Well, that's not exactly accurate. To be more precise, the consonant *y* can sometimes behave as a vowel. And, believe it or not, so can the consonant *w!* But don't try to use either of these consonants as vowels on Wheel of Fortune! Their game show rules aren't as flexible as language guidelines.

In words such as *low* and *way,* the *w* and *y* appear as silent vowels. The strength of *y* and *w* lies in their silence. By their presence and their silence, the first vowel becomes long.

introduce you and your child to the *w* and *y* vowel, see the following word
Have your child read the words in the list, and then show him how the
sence of these letters creates a long vowel sound:

bow	play	slay	throw
day	pray	slow	tray
flow	Ray	snow	tow
know	row	stay	way
May	say	stow	
mow	show		

Have your child read these sentences for practice:

She set the tray on the low bench.

Mom, can I play with Steve?

Row the old boat with your oars.

Ending Words with Long Vowels

What happens when long vowels appear at the end of words? Here's a little
gem for you to contemplate: When a word or syllable has only one vowel and
that vowel comes at the end, the vowel is usually long.

Have your child read the words with vowels at the end in the next word list.
Tell your child that the *y* at the end of these words is used as a vowel and represents the long sound of *i*, as in *my*. These words are fairly easy for kids to
read, but harder for them to spell.

Oh, I almost forgot: Exception alert! For the sake of simplicity, the *y*-ending
words in the following word list all make the long *i* sound at the end (not to
be confused with the Long Island Sound which is an estuary — where fresh
and saltwater mix — near Hoboken). You may want to mention to your child
that not all *y*-ending words end with the long *i* sound. Rascally exceptions
include the word *lazy*, where the *y* at the end sounds like a long *e*.

be	go	she	thy
by	he	shy	we
cry	hi	sky	why
dry	me	so	ye
fly	my	spy	
fry	no		

Have your child practice these sentences using long vowels.

We came to fry an egg.

Did he go to see the white duck?

My dad paid a dime for the kite.

He got in the dry, brown hole.

Why does the dog like the bones?

The fire is low in the sky.

Why does he have tears on his cheeks?

By lunch Pete was fine with the plans.

She is to keep the shy pup.

Joe goes here to wade with me.

The gray twig will float to dry land.

The red cloak was clean.

Chapter 8

Presenting Diverse Vowel Sounds of a, o, and u

*O*f the many sounds you explore in phonics, this chapter presents the most diverse sounds. This chapter sounds a bit like a rain forest with all the animals chirping or crowing or growling. Here I present the *third sound* of the letters *a, o,* and *u.*

Third sounds can be spelled in many different ways. Words that contain third sounds are often taught collectively as "nonphonetic." This chapter helps your child recognize when the third sounds of the letters *a, o,* or *u* appear in words and how to pronounce them correctly.

Part of the fun of this chapter is recognizing sounds that are spelled oddly. Words like *shoe* and *zoom* and *bush* and *crook* have the same vowel sound, although you wouldn't know it from looking at them. Being able to recognize and pronounce these third vowel sounds will definitely raise your child's level of reading proficiency. Refer to the vowel chart in Chapter 2.

Saying ä before u, w, r, ll, and lt

When the letter *a* is followed by *u, w, r, ll,* or *lt* in the same syllable, it usually has the third sound of *a,* or *ä.* This *ä* sound is heard in the words *haul, raw, car, call, salt,* and *squall.* The third *a* makes the *aw* sound. The sound with its particular consonants and vowel can be daunting, but when your child sounds out the words, he hears the *aw* sound, and after you teach your child the sound, you can apply it to the various groupings of words that have it.

Some phonics experts agree that whenever you use the *r* with a vowel, the *r* sound has a great influence over the vowel preceding it. Most experts say that the American *r* is a very bossy letter! When it follows a vowel you really can hear the *r* sound. However, people in Boston say, "Pahk the cah," people in Detroit say, "Parrk the carr," and still other people say "Park the car." Accents and regional dialect dictate the sounds of many words. The standard presented in this book uses the sound of *är* similar to saying the letter *r*.

The vowel guidelines, mentioned throughout this book, cover roughly 75 percent of all vowel sounds. Appendix A outlines some basic guidelines, but to spare you a trip to that appendix, here's an overview of the guidelines:

- When a word or syllable has only one vowel, and the vowel comes between two consonants, the vowel is usually short.

- When a word or syllable has only one vowel, and that vowel comes at the beginning of the word, the vowel is usually short.

- When a word or syllable has only one vowel, and that vowel comes at the end of the word, the vowel is usually long.

- When the letter *a* is followed by *u, w, r, ll,* or *lt* in the same syllable, it usually has the third sound of *a*, or *ä*.

Teaching ä: The /aw/ sound

In order to teach the third sound of *a*, or *ä*, you have to distinguish between it and the two other sounds for the letter *a*:

- The first sound of *a* is the short *ă*, as heard in the word *apple*.

- The second sound of *a* is the long *ā*, as heard in the word *ate*.

- The third sound of *a* makes the *ä* sound, as heard in the word *father*.

This sentence includes all three letter *a* sounds: *His fäther āte the ăpples.* (For more information about short *a* vowel sounds, see Chapter 4; for more about long *a* vowel sounds, see Chapter 7.)

To help your child understand the third sound of *a*, be sure to distinguish between the short *o* (as in *ostrich*) and the third sound of *a* (as in *all*). Facing your child, urge him to watch your lips. Then exaggerating each sound, say, "ŏ, ostrich, ŏ" and "ä, all, ä." Practice saying this phrase until your child can distinguish between the short *o* and *ä*.

For the corresponding sound on the CD, listen to Track 35 for *ä*.

Examining the umlaut

The umlaut (¨), a diacritical mark, consists of a pair of dots placed over a letter. An umlaut over an *a* (ä) makes the /aw/ sound in *au, aw, all, alt* — the sound you hear in the word *cause*. The umlaut commonly appears in the German language. Linguists borrowed it from German to indicate how to pronounce the /aw/ sound.

The third sound of *ä* is an umlauted vowel, as in *bar*. Some dictionaries still use the umlaut over the *ä* to describe the /aw/ sound, as I do in this book. It serves very well as a diacritical mark for phonics.

Putting ä to good use

Look at the vowel chart in Chapter 2 and notice the third sound header. See **a³** there? You can tell your child that it's the third sound of *a*, and it's the *a* with an umlaut (ä).

You may notice that I describe and use the *ä* sound three different ways. I use them interchangeably and they all refer to the /aw/ sound that presents itself in the *au, aw, ar, all, alt* words in the following word list.

As you look at the following word list, ask your child to say the *aw* sound before she starts. In general, children don't have a problem with this sound. You can also ask her to spell some of the patterns she sees in the list:

ball	farm	malt	small
bark	fault	Maud	squall
call	flaw	part	stall
car	fraud	Paul	starch
cause	halt	pause	start
clause	hard	pawn	taunt
crawl	haul	raw	vault
daunt	haunt	salt	wall
dawn	jaunt	saw	Walt
drawl	jaw	scar	yarn
drawn	lark	scrawl	yaw
garb	launch	shark	yawn
gauze	law	sharp	
fall	lawn		

Now have your child practice these sentences.

The ball of dark yarn is small.

Paul had a scar on his jaw from the fall.

He saw the sharp pause near the launch.

Activity: Completing the Sentence with the Third Sound of A

Preparation: You need pencil and paper.

To play: Read the following sentences. Choose the word that correctly completes the sentence from the word bank after each sentence. Write the word you choose on the line provided.

1. Dan went to swing at the _____. (park, pack, peck)

2. Stan and Jane saw a big _____ in the sky. (scar, star, soar)

3. After the war, Don had a scar on his _____. (chap, coat, arm)

4. Paul began to throw the small blue _____. (ball, barn, scale)

5. He asks his mom if he can play from _____ to dusk. (Don, dawn, sun)

6. Dad had to _____ up the car before work. (heat, warm, wing)

7. Baby Jake began to _____ at bedtime. (year, eat, yawn)

8. They gave the lead _____ of the play to Shawn. (paint, part, past)

9. The _____ of the leak was a bad patch. (fault, flow, farm)

10. The _____ swam in the deep to look for fish to eat. (mole, shark, shack)

Answer Key: 1. park 2. star 3. arm 4. ball 5. dawn 6. warm 7. yawn 8. part 9. fault 10. shark

Activity: Word Strips: ä

Preparation: You need pencil and paper.

To play: Sit next to your child, and read the following word strips (Chapter 2 explains how to teach with and create word strips):

are, bar, car, far, gar, jar, mar, par, star, tar, war, scar, char

part, Bart, art, dart, mart, start, tart, wart, chart

ball, call, fall, gall, hall, mall, pall, tall, wall, small, squall, thrall, stall

draw, jaw, claw, straw, flaw, paw, raw, saw, law, thaw

paunch, launch, staunch

taunt, daunt, jaunt, flaunt

bark, dark, stark, hark, lark, mark, park, shark, spark

yarn, barn, darn, warn

salt, halt, malt, paltry

Activity: Tongue Twister

To play: Read the following tongue twister with your child. Besides having fun, it's a great exercise for smooth reading and practicing the /aw/ sound.

Mr. See and His Saw

Sam Soar owned a seesaw. Now, Shawn See's saw sawed Soar's seesaw, before Sam Soar saw Shawn See. That made Soar mad. Had Soar seen See's saw before See sawed Soar's seesaw, See's saw would not have sawed Soar's seesaw. So, See's saw sawed Soar's seesaw. But it was sad to see Soar so mad just because See's saw sawed Soar's seesaw.

Activity: Poems

To play: Read the following poems to your child. After discussing how silly the poems are, ask her which words sounded like the /aw/ sound. Ask her to spell the words out loud.

There was a young lady whose chin

Resembled the point of a pin;

So she had it made sharp,

And purchased a harp,

And played several tunes with her chin.

—Edward Lear

Answer Key: sharp, harp

The North Wind Doth Blow

The north wind doth blow,

And we shall have snow,

And what will poor robin do then,

Poor thing?

He'll sit in a barn,

And keep himself warm,

And hide his head under his wing,

Poor thing.

—Mother Goose

Answer Key: barn, warm

Jerry Hall

Jerry Hall, he was so small,

A rat could eat him, hat and all.

—Mother Goose

Answer Key: Hall, small, all

Activity: Joke

Preparation: You need a dictionary.

To play: Read the joke with your child and find the word with the third sound of *ä*. Then go find out what an aardvark is and what it looks like.

Knock, knock!

Who's there?

Aardvark.

Aardvark who?

Aardvark a million miles, for one of your smiles.

Answer Key: Aardvark

Studying the Third Sounds of o and u

The letter *ä* isn't the only letter that makes a third sound — the letters *o* and *u* have a third sound, too. You can hear the third sound of the letter *o* in the word *move;* you can hear the third sound of the letter *u* in the word *bush.* What appears in this section is an organization of tons of words under the banner of the third sound of *o* and *u.*

It's a confusing bit of phonology. The words are mostly easy and common; it's the diacritical marks and the cross-descriptions of the *o* and *u* in words and sounds that get you crazy with confusion. Here's some background information that you may find useful:

✔ The vowels *a, o,* and *u* have three sounds. They're organized and systematized on the vowel chart in Chapter 2. Phonics expert Monica Foltzer thought that because the English language has so many words with the *a* (ä) sound as in *all,* the *o* (oo) sound as in *too,* and the *u* (u̇) sound as in *put,* she would classify as many as she could and place them into third a^3, o^3, and u^3 sounds.

✔ Webster's uses the long *oo* as in *too* and the short *oo* as in *put* for their phonetic spelling. The Thorndike and similar dictionaries use the two dot u (ü) for *too,* and one dot u (u̇) for *put.* School text glossaries use one or the other, so teaching these sounds originally as the third sounds of *o* and *u* gives you a practical bridge to link the two types of diacritical marks.

Long *o,* as in too, can be written as ōō, ü, and o^3.

The first column of Table 8-1 lists words that make the third sound of *o;* the second and third column list words that make the third sound of *u.* The words in column three follow no guideline and are partially nonphonetic words. Have your child read these words, making sure that she pronounces the third sound of *o* and *u* as necessary. Make flashcards for the most common words if they cause difficulty for your child, but don't worry about the uncommon words.

The letters in the table that are crossed out are "silent" letters, so they don't add any sounds to those words.

Table 8-1	The Third Sounds of o and u	
Third Sound of o	*Third Sound of u*	*Third Sound of u, Partially Nonphonetic*
do	put	sho̶u̶ld
to	push	b<u>u</u>ll<u>e</u>t

(continued)

Table 8-1 *(continued)*

Third Sound of o	Third Sound of u	Third Sound of u, Partially Nonphonetic
lose	pull	b<u>u</u>sh<u>e</u>l
move	bush	p<u>u</u>sh<u>i</u>n<u>g</u>
~~w~~ho	puss	p<u>u</u>lp<u>i</u>t
shoe	bull<u>y</u>	p<u>u</u>ll<u>e</u>t
t~~w~~o	full	b<u>u</u>llfr<u>o</u>g
~~w~~hom	bull	p<u>u</u>dd<u>i</u>n<u>g</u>

Have your child practice by reading these sentences.

> Who will lose the ball?
>
> Do Walt and I push and pull?
>
> Whom did she see with a shoe?

Pay special attention to the word *should* in Table 8-1. The *-ould* words can be problematic because of their unusual spelling. Make a separate flashcard with these words: *would, could,* and *should.* They're common words and easy to sight. Learning them now puts your child ahead of the game.

Mixing the third sounds of o

Throwing you another curve ball, the words in next list fit so well with *o,* because they say the same sound (the third sound of *o*). Ask your child to read these easy and fun words, which say the ōō sound:

boom	fool	pool	sloop
boot	hoop	roof	soon
broom	loop	room	spoon
cool	loose	root	stool
coop	moon	school	tool
drool	noon	scoop	toot
food	ooze	shoot	zoom

Now have your child practice by reading these sentences:

Joe will scoop a spoon of food.

Little Scott will zoom his cars on the rug.

Dad will loop his bootstrap.

For the corresponding sound on the CD, listen to Track 36 for ōō.

Activity: Word Strips: Words with the Third Sound of *o*

Preparation: You need paper and pencil.

To play: Sit next to your child and read the following word strips (Chapter 2 explains how to teach with and create word strips):

boo, coo, moo, too, woo, shoo, zoo

who, do, to, two

boom, broom, groom, bloom, doom, loom, room, zoom, gloom

proof, roof, hoof, spoof

shoot, boot, root, hoot, loot, coot, scoot, moot

cool, fool, stool, spool

troop, loop, hoop, snoop

goose, noose, loose, moose

boon, coon, goon, loon, moon, noon, soon, spoon

Activity: Completing Sentences with the Third Sound of *o*

Preparation: You need paper and pencil.

To play: Read the following sentences and choose the word that correctly completes the sentence from the word bank after each sentence. Write the word you choose on the line provided.

1. Scott fed the little lad with a _____. (spite, soot, spoon)

2. Let's go to the _____ and splash each other! (pain, pool, wet)

3. Kate and John need to find _____ for the rain. (boots, bite, bath)

4. The gray stone slab was _____ to the touch.
   (cane, shine, cool)

5. My mom said, "Taste your _____ when it's still warm."
   (fell, food, beam)

6. Steve lost his _____ at the beach. (shut, make, shoe)

7. Jane said, "I don't know _____ was at the door."
   (hoot, who, when)

8. Let's _____ the bandstand to the park. (move, chum, mat)

9. Don't _____ your cash at the show, Stan. (flat, jet, lose)

10. Joe has matchbox cars that he can push and _____.
    (shade, zoom, drip)

Answer Key: 1. spoon 2. pool 3. boots 4. cool 5. food 6. shoe 7. who 8. move 9. lose 10. zoom

Activity: Poem

Preparation: You need paper and pencil.

To play: Ask your child to read the following poem. Have her pick out the words that have the third sound of *o* and write them on a printing tablet.

Cock-a-doodle-doo

Cock-a-doodle-doo!

My dame has lost her shoe;

My master's lost his fiddling stick,

And don't know what to do.

Cock-a-doodle-doo!

What is my dame to do?

Till master finds his fiddling stick,

She'll dance without her shoe.

Cock-a-doodle-doo!

My dame has found her shoe,

And master's found his fiddling stick,

Sing doodle-doodle-doo!

Cock-a-doodle-doo!

My dame will dance with you,

While master fiddles his fiddling stick

For dame and doodle-doo.

—Mother Goose

Answer Key: doodle-doo, shoe, do, you

Activity: Joke

Preparation: You need only this activity.

To play: Read the joke to your child and ask her to shout when she hears the ōō sound. See whether she understands the joke (a little science lesson).

Q: What is the definition of a goose?

A: An animal that grows down as it grows up!

Studying another way with u (ŏŏ)

The following word list deals with the o sound that says ŏŏ, as in the word *put*. This sound, which looks like the ōō, as in *boom,* deserves the same amount of care and attention. In this case the spelling is easy, but the pronunciation can be tricky. Most kids self-correct when they're familiar with the words. This list is designed to help your child read, recite, and remember the third sound of *u:*

book	good	poor	stood
brook	hood	precook	took
cook	hook	shook	unhook
crook	look	soot	wood
foot	nook	songbook	wool

Have your child practice by reading these sentences:

The crook ran off with the blue book.

Tom and Bill had to stack all the wood.

The poor man stood in the nook of the tree.

For the corresponding sound on the CD, listen to Track 37 for ŏŏ.

Word Strips: ŏŏ Words that Make the Third u Sound

Preparation: You need paper and pencil.

To play: Sit next to your child and read the following word strips (Chapter 2 explains how to teach with and create word strips):

> book, cook, brook, crook, hook, look, took, shook, nook
>
> good, wood, stood, hood
>
> hooks, looks, brooks, nooks, crooks, cooks, books

Activity: Filling in the Blanks

Preparation: You need paper and pencil.

To play: Read each of the following sentences, and then choose a word from the word bank after the sentences to correctly complete them. You may copy these sentences or rewrite the exercise for your child.

1. Butch and Bud _____ by the oak tree. (stand, stood, side)

2. Mom _____ for the kids at camp. (cake, cried, cooks)

3. Dad said, "Mitch and Jake! Clean up the _____ pile." (zoom, wood, dawn)

4. Beth ran track and has a sore _____. (fate, good, foot)

5. My brown _____ coat was wet from the snow. (wood, wool, catch)

6. My little gray dog _____ his wet tail. (rats, shine, shook)

7. Grandpa went to the bait shop to get a fish _____. (hide, pin, hook)

8. Here we go! Let's hide by the _____. (sky, bush, brood)

9. _____ aunt is pretty in her red dress. (Sal, Mine, Your)

10. I want a _____ of apples to keep in the cool box. (tin, bushel, tree)

Answer Key: 1. stood 2. cooks 3. wood 4. foot 5. wool 6. shook 7. hook 8. bush 9. Your 10. bushel

Activity: How Smart Is Your Foot?

To play: Read this story with your child and do the exercise. This is a reading, phonetic, and kinesthetic exercise all in one. While you're busy doing the foot/hand thing, notice the third sound of *u* (ù) in the exercise. The words that are underlined refer to the third sounds of *a, o,* and *u*.

1. While you sit at <u>your</u> desk, lift <u>your</u> right <u>foot</u> off of the floor. Make clockwise circles with it.

2. While you <u>do</u> this, <u>draw</u> the number six in the air with <u>your</u> right hand. <u>Your</u> <u>foot</u> will change direction.

Sight words: circle, right

Activity: There Was a Crooked Man

Preparation: You need paper and pencil.

To play: Ask your child to read this poem and write down the one word that has the third sound of *u*.

> There was a crooked man and he walked a crooked mile,
>
> He found a crooked sixpence upon a crooked stile.
>
> He bought a crooked cat, which caught a crooked mouse.
>
> And they all lived together in a little crooked house.
>
> —Mother Goose

Answer Key: crooked

Activity: Jokes

To play: Read the jokes with your child and ask her to shout when she hears the third sounds of *a, o,* and *u*. You can also dictate spelling words to your child from the lists in this chapter.

Q: What do you call a bull who tells jokes?

A: Laugh-a-bull!

Q: Why did the bull rush?

A: Because it saw the cow slip!

Answer Key: call, bull, who, because, saw

Going to the third vowel sound roundup

The next word list gives you and your child one last opportunity to explore the third sounds of *a* (paw), *o* (boom), and *u* (bush). Think of this list as a third vowel sound roundup. The idea is for you and your child to wallow in the various third vowel sounds:

ball	gaunt	Paul	stood
boot	gloom	poor	tomb
bullfrog	hark	put	two
do	hood	spool	who
drawn	lose	spoon	your
fawn	mall	sprawl	zoom
full	move	stark	

Activity: Story

Preparation: You need paper and pencil.

To play: Read this story with your child and pick out the *a, o,* and *u* words. Write the words on a separate piece of paper.

Under the Bed

Little Jake had a pair of red Keds,

But lost them today under his bed.

His mom said, "Find them!"

Look till you do.

Look and look for each little shoe.

Dive down in the dark, slip under and see,

Slip under and see,

What is there that shouldn't be.

He saw trucks and trains,

Slippers and socks,

And even a great big box of rocks.

In that dark place under his bed,

Little dust bunnies danced on his head.

It got a bit spooky there in the dark.

Was that a monster he heard give a bark?

He jumped up too fast and hit his fool head,

He hit his fool head on the springs of the bed.

He cried and he cried and raised such a fuss,

He couldn't find his red Keds in all that muss.

Out from under he came from that under-bed mess.

He'd rather confess and today just go shoe-less.

Answer Key: do, shoe, dark, shouldn't, saw, dark, spooky, bark, fool, too, couldn't

Sight Words: bunnies, find, place, dance, spooky, heard

Chapter 9

Delving into Diphthongs and Shortcuts

In This Chapter

▶ Finding out what diphthongs are

▶ Understanding diphthongs

▶ Murmuring about some diphthongs

▶ Handling shortcut contractions in your speech and reading

This chapter looks into the *ow, oy,* and *er* diphthongs in one- and two-syllable words. You may have seen the word *diphthong* lurking around in a dusty grammar or spelling book. Or maybe you remember your grade-school buddies calling each other "dip-thongs." It's a funny word that Webster's uses to describe three common sounds that you use every day in your speech and writing.

In this chapter you discover a section on shortcuts in your speech — like putting two words together with an apostrophe. The apostrophe stands for the missing letters and gives you a compacted version of the two words. For example, you see words such as *I am, you will,* and *I would* squeezed together to form *I'm, you'll,* and *I'd.* Contraction usage comes early in reading, and discovering it now can really come in handy.

Introducing Diphthongs: When Vowel Sound Meets Vowel Sound

A *diphthong* is a blend of two vowel sounds in one syllable that's pronounced as one speech sound. Diphthongs are sometimes called *gliding vowels.* Examples of diphthongs include the *ou* sound in *house,* the *ow* sound in *cow,* the *oi* sound in *join,* and the *oy* sound in *toy.* The word *diphthong* comes from the Greek *di,* which means *two,* and *phthong,* which means *tone.* Pronouncing a diphthong involves making a quick, smooth movement from one vowel sound to another; it requires assuming two different mouth positions.

The two types of diphthongs are

- **Plain diphthongs:** The plain diphthong is two vowels in one syllable making a completely new sound. Examples of words with plain diphthongs include *out, boy, down,* and *noise.* (This would be a good time to look at the vowel chart in Chapter 2 and give up a big hurrah, because these are the last classified vowel sounds. See the next section in this chapter for information about plain diphthongs.)

- **Murmur diphthongs:** A murmur diphthong is a vowel and the letter *r* in one syllable, making the *ur* sound. In this case, the *r* is called a half-vowel, because it controls the murmur diphthong in the word. For example, say the word *burn.* You surely don't hear the sound of *u* in any way, but you can hear the modified *r* sound. Examples of these words include *perk, bird,* and *fur.* (See "Exploring Murmur Diphthongs" later in this chapter for information about murmur diphthongs.)

A diphthong has two different mouth movements, but not necessarily two different sounds. For example, in the diphthongs /oi/ or /oy/, the mouth has two different movements, but you hear only one sound.

Teaching diphthongs by reading lips

Reading lips — that is, watching another's lips closely — is an excellent way to commit diphthong sounds into memory. As your child watches your lips move, he can clearly see the mouth movements you use to form the diphthong.

Face your child face and tell him to watch your lips as you read the following sentences. Exaggerate the sounds of the diphthongs as you read the sentences, and notice that your lips move in different ways to make the sounds. Wait for your child's response before moving on to the following numbered sentences.

1. Watch my lips as I say *ow.* Can you see my lips?

2. Do you notice the two positions that my lips form as I say this sound: *ow?*

3. Can you say this sound, *ow,* and feel your lips move to two separate positions?

4. Say the *ow* sound fast! Do you notice that this sound, *ow,* becomes one vowel sound?

5. Now say *powder* at a regular speed. Can you hear that the *ow* sound is there, but toned down by the consonant sounds of *p* and *d?*

When you finish this exercise, substitute the *oi/oy* sound for the *ou/ow* sound in the script. This script is a fast, cute way for kids to learn the two diphthongs.

Sounding Out ou/ow and oi/oy

Diphthongs that make the *ou/ow* sound and the *oi/oy* sound are kind of tricky. Notice in these diphthongs that the *y* and *w* act as vowels. Consider the following about plain diphthongs:

- Each diphthong contains two vowels with regard to its spelling, but makes one new sound.

- The *ou/ow* diphthong makes one sound but can be spelled in two different ways. For example, you pronounce the diphthongs in *house* and *cow* the same way.

- The *oi/oy* diphthong also makes the one sound but can be spelled in two different ways. For example, you pronounce the diphthongs in *soil* and *boy* the same way.

- Your lips assume two different positions when you pronounce a diphthong. You notice this when you exaggerate the sound of a diphthong as you pronounce it.

Getting to know the ou/ow diphthong

Table 9-1 gives your child sufficient practice with the *ou/ow* diphthong. Have your child read the words carefully. Start with the first two columns (the *ow*s) before doing the last two columns (the *ou*s).

Table 9-1		The ou/ow Diphthong	
bow	gown	bound	out
brow	how	cloud	pound
brown	howl	count	pout
clown	now	found	round
cow	owl	hound	shout
cowl	plow	house	sound
crown	prow	mount	sour
down	prowl	mouse	south
drown	town	mouth	spout
fowl	vow	our	wound

Have your child read these sentences silently and then say them aloud for practice:

> Mom, is our milk sour now?
>
> Can Howard come to our house?
>
> How did Kate count the brown cows?

For the corresponding sound on the CD, listen to Track 38 for *ou*.

Recognizing two ways to use ow

Besides being a diphthong (as in *how*), *ow* is also a digraph. For example, you see it in the words *flow* and *show*. If you say the words *how* and *flow* one after the other, you can hear that the *ow* makes a different sound in the words. These words don't rhyme even though they both have the *ow* ending. They don't rhyme because the *ow* in *how* is a diphthong and the *ow* in *show* is a vowel digraph. See Chapter 5 for more information about digraphs.

How do you know when *ow* is a diphthong and when it's a digraph? I wish I could give you a hard and fast rule, but only the context of the sentence can give you a clue as to the correct pronunciation.

Table 9-2 contains words with *ow* digraphs and diphthongs. Have your child read these words aloud.

Table 9-2	Digraphs and Diphthongs
Digraphs	*Diphthongs*
shown	shower
follow	allow
crow	prow
flow	flower
bow	bow
sow	sow
row	row

Have your child read these sentences silently, and then have him say them aloud for practice. Have your child point out the differences in the sounds as he reads.

1. Mother tied a blue <u>bow</u> in my hair.
2. The star of stage and screen took a <u>bow</u>.
3. The farm hand began to <u>sow</u> the crop.
4. Mother <u>sow</u> fed three pigs.
5. Dale began to <u>mow</u> the grass.
6. She put rose <u>powder</u> on her cheeks.
7. White Oak Creek had a strong <u>flow</u>.
8. The master stood at the <u>prow</u> of his ship.

Getting to know the oi/oy diphthong

The *oi/oy* diphthong can appear in the middle (*royal*) or at the end (*toy*) of a word or syllable.

Table 9-3 presents words that contain the *oi/oy* diphthong. To make it easier for your child to master this sound, I divide the table into three columns — each group of words is successively harder to read. Your child may come across the words in the third column in his reading.

Table 9-3	The oi/oy Diphthong	
boil	avoid	ahoy
coil	boy	annoy
coin	broil	busboy
foil	buoy	convoy
foist	charbroil	decoy
hoist	coy	destroy
join	doily	employ
moil	joy	enjoy
oil	loin	loyal
oink	ploy	royal
point	recoil	Troy
poise	roil	voyage
quoit	Roy	deploy

Have your child read these sentences silently, and then ask him to say them aloud for practice.

Will Roy shout with joy?

That toy had to be found.

Can I join you for a card game?

For the corresponding sound on the CD, listen to Track 39 for *oy*.

Activity: Story

Preparation: You need paper and pencil.

To play: Read this story with your child. After you read it, have him read it to you. If you can, make a copy and ask him to draw a line under all the diphthongs in the story.

The Town Mouse and the Country Mouse

A country mouse did ask a town mouse, who was a good chum, to pay him a visit and eat of his country fare. They began to eat on the bare plow lands. They ate wheat-stocks and roots from bushes. The town mouse said to his friend, "You live the life of the ants out here, while my house in town has the horn of plenty. I have everything that I need, and if you will come with me, and I wish you would, you will have a great share of my food stock." With much joy Country Mouse joined his friend as they made their way to South Brown County for a jolly good feast. When they got to the large and rich-looking house, Town Mouse led the way to a sun-filled kitchen through a small crack in the wall. There lay before them good treats of all kinds. The country mouse sat down as Town Mouse set before him bits of pork, sour grapes, sweet corn, dried figs, and best of all a sweet hunk of cheese from a round tin. Country Mouse was glad to feel such good cheer. He said thanks in warm terms, sad that his life was so hard in the country.

They began to put some food in their mouths when the maid came in to get a plate and saucer from the cupboard. She spoiled their feast! The two mice ran and were more scared than they had ever been in their lives.

Country Mouse did still feel quite hungry, and in a bit of a pout, said to his dear friend, "Although you set before for me a feast of great taste, I must leave you to eat it by yourself. Your life has too many pitfalls to please me. I just like to live my plain life in the country with my roots from the bushes and wheat-stocks from the plow lands. I can be safe there and not be in fear. Please come and visit sometime soon out in my country. I vow to show you a smooth night and a safe day void of stress and fear. Good-bye my dear friend."

—Adapted by Marilyn Johnson

Answer Key: town, house, mouse, plow, joy, join, out, south, brown, county, terms, pork, sour, corn, round, bounty, noise, mouth, spoil, pout, void

Sight Words: country, plenty, through, heard, open, cupboard, out, night, hungry

Activity: Poems and Tongue Twisters

Preparation: You need paper and pencil.

To play: Have your child read these poems and tongue twister for pleasure. After he reads them, go over them and have him write down the *ou/ow* words.

> **Daffy-down-dilly**
>
> Daffy-down-dilly has come to town
>
> In a yellow petticoat and a green gown.

> **A Sunshiny Shower**
>
> A sunshiny shower
>
> Won't last half an hour.

> **The Boy in the Barn**
>
> A little boy went, into a barn,
>
> And lay down on some hay.
>
> An owl came out, and flew about,
>
> And the little boy ran away.

> **Robert Rowley Rolled Around**
>
> Robert Rowley rolled around a rolled round, and if Robert Rowley rolled around a rolled round, where is the round roll Robert Rowley rolled round?

Answer Key: down, town, gown, shower, hour, owl, about Rowley, around, round

Exploring Murmur Diphthongs

Murmur diphthongs make the *ur* sound. As far as spelling goes, the murmur diphthong can be rendered with the letters *ur, ir,* or *er.* No matter which spelling you use, the diphthong makes the *ur* sound, as in the word *urn.* These *r*-controlled diphthongs are simple to read, but harder to spell. Some memorization of spelling applies here.

Making sounds with r-controlled diphthongs

Table 9-4 lists words with murmur diphthongs. I sorted them into three columns to make these diphthongs easier for your child to absorb. Make sure your child understands that all three spellings (*er, ir,* and *ur*) represent the same sound. Children can test their memorization skills to see whether they can spell these words correctly. Later, your child will also learn that on occasion, *ar* (dollar) and *or* (doctor) can also make the *ur* sound.

Table 9-4	Words with the ur, er, and ir Diphthong	
blurt	berm	dirt
burn	clerk	fir
burr	fern	firm
burse	her	flirt
curb	herm	gird
curl	insert	girl
curt	jerk	quirk
fur	nerve	sir
hurt	perk	skirt
nurse	perm	squirt
purr	pert	stir
purse	serve	twirl

Have your child read these sentences silently, and then have him say them aloud for practice:

Her pert bird began to scratch in the dirt.

The nurse took the boy to the lab.

The stern dad said, "Say 'sir' when you speak to me."

Activity: Sentence Completion (Advanced)

Preparation: You need paper and pencil.

To play: Read each sentence in the following list, and choose the correct word to complete each one from the word bank to the right of each sentence. Write the word on the line. You may copy these sentences or rewrite the exercise for your child.

1. The _____ in the yard was a finch. (bark, bird, bride)

2. He used the _____ to catch the fish. (cork, boot, cake)

3. The cat began to _____. (bark, purr, pot)

4. Ferd went to the _____ field to pick the ripe ears. (sty, corn, store)

5. Joy and Chet sat on the _____. (porch, fish, wig)

6. That child is on my last _____. (egg, blank, nerve)

7. The _____ gave me a back rub. (bird, nurse, name)

8. Use your _____ to eat the cake. (fork, leg, stir)

9. He was _____ on the fourth of July. (sang, born, blurt)

10. Will Paul _____ Steve sing that song? (or, her, fir)

Answer Key: 1. bird 2. cork 3. purr 4. corn 5. porch 6. nerve 7. nurse 8. fork 9. born 10. or

Activity: Stories

To play: This a funny story for you to read to your child. Ask him to shout when he hears an *ow, oy,* or *er* sound.

Grandma and the Cowboy

Did you hear about Grandma Turner, who tried to help her grandson, Howie, dress for school? Howie needed Grandma to help him with his brown and tan cowboy boots. He asked for help and she could see why. Even with her pulling and him pushing, the little boots still didn't want to go on his feet.

Finally, when she got the second boot on, she was tired. She almost cried when the little boy said, "Grandma, they're on the wrong feet." She looked and she said, "Yep! They are!" So, she pulled the boots off, which wasn't easy.

She kept her cool as they both worked to get the boots back on the right feet. She said, "Now your boots are on the right feet!" The little cowboy said, "These aren't my boots, Grandma." She was fit to be tied!

Once again she tried to help him pull the boots off his little feet. When they got the boots off, Howie said, "They're Ferd's boots. He made me wear them." Now she didn't know if she should laugh or cry. But, being a grandma with staying power, she helped him into his coat and asked, "Now, where are your mittens?" He answered, "I stuffed them in the toes of my boots."

Answer Key: cowboy, Turner, Howie, brown, Ferd, power

Sight Words: even, almost, finally, easy, right, laugh, being, staying

Activity: Poem

To play: Read the poem with your child have him pick out the *ow, er,* and *or* words.

Gloucester is a two-syllable word (Glouce-ster) and is pronounced "Gloster," rhyming with Foster.

> **Doctor Foster**
>
> Doctor Foster
>
> Went to Gloucester
>
> In a shower of rain.
>
> He stepped in a puddle,
>
> Right up to his middle,
>
> And never went there again!
>
> —Mother Goose

Answer Key: Doctor, Foster, Gloucester, shower, never

Checking on a few or words

The *or* murmur diphthong can be confusing. It makes the *or* sound you hear in *fork,* but it has the same spelling as the long sound of *or* you hear in the word *shore.* The tip-off is when you see the word *shore,* you see the magic *e* on the end. Most of the time *or* makes the long *o* sound, so knowing when to pronounce the *or* diphthong takes practice. Moreover, this sound varies depending on what part of the United States you're in.

The following list contains *or* words that are diphthongs. All these words make the *or* sound you hear in the word *fork.* Have your child read these words for practice:

born	horn	port	stork
cord	lord	scorch	storm
cork	morn	scorn	sworn
corn	nor	shorn	thorn
dorm	norm	short	torch
for	or	snort	torn
fork	porch	sort	worn
form	pork	sport	york

Have your child read these sentences silently, and then have him say them aloud for practice:

Norm had a fork in his hand.

I saw a stork at the zoo.

The storm began to form in the south.

Activity: Stories

Preparation: You need paper and pencil.

To play: Read the story with your child and have him pick out the diphthongs. Write the words he picked out on a separate piece of paper and have him read them to you.

Roy Rogers

Roy Rogers was a famous TV cowboy. Roy was born in Cincinnati, Ohio, in 1911. His family was poor and wanted a good life on the farm. His dad and Uncle Will took a houseboat upriver and floated to Portsmouth, Ohio. Dad Slye (Roy's real name was Leonard Slye) and the family lived on a farm in Duck Run. The farm soil did not help the family much even though Mr. Slye used a plow. The dad went to work full time to make shoes for the family in Portsmouth. He purchased a horse for Roy. That is how Roy became such a good rider.

The family returned to Cincinnati, and the father went to work on shoes there. Roy joined his dad at the shoe factory, too.

The family left the city, and went to California to work as truck drivers. That didn't happen, because there were no jobs to be had. Roy and his father became workers who went from farm to farm picking fruit and toiling in the soil.

After that, Mr. Slye went to Los Angeles to work at another shoemaker's job. Roy stayed on the farms. He sang and played his guitar at night around the campfires. Seeing the joy that his guitar and singing gave to the men, he wanted to become a singer.

He and his cousin Stan went to Los Angeles to start their music job. They called their group Sons of the Pioneers and became famous. Roy Rogers took his men to TV, and everyone knows Roy as the TV cowboy of the 1950s. He had a horse, Trigger, and a dog, Bullet. Children in the '50s would not miss watching the TV show, which was on every Sunday.

Roy and his wife, Dale, had children of their own and several adopted children. They had a big ranch in Apple Valley, California. He and Dale were well loved by many and he is in the Country Music Hall of Fame.

—Susan Greve

Answer Key: cowboy, Roy, born, return, father, there, join, California, driver, were, soil, after, another, factory, maker, joy, singer, horse, Trigger, Country

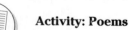

Activity: Poems

To play: Ask your child to read these poems with you. Even though you're reading the poems for enjoyment, ask him to pick out the words that have diphthongs.

The Man in Our Town

There was a man in our town,

And he was wondrous wise,

He jumped into a bramble bush,

And scratched out both his eyes;

But when he saw his eyes were out,

With all his might and main,

He jumped into another bush,

And scratched 'em in again.

—Mother Goose

Wee Willie Winkie

Wee Willie Winkie runs through the town,

Upstairs and downstairs, in his nightgown;

Rapping at the window, crying through the lock,

"Are the children in their beds?

Now it's eight o'clock."

—Mother Goose

Curly Locks

Curly-locks, Curly-locks, wilt thou be mine?

Thou shalt not wash the dishes, nor yet feed the swine;

But sit on a cushion, and sew a fine seam,

And feed upon strawberries, sugar, and cream.

—Mother Goose

The Wise Old Owl

A wise old owl sat in an oak,

The more he heard the less he spoke;

The less he spoke the more he heard.

Why aren't we all like that wise old bird?

—Anonymous

There Was a Little Girl

There was a little girl,

Who had a little curl,

Right in the middle of her forehead.

When she was good,

She was very good indeed,

But when she was bad she was horrid.

　　　　—Henry Wadsworth Longfellow

Answer Key: our, town, out, another, down, now, gown, curl, thou, nor, owl, more, bird, girl, forehead, horrid

Discovering How Vowel Sounds Change in Contractions

I'm taking a small detour here to tell you about contractions. I've found that kids start to notice contractions, such as the word *don't,* very early in reading. The contractions at the stage that I've reached in this portion of the book are small, one-syllable words, mostly, and certainly aren't advanced phonics.

A *contraction* is a word made from two words that have been joined together and made shorter. Contractions are basically speech shortcuts. Three things happen when we contract or squeeze words together: Letters disappear, sounds disappear, and an apostrophe (') appears in the place of the missing letters and sounds to mark their absence. An *apostrophe* is a punctuation mark that shows the omission of one or more letters.

Here are two examples or contractions:

- ✔ **What's:** This is a contraction of "what is," with the apostrophe taking the place of the *i.*
- ✔ **I'd:** This is a contraction of "I would," with the apostrophe taking the place of the *woul.*

This discussion about contractions is mainly about reading and spelling — not grammar.

Table 9-5 includes the most commonly used word contractions, with an example of each contraction in a sentence. Have your child read each set.

Protecting and preserving the apostrophe

John Richards started the Apostrophe Protection Society in 2001 with the "specific aim of preserving the correct use of the much abused punctuation mark." Here are the Society's guidelines for the correct use of apostrophes:

✔ Use an apostrophe to denote a missing letter or letters (*it is, it's*).

✔ Use an apostrophe to denote possession by a single person or thing (*the dog's bone* or *the dog's bones*). In this case, the apostrophe comes before the *s*.

✔ Use an apostrophe to denote possession by more than one person or thing (*the dogs' bone* or *the dogs' bones*). In this case, the apostrophe comes after the *s*.

Table 9-5		Contractions
Commonly Used Words	*Contraction*	*Sentence Usage*
I am	I'm	**I'm** about to go to the farm for some eggs.
you are	you're	**You're** home at last and safe.
he is	he's	**He's** in the backyard to help his dad.
it is	it's	**It's** not fair to grab too much.
she is	she's	**She's** at bat for her team at last.
we are	we're	**We're** in the house to get warm.
they are	they're	**They're** not working hard at the job.
are not	aren't	**Aren't** the boys in line for the ballgame?
is not	isn't	He **isn't** in the park with Rick.
did not	didn't	**Didn't** she hear the loud noise?
does not	doesn't	**Doesn't** that hat fit her well?
do not	don't	**Don't** go to this store for meat or milk.
I would	I'd	**I'd** see to that at three if I could.
you would	you'd	**You'd** thank him first if you're smart.
she would	she'd	**She'd** take the dishes to her dad.
it will	it'll	**It'll** be dark when you finish math.

(continued)

Table 9-5 *(continued)*

Commonly Used Words	Contraction	Sentence Usage
he will	he'll	**He'll** see the nurse for his bad cut.
we will	we'll	**We'll** go to his boss about the card.
they will	they'll	**They'll** try to get to work by nine.
will not	won't	I **won't** stay here for the meal.
can not	can't	He **can't** swim that far as yet.
must not	mustn't	She **mustn't** take her plane trip.
what is	what's	**What's** in the glasses on the shelf?
where is	where's	**Where's** the next train to leave for town?
there is	there's	**There's** more warmth in the back row. Go there.

Activity: Placing the Apostrophe

Preparation: You need paper and pencil.

To play: Read the following sentences and place the apostrophe in the right spot in each sentence. You may copy these sentences or rewrite the exercise for your child.

1. I ll go with you.
2. Let s go to the park.
3. Don t you think she is pretty?
4. It s dark out there.
5. I m in the back room.
6. He s a good boy.
7. I can t come out to play.
8. We re on our way to the farm.

Answer Key: 1. I'll 2. Let's 3. Don't 4. It's 5. I'm 6. He's 7. can't 8. We're

Activity: Sentence Completion (Advanced)

Preparation: You need paper and pencil.

To play: Read each of the following sentences, and choose the proper word to complete each one from the word bank to the right. Write the word on the line. You may copy these sentences, or rewrite the exercise for your child.

1. _____ see the nurse for her cut. (What's, She'll, I'm)

2. I _____ stay here by myself. (where's, can't, you'll)

3. Tim _____ go to the store with Mom. (didn't, isn't, aren't)

4. _____ be dark when the cows come home. (It'll, I'm, It's)

5. _____ at bat for his team at last. (Didn't, He's, They'll)

6. I _____ care if he said that. (it's, don't, isn't)

7. _____ play ball! (Let's, We're, Aren't)

8. Today _____ cut the grass. (didn't, I'll, weren't)

Answer Key: 1. She'll 2. can't 3. didn't 4. It'll 5. He's 6. don't 7. Let's 8. I'll

Activity: Joke

To play: Have your child read the following joke and pick out the diphthongs.

Q. Do you know how Roy Rogers put his boots on?

A. He put them on with a long horn.

Answer Key: how, Roy, horn

Part III
Moving Beyond the Phonics Basics

The 5th Wave   By Rich Tennant

©RICHTENNANT

"Hi! We're in the kitchen learning to read words that begin with 'TH.'"

In this part . . .

*H*ere is where I delve deeply into pronunciations and the structure of words. I also give you tips on mastering some basic vowel guidelines and patterns. (Not to worry! They're common and easy to follow.) I also ease into lessons that help your child master *c* and *g*, dabble in *x* and *z*, and dip into the muck and mire of vowel combinations.

Chapter 10

Stepping Through the Pronunciation Process

In This Chapter

▶ Working through the process of pronunciation

▶ Uncovering the syllables

▶ Getting the emphasis right

▶ Seeing *y* in different ways

*I*n this chapter you discover how to teach your child good pronunciation by looking at the composition of multisyllable words and seeing how to apply accents (stressed or emphasized syllables). You also look at root words and the versatile letter *y.*

When your child is able to read multisyllable words, you need to understand the how's and why's of pronunciation. Your work is mainly with two-syllable words ending in *y.* This is a pretty big jump, so take your time.

Unlocking the Sounds of Words

To *pronounce* means to utter a word or sound in a particular way, especially with a certain accent or according to an accepted standard. You've probably heard this before, but didn't you wonder why the people across the river, up the road, or in another state talk differently than you?

American English words are spelled the same all over the United States, but regional inflections (distinctive ways words are spoken) change the way some words sound. The way words are spoken, which determines how they sound, depends upon how they're pronounced. And the way words are pronounced is called pronunciation! Now isn't that clever?

You may have heard people speak with a New England drawl or a Kentucky twang or a Minnesota clip. Although regional differences of pronunciation may cause words to sound different from place to place, the meanings remain the same. And in most instances, what a person is saying is discernible with careful listening, no matter where you're from.

Proper pronunciation of English words follows basic guidelines, patterns, and structures of language. You may say *two-MAY-toes,* and I may say *toe-MA-toes,* but we both know we're talking about tomatoes and not feet!

Although the exploration of regional dialects is interesting, it's beyond the scope of this book. However, wherever you live or were born in the United States, good pronunciation is important for building good reading and spelling skills. And that *is* what this book is about! Good pronunciation encompasses recognizing long and short vowels, understanding the parts of words called syllables, and knowing which part of a word is emphasized.

Finding the syllables to say

A *syllable* is a word or a part of a word that's pronounced with a single uninterrupted sound of the voice. Some people say that syllables are broken parts of words.

Some facts about syllables are:

- Syllables can be considered building blocks of multisyllable words.
- A syllable is a word or part of a word with one vowel sound.
- At least one vowel is present in a syllable.

After all that, sometimes it's still easier to show a child examples to help her catch on. Say some three-syllable words and slap your hand down, counting each syllable. Children usually get the hang of it quickly, but remember that they do need to understand what a syllable is. For example, say these words and slap your hand on the table as you speak each syllable:

- Syllable (syl-la-ble)
- Tomato (to-ma-to)
- Strawberry (straw-ber-ry)

Setting up a pronunciation key

Accents and diacritical marks are characters or signs that are added to a letter to indicate a special pronunciation.

The following presentation of diacritical marks and their definitions is a specifically drawn pronunciation key for *Phonics For Dummies:*

✔ Short vowel: breve (˘) as in pĕn

✔ Long vowel: macron (¯) as in nāme

✔ Third sound of a: umlaut (¨) as in säw

✔ Third sound of o: ōō or umlaut (ü) as in move or zoom

✔ Third sound of u: one dot u̇ or ŏŏ as in put or wood

✔ Diphthong sound: slur (˘) as in out, boy, ow/ou, oi/oy, pert, irk, er/ir/ur, and or as in fork.

✔ Stressed vowel or syllable: accent mark (á) as in ba´by

✔ Vowel sound: schwa (ə) as in lo´cəl

✔ Line: hyphen (-) joins or separates syllables as in mix-up

Accenting syllables for proper emphasis

If you're looking at words in a dictionary, you see definitions as well as visual representations (which are letters and symbols) of how the spoken parts of the sounds of a word (sounds) are pronounced. But wait, there's more! Interspersed among those letters are diacritical marks. No, diacritical isn't a curse that an actor places on a movie critic who panned his latest film! *Diacritical* simply means to distinguish or show differences. You may also know about phoneme and grapheme, but I don't recommend teaching them to your kids at this point. I choose not to use those words.

Hey, just for fun, why not get out your dictionary right now and look up some of these new terms to see the syllables and the marks used with the syllables? Also check out the sidebar in this chapter, "Setting up a pronunciation key," for more on diacritical marks.

An important mark, and the one I'm most concerned with in this chapter, is the accent mark (´). The accent indicates an emphasis or stress in a word or syllable.

For example, look up the word *diacritical* (or *diacritic,* which is the root word) in your dictionary. You will see that the syllables are di-a-crit-i-cal. Now, where's the accent mark? You may see two — one skinny and one fat. You're looking for the fat one because it shows which syllable gets the emphasis: diaCRITical. If you already have your dictionary out, look up these words with your child and find the fat accent mark for each. Say the words together out loud, putting extra oomph on the accented (stressed) syllable: *express, Halloween, lacing, medicine,* and *vitamin.*

When you speak the words of the English language, the accented syllable is often determined by where on the planet you live.

Even the people of different regions in the same country may speak with a different accent.

Accenting syllables for proper meaning

The way you pronounce multisyllable words depends upon the way you say the sounds of the letters and the stress (accent) that you place on a specific syllable. The syllable that you stress in pronunciation is called the accented syllable.

Now, here's the twist! As you know, the wonderful English language has words that sound the same but aren't spelled the same. In addition, English has those tricky words that *look* the same yet sound and mean something completely different. What's the distinguishing factor? Yes! The accent mark!

These nefarious words even have their own name: heteronyms. (Go ahead, feel free to look up nefarious and heteronym in the dictionary. I know you're dying to! Stopping to look up new words is a good habit for you and your child to get into. And you'll see that I'm exaggerating a bit by describing heteronyms as nefarious.)

So how do you know which way to pronounce a heteronym when you bump into one in a sentence? In a word: context. Consider the word within the context of the entire sentence or sometimes the whole paragraph. But for now, focus on words, because if you don't know the words, context (and all that advanced stuff) won't help you.

The accent can even change the definition of a word, such as ob' ject and ob jećt. These words are spelled the same, but have different meanings, merely because of the placement of the accent mark. Table 10-1 highlights a few *heteronyms,* or words that have the same spelling but different pronunciations and meanings. You can read them to your child with a brief explanation. Read these listings from left to right.

Table 10-1	Heteronyms
Con' duct: Behavior	Con duct': To lead
Con' flict: A fight or disagreement	Con flict': Disagree
Con' sole: An upright case	Con sole': To comfort
Con' tent: The amount contained	Con tent': Satisfied
Con' test: A match of skill	Con test': To argue
Ob' ject: A thing	Ob ject': To complain
Per' fect: Exactly correct	Per fect': To make correct
Per' mit: Formal consent	Per mit': To allow an event to occur
Proj' ect: A task	Pro ject': To show a movie
Reb' el: A resister	Re bel': To resist
Sub' ject: A theme	Sub ject': To force upon someone

Discovering some accent strategies

Although it's impossible to create nice and neat, hard and fast rules for reading accents, syllables, and vowel sounds, here are some helpful general guidelines:

- Look for accents on the first syllable. (ba' by, stud' y)
- The accent is usually on the main root word when the word has a prefix or suffix. (un did', thank' ful)
- If prefixes such as de-, re-, in-, pro-, or a- are the first syllables in a word, the word usually isn't accented. (de cide', re group', in sist', pro pel', a gain')
- If you have two vowels together in the last syllable of the word, the combination often shows that the accent is on the last syllable. (de rail', com plain')
- If you have two consonants that are the same letter, the syllable that comes before the two consonants is usually accented. (fret' ted, rot' ted)
- If you have a word with three or more syllables, one of the first two syllables is usually accented. (ex ten' sion, con di' tion)

Exposing root words with suffixes and prefixes

A *root* is a word or word part to which you add suffixes and prefixes to make new words. For example: *Faith* is the root word of *faithful.*

A *prefix* is a syllable added to the beginning of a word, or root, to change its meaning to form a new word. For example: *Re-* is the prefix in the word *return.*

A *suffix* is almost always a syllable or syllables added to the end of a word to form another word of different meaning or function. For example: The suffix *-er* is at the end of the word *paint,* changing it to *painter.* See Chapter 14 for more on root words.

Understanding y in Syllables

The letter *y* has many faces; in other words, it's a really versatile letter. For example, here are some of the variations a *y* exhibits in different words:

- ✔ It can be a consonant at the start of a word: yam
- ✔ It can be a silent vowel at the end of a word: play
- ✔ It can be a long vowel at the end of a word: dry, lady
- ✔ It can be a long vowel inside of a word: eye, embryo

In fact, the *y* can be called a chameleon letter because it makes different sounds (or no sound) in different words. (For more on *y,* see Chapters 7 and 13.)

Some examples of the *y* as a long *i* are: *by, cry, thy, my, fry, try, dry, why, shy, sty, sky, spy, fly, pry, ply, sly, spry, bye, aye, eye, rye, lye,* and *dye.* Making word strips here provides some reinforcement before the next table.

The letters *x, u, y,* and *w* are often called *chameleon letters* because, like the chameleon lizard that can change its skin to many different colors, they have different sounds.

Eek! It's a y!

The letter *y* also works beautifully in multisyllable words and displays more of its chameleon-like qualities. Look closely at the two-syllable words in the next list. The words all end with a *y* that you pronounce like a long *e* (ē) sound. When *y* comes at the end of a word with two or more syllables, and the *y* syllable isn't accented (meaning it isn't the stressed syllable), then the *y* has the sound of a long *e* (as in happy!). Make a note of this because lots of kids tend to write what they hear. You may want to remind your child to go from vowel sound to vowel sound in the words. That's why these vowels have been underlined. Although some of these words look a little difficult, she'll soon enjoy being able to sound out the three- and four-syllable words.

To help your child become familiar with the long *e* sound of *y,* have her read through each of the words in the following list.

ba´by	fla´ky	po´ky	smo´ky
bea´dy	fris´ky	po´ny	stick´y
bee´fy	fun´ny	pop´py	sun´ny
bug´gy	gra´vy	pu´ny	ti´dy
bun´ny	han´dy	pup´py	ti´ny
can´dy	jum´py	ris´ky	ug´ly
chee´ky	la´dy	rus´ty	wa´vy
dad´dy	lob´by	sha´dy	wee´py
dai´sy	na´vy	shi´ny	
dol´ly	nee´dy	slee´py	
dus´ty	pen´ny	slop´py	

Have your child read these sentences for practice:

The funny baby has wavy hair.

Penny had a pony named Smoky.

A tidy lady likes to clean.

Aye, I see y!

In this section, you look at what happens when *y* is attached to an ending syllable that's stressed. For example, in the word *multiply,* the chameleon *y* sounds like a long *i.* Why? Because the emphasis falls on the final *y* syllable (mul-ti-ply´).

When *y* comes at the end of a word with two or more syllables, and the *y* syllable is accented, *y* has the sound of long *i* ($\bar{i}$).

Here's a great way to gain a tactile and audible sense of the syllables and the emphasis (accent). Lay your hand flat on the table. Starting with the little finger, tap one finger per syllable while saying the words in Table 10-3. Tap with a heavier beat on the accented syllable. Show your child how to do this as well and do it together if you want.

Here's another way to feel stress: Put your hand, back side up, under your chin. Pronounce the word naturally. The syllable that causes your chin to drop the most is the stressed syllable. When "feeling for stress" you must pronounce the word naturally.

If you see that your child is feeling stressed when you work through the table, stop and circle each syllable in each word, and then have her go from vowel sound to vowel sound.

Now you're ready to apply this new insight. Have your child read through the words in the following list. You want to hear the long *i* sound, as well as the proper emphasis on the final syllable:

ally'	dig'nify'	mag'nify'	reply'
apply'	ed'ify'	mul'tiply'	sig'nify'
comply'	elec'trify'	oc'cupy'	supply'
defy'	ident'ify'	rat'ify'	

Have your child read these sentences for practice:

Her pony will occupy the shady stall.

The baby will reply with a happy smile.

Henry will multiply seven times seven.

Activity: X's and O's

Preparation: Copy or rewrite this exercise.

To play: Put an X on the words ending with the long *i* ($\bar{i}$) sound. Draw a circle, or O, around the words ending with the long *e* ($\bar{e}$) sound. Then ask your child to print the words in the correct rows.

by	cry
lady	try
funny	puppy

y sounds like long *i* (ī)   *y* sounds like long *e* (ē)

1. _____   1. _____

2. _____   2. _____

3. _____   3. _____

Answer Key: Long *i* sound: by, cry, try; Long *e* sound: lady, funny, puppy

When the y flies and plays!

Now that you and your child have a somewhat solid grip on the slippery *y*, here's more information to round out your understanding. How do you make a word ending in *y* plural? Here are a couple of guidelines:

✔ All names or nouns ending with *y* when preceded by a consonant form their plurals by changing *y* to *ies*. Examples include changing *cherry* to *cherries* and *fly* to *flies*. You may have heard this guideline stated as "Change the *y* to *i* and ad *-es*."

✔ If *a*, *e*, or *o* precedes the *y*, the plural is formed by adding only an *s*. For example, *day* becomes *days*, *ploy* becomes *ploys*, and *key* becomes *keys*.

Read the words in Table 10-4. Do you see what happens when you make a plural out of the word? You drop the *y*, change it to *i* and add *-es*.

Table 10-4	Singular to Plural
Singular	*Plural*
ally	allies
bunny	bunnies

(continued)

Table 10-4 *(continued)*

Singular	*Plural*
fairy	fairies
lady	ladies
navy	navies
penny	pennies
pony	ponies
poppy	poppies
puppy	puppies
supply	supplies

Accessing Opened and Closed Syllables

As your child advances in reading and writing skills, she needs to know basic syllable division (also called *syllabication*). Syllable division can be helpful for decoding multisyllable words. Syllable division looks at the position of the vowels and consonants, and whether the vowel is long, short, or a vowel pair.

A hyphen (-) is the punctuation mark used either to join words or to separate syllables. This isn't the whole story, but it's good for starters. Right now, you're going to learn how it separates syllables. Just two for now: syllabication division. You can check out Appendix A for a complete unit on syllabication division. However, right now is a good time to learn two important things about syllabication division:

- ✔ If a word has one consonant between two vowels, and the first vowel is short, the word is usually divided after the consonant. This is called a *closed* syllable. For example: rob-in, com-ics, grav-el, pol-ish.

- ✔ If a word has one consonant between two vowels, and the first vowel is long, the word is usually divided after the first vowel. This is called an *open* syllable. For example: mu-sic, la-bor, pa-per, Po-lish.

If you're wondering why these syllables are referred to as open or closed, I offer a little more explanation:

- Closed syllables went into lockdown because of the consonants.

- Open syllables have a vowel left hanging.

- If you hear a short vowel in the first syllable, you close the syllable with a consonant, as in the word *ro_b_-in*.

- If you hear a long vowel in the first syllable, as in the word *mo̱-tel,* the vowel is the last letter of the syllable, keeping the syllable open.

Although this generalization is less than perfect, it's a good guideline.

With the exception of the word *occupy,* the words in Table 10-3 all contain at least one schwa sound (a quick *ŭh*), that is, an unaccented syllable. The schwa (ə) is also in the earlier sidebar "Setting up a pronunciation key." If you introduce the schwa now, your child will have an easier time understanding it when you encounter it in Chapter 15.

Unaccented syllables (marked by the schwa in the dictionary) seldom have a definite long- or short-vowel sound, and you really need to play by ear and syllabicate accordingly. If you want to, you can introduce your child to the dictionary at this juncture and hunt for some two-syllable words for practice.

After your child masters the words in Tables 10-2 and 10-3, she's ready to divide more difficult words (three and four syllables) as she meets them in her reading.

Activity: Stories: *y*

Preparation: You need paper and pencil.

To play: Ask your child to read these stories out loud to find out how fluent she is. You want your child to read with expression and, above all, be smooth. When you get to the last story in this section, ask your child to write all the two-syllable words that end in *y* on a separate piece of paper.

A Visit to the Park

One day, Sally, Bobby, and Danny asked Mommy and Daddy Hardy if they could go to the park. There was a park five streets from their house. The family lived in a two-story house on Purdy Drive. It was near the railroad tracks. Mommy said they could go if they would be home for lunch. Sally was very happy and thanked Mommy.

The children left for the park with their wide-awake dog, Smoky, who was barking at their feet. The first thing they saw was a lost puppy. Smoky barked at the funny, wiggly puppy, and the scared little puppy ran away from them.

When they got close to the main street, which led to the park, a neighbor stopped to talk with them. Her name was Mrs. Ann Rally. She had a happy little baby in her buggy. She told the children to be safe when they crossed the busy street.

So far, they were having fun. Bobby and Danny began to run away from Sally. She said that they should stay by her, because she was ten and they were not as old as she.

When Sally ran after them, the boys were already on the swings. The Hardy children had a good time that sunny day.

Fun on the Farm

The Duffy family lived on a big farm of fifty acres. They had four peppy children named Jack, Jamie, Polly, and a rosy-cheeked baby whose name was Lizzy. There was a puppy called Floppy and a kitty named Fluffy. They could hear the pony, Tawny, whinny in the barn.

Sometimes little Lizzy was fussy, but most of the time, she had a sunny way about her. Polly always had her dolly with her, and the boys told her that she was silly.

One day they asked Mommy if they could have a party outside on the grassy spot in the backyard. It was a shady yard, but it was hilly and rocky. Jack said it was fine and they could still have plenty of fun.

Mommy gave the children a pretty cloth to lay on the ground. Jamie got some jelly and ham. Polly got a bag of cookies, and Jack had plates and napkins. The lunch was yummy even if their hands were sticky from the messy jelly. Mommy gave them candy, too.

With her tummy filled, the baby got sleepy and took a nap in her buggy. The boys ran off to play, and Polly and her dolly went to the swing and sat down.

Daddy Duffy got back from town and sat on a grassy spot for lunch. All in all the Duffy family was a jolly bunch.

A Lucky Pony

My name is Henry, and this is the story of Rocky, my pony, and how I came to be his happy master.

One lucky day, a lost and muddy pony walked slowly down our lane. His mane was shoddy and looked as if it had not been brushed for a long time. There was a navy blue rope tied around his neck. Rocky was smelly and his hide was saggy. Did he run away or had some person turned him loose? He was in a needy shape, and I was happy to take care of him.

Daddy felt it was his duty to ask many people around our homey little town if they knew anything about Rocky. No one came forth, so from that misty morning on, Rocky stayed.

Our family fed him a bounty and he drank from the pond for many years. Rocky's coat was always shiny and he was full of energy. He lived for twenty years or more.

In those days, the best part of every day was when I swiftly jumped upon his back and rode around the town. Rocky and I were best buddies until I went into the army.

Activity: Counting Syllables

Preparation: You need pencil and paper.

To play: Read each word in Table 10-5. Count the number of syllables in the word, and write the number on the line next to the word. You may copy this table, or rewrite the exercise for your child.

Example: navy __2__

Table 10-5		Counting Syllables		
shaky ____	sandy ____	Davy ____	navy ____	multiply ____
reply ____	puppy ____	defy ____	electrify ____	kitty ____
wavy ____	poppy ____	identify ____	happy ____	apply ____
tidy ____	solidify ____	funny ____	supply ____	comply ____
baby ____	pony ____	dignify ____	shady ____	ally ____

Answer Key: All words in the table are two-syllable words, except for solidify, identify, and electrify (four-syllable words), and dignify and multiply (both three-syllable words).

Mega-testing your word skills

Strengthening these word skills in this chapter brings you to the advanced level in phonics. By this time, your child should be able to read fluently with some expression in her voice. She should be able to tackle most two-syllable words, especially the keywords you use for the letters of the alphabet. Use the following assessment tools to tell whether or not she's ready to move on. If you think that she needs more time, go over the material. Note that this is expected to be a difficult exercise.

Activity: Drop the *y* and Add *ies*

Preparation: You need pencil and paper.

To play: Read each word in the following list. Drop the *y* at the end of the word and add *ies.* Write the word on the line. You may copy these sentences, or rewrite the exercise for your child.

Example: penny <u>pennies</u>

1. baby _____
2. fly _____
3. candy _____
4. lily _____
5. pony _____
6. story _____
7. bunny _____
8. lady _____

Answer Key: 1. babies 2. flies 3. candies 4. lilies 5. ponies 6. stories 7. bunnies 8. ladies

Activity: Suffixes

Preparation: You need pencil and paper.

To play: Read the following sentences. Finish each sentence by printing the plural form of the word in parentheses. The suffixes you're choosing from are *-s, -es,* and *-ies.*

Example: Mom and Sis baked <u>pies</u> this week. (pie)

1. Joy gave her mother two _____ of lunchmeat. (pound)

2. Tim and Sue went to the farm to pick _____. (berry)

3. Four men on horses chased the _____. (fox)

4. The _____ went out to lunch together. (lady)

5. The children painted the park _____. (bench)

6. The little boy collected ten _____. (penny)

7. The man used the _____ for his car. (part)

8. Sadie looked for _____ in the garden. (rose)

Answer key: 1. pounds 2. berries 3. foxes 4. ladies 5. benches 6. pennies 7. parts 8. roses

Chapter 11

Finding Happy Endings with Suffixes

Are you up for a little challenge? Great! In this chapter, you take on two- and three-letter word endings (called *suffixes*) that present some twists. A suffix is added on to the end of a word, and it can change the sound of the word, its meaning, and even the number of syllables. In fact, a suffix can even make a word travel through time from the present into the past!

This chapter looks at how you pronounce and spell words with the *ed, ing,* and *er* suffixes. These suffixes can be attached to almost any verb. For example, *skate* can become *skated, skating,* and *skater.* And *rub* can become *rubbed, rubbing,* and *rubber.*

As an adult, you may tend to take these suffixes for granted, but if you look closely at them, you notice that attaching a suffix to a word can change it in subtle ways. Take *skate,* for example. Adding a suffix to this word gives it an additional syllable, which isn't necessarily true of all verbs with suffixes. *Dropped,* for example, is still a one-syllable word after you add the *ed* suffix. As for *rub,* notice how it gains an additional *b* when you attach a suffix to it.

This chapter helps you and your child explore suffixes, pronounce words with suffixes, and learn how to spell these words. Don't tense up! It'll all work out in the end.

Exploring the ed Suffix

The *ed* suffix offers challenges in meaning, tense, and sound. In grammar, *tense* isn't about being uptight, but rather refers to the form of a *verb* (an action word) that shows when an action takes place. The verb's tense tells you whether an action happened in the past, present, or future. The simple past tense describes actions that happened sometime in the past.

You form the simple past tense by adding the letters *ed* to the end of a verb. For example, the past tense of the verb *stop* is *stopped.* (I tell you where that extra *p* comes from in a minute.) Sometimes adding the *ed* suffix to a verb to form the past tense adds another syllable to the word. For example, *rented,* the past tense of the verb *rent,* is two syllables long.

The *ed* suffix also has three different sounds. Isn't the English language gloriously complicated? These sounds are *ĕd* (as in *listed*), *t* (as in *trapped*), and *d* (as in *robbed*).

Tables 11-1, 11-2, and 11-3 demonstrate the three phonics patterns that occur when you add *ed* to a verb to form the past tense. These three phonics patterns are:

- ✔ **The *ĕd* ending:** After verbs ending in *t* and *d,* the letters *ed* make the *ĕd* sound (see Table 11-1). When you add the *ed* suffix to words ending in *t* and *d,* the word gains an additional syllable.

- ✔ **The *t* ending:** After verbs ending in *s, x, k, ck, sh, ch, p,* and *f,* the *ed* suffix makes the *t* sound (see Table 11-2). When you add the *ed* suffix to words ending in these letters, you don't add an additional syllable.

- ✔ **The *d* ending:** After verbs ending in all other letters of the alphabet, the letters *ed* make the *d* sound (see to Table 11-3). These words also don't get an additional syllable when the *ed* suffix is added.

The past-tense suffix here and now

To understand what past tense means, a child must understand the difference between the past and the present. Don't take it for granted that children understand the difference; the concept of past and present tense can be hard for a young child of 4 or 5 to understand. Sometimes young kids can read like nobody's business, but concepts like the past tense are too abstract for them to grasp initially.

Children on the young side can usually read the words presented in this chapter, but they may not fully grasp how the words are spelled or the grammar associated with the past and present tense. Don't worry about it. As children progress beyond the basics in phonics, they pick up new concepts at their own pace. Eventually children understand the past tense as long as they keep practicing.

Having three sounds for one suffix can be confusing at first. For most children, adding *ed* comes naturally as their speech progresses, beginning around age 2. The confusion lies only in spelling past-tense verbs correctly when they begin to read.

Working with the ed suffix

When teaching the past-tense *ed* words, pronounce the words as your child looks at them on the printed page. This technique helps reinforce the sound represented by the *ed* and also what the letters *ed* do to the end of a word. Before your child reads the words in the tables in this chapter, choose a handful of words from each table, write them down, and say the endings in an exaggerated fashion.

Exaggerating the pronunciation of past-tense verbs can help your child hear the difference among the *ed* sounds. For example, if you say *worked,* make sure your child hears the *t* sound; if you say *stunned,* make sure he hears the *d* distinctly; if you say *listed,* he should clearly hear the *ed.*

Notice in all three tables (Tables 11-1, 11-2, and 11-3) that the vowel in the first syllable in every word (the root word) makes the short sound. Beyond that, the words in Table 11-1 are two-syllable words (for example, *tinted, planted,* and *ended*), whereas the words in the other two tables are one syllable long. Watch out! The one-syllable words in Table 11-2 and Table 11-3 are the confusing ones. Even though these words have the *ed* suffix, they contain only one syllable. *Mixed* and *scrubbed,* for example, are only one syllable.

Ask your child to read the columns. Refer to the columns as column 1, column 2, and so on. It enhances the child's ability to follow directions. For example, the parent instructs the child to the number of the column. This preparation can take place even before the parent sits down. Maybe the lesson is going to be brief, so the parent says, "Put your finger on the third column; we're only going to do this one now."

Table 11-1	ed Words that End in the ĕd Sound	
tinted	rested	listed
sifted	blended	nested
drifted	rented	rusted
blotted	ended	hinted
misted	rotted	planted
wended	welded	halted

Table 11-2	ed Words that End in the t Sound	
mapped	pecked	mixed
huffed	licked	stressed
snapped	zapped	puffed
inched	stripped	topped
slashed	trapped	dressed
dropped	slapped	capped

Table 11-3	ed Words that End in the d Sound	
fanned	planned	sobbed
mobbed	flagged	dimmed
dammed	thrilled	scrubbed
hugged	bobbed	manned
tilled	stilled	tugged
robbed	filled	milled

After your child masters the words in Tables 11-1, 11-2, and 11-3, have him read these sentences for practice. The goal is for him to be able to read as he speaks, so you want him to read each sentence to himself and then say it out loud with expression, naturally speaking the words in the sentence.

The boy wended his way on the rented pony.

We sifted and blended the mix.

I scrubbed and mopped the dirty floor.

Mastering the ed suffix

Adding *ed* isn't a difficult process, so the exercises in this section are stimulating but not difficult. These skill boosters enhance your child's ability to spell and read well.

Activity: Sentence Completion: *ed*

Preparation: Make a copy of or rewrite the sentences. Your child also needs a pencil.

To play: Read each sentence. Choose the correct word to complete the sentence from the word choices to the right of the sentence. Write the word on the line.

Example: Dave and Tony _____ at Day Hill Farm today. (played, plot)

Answer: played

1. Sally and Dan _____ at the toy store. (worked, works)
2. Sammy _____ the busy street. (pasted, passed)
3. Ann _____ for a green car. (looked, locked)
4. Tony _____ for his tired dad. (wiped, waited)
5. Rob _____ the slick ball. (tossed, toasted)
6. Rosy _____ her pretty mother. (hoped, helped)
7. Kathy _____ the old house. (rented, read)
8. Beth _____ the thick rope. (twin, twisted)
9. Sally _____ the pen to Ben. (hunted, handed)
10. The kitty _____ across the street. (stopped, darted)
11. Daddy _____ to catch the ball. (rushed, crushed)
12. Grace _____ hot dogs for the party. (roasted, lasted)
13. Danny _____ his mother for some candy. (asked, boxed)
14. The clock _____ away as we rested. (tacked, ticked)
15. Who _____ the cake for the picnic? (baked, waxed)
16. The class _____ papers on three trucks. (lasted, loaded)
17. The bike _____ when it was left in the rain. (rusted, tested)
18. We _____ our way around town. (taxed, wended)
19. We _____ the letters into 20 stacks. (nested, sorted)
20. Pete _____ his bike into the wall. (slammed, dreamed)

Answer Key: 1. worked 2. passed 3. looked 4. waited 5. tossed 6. helped 7. rented 8. twisted 9. handed 10. darted 11. rushed 12. roasted 13. asked 14. ticked 15. baked 16. loaded 17. rusted 18. wended 19. sorted 20. slammed

Activity: Self-Quiz: Using phrases in sentences

Preparation: Your child needs a piece of paper and a pencil.

To play: Ask your child to read the following phrases and to use these phrases in sentences. You can do this exercise orally and/or have your child write the sentences on a separate piece of paper.

1. listed by name
2. ended quickly
3. snapped at
4. lacked the time
5. smashed his hand
6. tilled the soil

Activity: Identifying the *ed* Suffix

Preparation: Make a copy of or rewrite the words in this table. Your child also needs a pencil.

To play: Ask your child to read the words in Table 11-4 and circle the *ed* suffixes. Have him print the letter of the sound he hears at the end — *ed, d,* or *t.*

Table 11-4		Identifying the ed Suffix		
fixed __	pointed __	messed __	perched __	picked __
plotted __	wailed __	buzzed __	bleached __	cuffed __
lifted __	burned __	boiled __	dreamed __	twisted __
slammed __	played __	rowed __	boxed __	lasted __
braided __	mended __	splashed __	dusted __	penned __
kicked __	turned __	printed __	walled __	reached __
stopped __	cashed __	bragged __	beaded __	wheeled __

Answer Key: Moving down the columns from top to bottom: 1: t, ed, ed, d, ed, t, t; 2: ed, d, d, d, ed, d, t; 3: t, d, d, d, t, ed, d; 4: t, t, d, t, ed, d, ed; 5: t, t, ed, ed, d, t, d

Taking on Suffix Spelling Challenges

The difficulty with words having the suffixes *ed, ing,* and *er* lies not only in the reading, but also in the spelling. Adding the *ed* suffix to a word sometimes means adding an additional syllable, and that makes decoding and spelling words even harder. This section looks at the challenges of spelling words that end in *ed, ing,* and *er*.

Doubling consonants (or not) with suffixes

When the *ed, ing,* or *er* suffix is added to a one-syllable word and the last three letters of the word follow the consonant-vowel-consonant (cvc) pattern, you double the final consonant in the word. For example, the last three letters in the word *spot* (*pot*) follow the cvc pattern, so the final consonant, *t,* is doubled when a suffix is added to the word (*spot, spotting, spotted*). However, if the last three letters of the word follow the vowel-consonant-consonant (vcc) pattern, you don't double the last consonant. For example, the last three letters in the word *pump* (*ump*) follow the vcc pattern, so the final consonant, *p,* isn't doubled when a suffix is added to the word (*pump, pumped, pumping*).

Look at the pattern of the last three letters in the words in this list. Notice what happens or doesn't happen to the last consonant when a suffix is added to these words:

> **plan:** planned, planning, planner
>
> **drum:** drummed, drumming, drummer
>
> **jest:** jested, jesting, jester
>
> **scratch:** scratched, scratching, scratcher

You can choose from two approaches when teaching your child how to spell words with *ing, ed,* and *er* suffixes:

- ✔ Have your child look at the whole word (*popping,* for example), the root word (*pop*), and the suffix (*ing*). Point to the root word, and either show your child that the consonant after the vowel is doubled when the suffix is added or show him that two consonants appear after the vowel.

- ✔ When the *ed, ing,* or *er* suffix is added to a word whose last syllable is a short vowel, and the last three letters of the word follow the consonant-vowel-consonant (cvc) pattern, the final consonant in the word is doubled.

Reading short-vowel words with suffixes

In a word that ends with the suffix *ing, ed,* or *er,* the first vowel is usually short if it comes before two consonants. For example, listen to the short vowel in these words: *dipping, rubbed,* and *sitter.* This guideline can help your child correctly pronounce words that end in *ing, ed,* or *er.* When reading these words with your child, point out the short-vowel sound in the word's root. After some practice, your child will be able to decode these words by applying the short-vowel sound before doubled consonants.

Read the following list with your child. Point out how the first vowel in a word is short because it comes before two consonants.

bedding	fretting	printer	softer
bending	getting	quilted	splitting
bumping	helper	rammed	stopper
canned	hemmed	redder	swimmer
clicking	jested	render	tilted
costing	jigging	robber	tossing
dipping	jotting	rubbed	tramping
dragged	jumper	runner	trapping
drummer	landed	sitter	yelled
dulled	lisping	shutter	
fishing	pinned	skinned	
flatter	planting	snatching	

Have your child read the following sentences for practice. Ask him to read them silently to himself first, and then read them out loud with expression to you, naturally speaking the words in the sentence. The goal is for him to be able to read as he speaks.

She went camping and fishing near her home.

The runner in the race started to jog.

The swimmer kept ramming the sidewall.

Activity: Sentence Completion: *ed, ing,* **or** *er*

Preparation: Make a copy of or rewrite the sentences. Your child also needs a pencil.

To play: Read the sentences below. Fill in the word in each sentence by adding *ed, ing,* or *er* to the word listed to the right.

1. Mother put the corn in the _____. (pop)

2. Are you _____ the party dress for Jane? (pin)

3. The swimmer _____ sun block on his arms. (rub)

4. Are you _____ at me? (yell)

5. The child _____ down the lane. (skip)

6. Will Ben be _____ by for dinner? (stop)

7. A masked _____ held up the bank. (rob)

8. Tom was _____ his new puppy. (pet)

9. The farmer _____ his crops today. (plant)

10. The clerk was _____ the parts order. (check)

Answer key: 1. popper 2. pinning 3. rubbed 4. yelling 5. skipped 6. stopping 7. robber 8. petting 9. planted 10. checking

Activity: Spelling Add-Ons: *ing, er,* and *ed*

Preparation: Make a copy of or rewrite the list of words. Your child also needs a pencil.

To play: Have your child add the *ing, er,* and *ed* suffixes to the following words. Write the correctly spelled word on the lines next to the root word.

Example: blend: blending, blender, blended

1. **stop:** _____, _____, _____

2. **trap:** _____, _____, _____

3. **rub:** _____, _____, _____

4. **jog:** _____, _____, _____

5. **print:** _____, _____, _____

6. **quilt:** _____, _____, _____

7. **bump:** _____, _____, _____

8. **snatch:** _____, _____, _____

Answer Key: 1. stopping, stopper, stopped; 2. trapping, trapper, trapped; 3. rubbing, rubber, rubbed; 4. jogging, jogger, jogged; 5. printing, printer, printed; 6. quilting, quilter, quilted; 7. bumping, bumper, bumped; 8. snatching, snatcher, snatched

Adding suffixes to long-vowel words

Adding suffixes to words with long-vowel sounds involves a small disappearing act. Words with long vowels typically end in *e* (see Chapter 7 for an explanation of long vowels). The word *joke,* for example, makes the long *o* sound and ends with the letter *e*. When you want to add the suffix *ing*, *er*, or *ed* to one of these long-vowel words, the *e* has to disappear.

Have your child read the following list. It demonstrates how to pronounce long-vowel words that have the *ing*, *ed*, or *er* suffix. Tell your child to hear the long vowels — *a*, *e*, *i*, *o*, and *u* — inside the words as he says the words.

biter	hiker	shaking	taming
blazer	joker	sided	thriving
choked	liked	skated	user
craned	noted	skater	voter
cubed	miner	sliding	voting
cuter	naming	sloping	waiter
dared	probing	smiling	wider
filer	riding	smoker	wiser
flaming	riper	stating	zoning
fuming	safer	stroking	
grading	scraper	swiping	
hating	shaded	tamer	

After your child masters the words in the list, have him read these sentences for practice:

The hiker is daring as he scales the peak.

Smiling at the joke, Jane ended the game.

We liked riding the safer pony.

Grading papers is a hard task.

Reinforcing long-vowel words with suffixes

Dropping the *e* and adding *ing* is tough. If your child has a good background in long vowel reading and spelling, he should do these activities with ease.

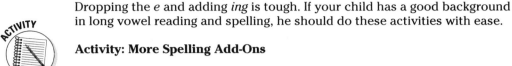

Activity: More Spelling Add-Ons

Preparation: Make a copy of or rewrite the list of words. Your child also needs a pencil.

To play: Have your child add the *ed, er,* and *ing* suffixes to the following words. Write the correctly spelled word on the lines next to the root word.

Example: hate: hated, hater, hating

1. **grade:** _____, _____, _____
2. **vote:** _____, _____, _____
3. **skate:** _____, _____, _____
4. **choke:** _____, _____, _____
5. **hike:** _____, _____, _____
6. **blame:** _____, _____, _____
7. **joke:** _____, _____, _____
8. **file:** _____, _____, _____

Answer Key: 1. graded, grader, grading; 2. voted, voter, voting; 3. skated, skater, skating; 4. choked, choker, choking; 5. hiked, hiker, hiking; 6. blamed, blamer, blaming; 7. joked, joker, joking; 8. filed, filer, filing

Activity: Self-Quiz: Similar words

Preparation: You need the following list of phrases. Your child needs a piece of paper and a pencil if you want him to write down some sentences for practice.

To play: Ask your child to read the following phrases and use each phrase in a sentence. You can do this exercise orally and/or have your child write the sentences on a separate piece of paper.

Example: mopped up, is moping

Answers: Mother mopped up after the dog. Bill is moping about the lost game.

1. at a dinner, in a diner
2. is sloping, is slopping
3. he scrapped, he scraped bottom
4. striped shirt, stripped the wall
5. tiled wall, tilled the soil
6. is bitter, is a biter
7. pined away, will be pinned
8. she moped all day, she mopped and moped
9. filed past a desk, filled a cup
10. is licking, liking dogs so much

Chapter 12

The Dual Personalities of s, c, and g

This chapter is kind of sweet. Why? Well, think about parfait desserts for a minute. You know, those desserts that have alternating layers of ice cream and fruit, or two different flavors of puddings stacked in a tall glass dish. You start eating and you taste strawberry. Then you hit the next layer and you taste lime. Then strawberry again. Then lime again. Yum! Just like the consonants *s, c,* and *g*. Each of them has two sounds, just like one parfait dessert has two flavors!

This chapter starts by reviewing how the letter *s* makes the *z* sound. Then it focuses on the sounds for the letter *c*. The letter *c* doesn't have its own sound (meaning it never says its name in a word), but instead sometimes sounds like *k* and sometimes like *s*. You also discover the hard and soft *g* sounds, such as the *g* sound in *gum* and the *g* sound in *gem*. These three consonants have more challenging consonant sounds.

Throughout this chapter, your child may encounter words that she doesn't know yet. Even though the primary focus of this book is decoding words through phonics, some words give you an excellent opportunity to teach your child vocabulary and comprehension. When she reads an unfamiliar word and asks what it means, explain the meaning of the word and use it in a sentence or two.

Consonants with two sounds

As you and your child work through this book, you get a good, solid look at the 26 consonants and vowels that comprise the alphabet. At this point, you know how different consonants and vowels really are. But, do you know what distinguishes consonants from vowels? Here are a few factoids:

✔ Pronouncing consonant sounds correctly requires you to use your lips, tongue, and teeth. They're considered *closed* sounds.

✔ Pronouncing vowel sounds doesn't require using your lips or teeth, and you move only the back of your tongue a little bit. Vowels are called *open* sounds because they come from the open mouth.

✔ Consonants are any letters in the alphabet that aren't vowels (*a, e, i, o,* and *u*). (*Y* and *w* are consonants that sometimes behave like vowels.)

✔ *Voiced* and *voiceless* refer to consonants; *open* and *closed* refer to vowels.

Sounding s As z in Words

If you read the heading to this section, you discover the two sounds an *s* can make. It can sound like an *s* (as in *sounding*) or a *z* (as in *words*).

Knowing when to pronounce *s* as a *z* is a little tougher to grasp, so that's what I focus on in this section.

"Z" clue to pronouncing the se ending

When words end in *se*, they almost always end with a *z* sound, like in the word *hose*. An example of an exception is the word *vise*, where the *s* sounds like *s*. However, put the prefix *ad-* in front of it, and *vise* becomes *advise* where the *s* sounds like *z*. Then you have the quirky word *grease;* the *s* is pronounced by some people as a *z*, and by others as an *s*.

Despite these examples, when you see *se* at the end of the word, think *z* first and you'll usually be right. Some exceptions include *course, horse,* and *Norse*.

The following list has words that end with the letters *se* and make a *z* sound. Have your child read the words for practice. You may also have her spell each word aloud after she reads the words. Point out that although these words end in the letters *se*, they make the *z* sound at the end.

cheese	hose	prose	these
close	nose	rise	those
ease	please	rose	wise
grease	pose	tease	

Have your child read the following sentences for practice. Ask her to read them silently to herself first, and then read them out loud with expression to you, naturally speaking the words in the sentence. The goal is for her to be able to read as she speaks.

Rose plays cards with me on Sunday.

If you grease the pan, the cake comes out well.

Please close the door, Roy.

"Z" clue of voiced consonants

Here's a fun fact: Although all consonants make sounds, not all consonants are voiced. What does that mean? Simply that to produce a *voiced consonant*, you use your voice; to produce a *voiceless consonant*, you expel air to produce the sound. (See Chapter 5 for more on voiced and voiceless consonants.)

The voiceless consonants are *t, p, k,* and *f.* When a word ends with a voiceless consonant followed by an *s,* the *s* sounds like *s.* For example, *hats, naps, picks,* and *doffs.*

However, when a voiced consonant is followed by an *s* at the end of a word, the *s* sounds like *z.* For example, *digs* is pronounced like *digz* because *g* is a voiced consonant.

Voiced consonants like the ones in this list are easy to read, but your child may have difficulty spelling them. Have your child notice in this table what sound the letter *s* makes when it follows a voiced consonant.

bells	crags	grids	rugs
bids	digs	grills	scrubs
brags	dogs	grubs	squids
brims	drugs	jags	webs
buns	fans	jells	weds
cars	frogs	pegs	wins
crabs	glens	rubs	yells

Have your child read the following sentences for practice:

Frogs breathe from their gills when they are tadpoles.

Mountains and crags form a pretty landscape.

The crabs crawled in the sand.

Tuning into Nice c Sounds

The letter *c* can sound like *k* (as in *cat*) or like *s* (as in *city*). When the letter *c* makes the sound of *k*, it is called a *hard c;* when the letter *c* makes the sound of *s*, it is called a *soft c*.

How do you know when to pronounce the hard or soft *c?* The letter *c* makes the hard *k* sound when it appears before the letters *a, o,* or *u*. For example, listen to the sound of *c* in these words: *card, cord, curd*. When *c* appears before the vowels *e* or *i*, or the consonant *y*, it makes a soft *c* sound: *certain, city, cycle*. The following sections give you and your child more practice with these sounds.

Hard c sound before a, o, and u

Make a flashcard with this statement:

Hard *c* says *k* before *a, o,* or *u,* as in *cat, come, cup*.

In this list, you see words that have the hard *c* sound before *a, o,* and *u*. Read the words in the list with your child.

cake	coal	core	cuff
came	coat	cost	cull
cane	cob	count	cup
cape	coin	cove	curb
card	cool	cowl	curd
case	cop	cube	cure
cast	cord	cue	cute

Have your child read these sentences to herself and then out loud:

> He stood at the curb for a bus.
>
> Please don't eat the apple core.
>
> We went on a picnic near the cove.

Soft c sound before e, i, and y

Make a flashcard with this statement:

> Soft *c* says *s* before *e, i,* and *y,* as in *cell, cite, cyst.*

Even though the letter *y* is a consonant, it behaves like a vowel when it comes after the letter *c.* In the word *cycle,* the *y* that follows the first *c* behaves like a vowel, so *c* makes the *s* sound.

Have your child read the words in the following list. Have her observe the position of the letter *c* in each word and the letter that follows *c.* You also see the versatile letter *y* pop up as a vowel in a cvc (consonant-vowel-consonant) pattern. Boy! That *y* really gets around!

bounce	circle	fence	prance
cease	cite	glance	price
cede	city	ice	prince
cell	civil	lance	since
cent	cyclone	mince	thence
center	cynic	nice	thrice
cider	cyst	pence	trace
cigar	dance	place	trounce
cinch	dice	pounce	

Ask your child to read the following sentences for practice:

> Wow! You paid a big price for that TV.
>
> I said it once; I said it twice; now I say it thrice!
>
> Cease what you're doing and get to bed.

Hard c sound before consonants

Make a flashcard with this statement:

> When the letter *c* comes before a consonant, it makes the *k* sound, as in *crab, clue, crimp.*

But when the letter *c* is followed by the consonant *h,* the two letters make the *ch* sound, as in *church.* (*Ch* is a *consonant digraph* — a combination of two letters that creates a new sound. I cover those in Chapter 5.)

This next list is full of words in which the letter *c* makes the *k* sound because it precedes a consonant. Have your child read the words in the list.

clad	clot	cram	cream
claim	clout	crash	creed
clap	clown	crass	creep
claw	cloy	crate	cross
clay	clue	crawl	crowd
clear	crab	craze	crush

After your child masters the words in this list, have her read these sentences for practice:

> The crass boy will claim the cream.

> The clown danced over the crawling crab.

> Will you cease creeping through the crowd?

Hard c at the end of words

Normally the letter *c* pairs with the letter *k* at the end of words to make the *k* sound (as in *back, crack,* and *sack,* for example). But this is the English language, so of course you have exceptions! Sometimes the letter *c* makes the *k* sound by itself at the end of words.

Have your child read the following words, focusing on the *k* sound at the end of the words. Even though the words are "big" words and have as many as four syllables, your child shouldn't have too much difficulty if she reads them one piece at a time. She should also be able to spell them without any trouble. All but three of the words contain short vowels.

antarctic	drastic	inorganic	rustic
antic	epic	magnetic	septic
arctic	fantastic	mimic	topic
athletic	frantic	plastic	toxic
cosmetic	hectic	public	tropic

Have your child read the following sentences out loud with expression. The goal is for her to be able to read the way she speaks.

Is it cold in the Arctic circle?

The use of a noun was a topic for English class.

The dump was a toxic waste place.

Challenging hard and soft c lessons

Before saying good-bye to the letter *c*, here's a bit of high-powered practice with this letter. If your child can get through the following list smoothly, she has a good grasp of how to pronounce the letter *c* in different kinds of words. Have her read aloud the words in the list, correcting her pronunciation if necessary.

accept	cinder	cord	cypress
bicycle	circle	cork	Cyprus
can't	circus	corpse	dunce
carpet	cistern	cove	face
cash	citrus	cull	France
cause	civic	curb	grace
cave	civil	curse	pencil
cedar	coach	curt	prince
cellar	coal	curve	since
center	coast	cycle	space
censor	coax	cyclone	thrice
census	code	cyclops	trance
cider	coil	cynic	twice

After your child reviews the words in the list, have her read these sentences for practice:

> The prince and the princess may arrive in the coach.
>
> The girl can't see the center of the circle.
>
> The coast is clear near the cave.

This list is full of more words that illustrate how to pronounce the letter *c*. Some words show up in later chapters. If they're too advanced for your child, you can always use them later in her course of study.

accept	cyclic	lacy	sentence
accident	cyclist	license	service
ace	cyclone	lucid	silence
acid	decent	merciful	since
advance	decision	mercy	slice
balance	difference	mice	space
biceps	distance	notice	specific
bicycle	embrace	pacific	spicy
brace	excel	placid	splice
cancel	except	precept	spruce
celebrate	excite	precise	Stacy
cellar	exercise	presence	stencil
cement	face	price	succeed
center	fancy	quince	success
census	grace	racing	surface
certain	gracie	racism	trace
cinch	grocery	rancid	trice
cinnamon	icicle	recent	triceps
circulate	icy	recess	truce
circumference	innocence	recite	twice
civil	instance	reference	vaccinate
conceal	intercept	resistance	vice
concept	introduce	rhinoceros	voice
concise	juice	romance	
convince	juicy	science	
council	justice	scissors	

You can use the previous list as a vocabulary list. Post one or two of the more difficult words on your refrigerator and encourage everyone in the family to use the words frequently. You also can print the words on flashcards. For example, write *vaccinate* on one side of a flashcard, and on the other side, draw a picture of the action. Put the definition and the word under the action.

Practicing the varied sounds of c

Your child is presented with a challenge in this chapter to learn some new sounds with unfamiliar words. The following exercises strengthen her knowledge of *c*. Also, she gets practice in decoding, sentence completion, and reading a good story.

Activity: Sentence Completion: *C*

Preparation: Make a copy of or rewrite the sentences. Your child also needs a pencil.

To play: Read each of the following sentences. Choose the proper word to complete the sentence from the word bank to the right of the sentence. Write the word on the line.

1. Bruce, roll those _____! (dice, done, deed)

2. Do you like corn on the _____? (core, cob, cube)

3. Someday your _____ will come. (then, prince, proud)

4. These storms come in a _____. (train, cart, cycle)

5. Jess and Beth went to the _____ with two brothers. (dance, down, dot)

6. I want to _____ skate for the rest of my life. (fond, pounce, ice)

7. There was a _____ of soap left in the sink. (trace, sop, seep)

8. Sue showed me the _____ with a lock. (glad, glance, case)

9. The _____ kept the puppy inside. (fence, stun, share)

10. _____ to ten before you run. (Many, Those, Count)

Answer Key: 1. dice 2. cob 3. prince 4. cycle 5. dance 6. ice 7. trace 8. case 9. fence 10. count

Activity: Stories to Reinforce the Soft *c*

Preparation: You need the following stories. Your child needs a pencil and a piece of paper if you want her to write down the soft *c* words.

To play: Read the fictional stories with your child for practice. Have her pick out all the soft *c* words. She can also print them on a separate piece of paper.

Magic in the Snow

It was late winter on the plains of Montana. Dad asked me to go out and check the fence line in the north corner. The sky began to shower me with white snow that had not been forecast. My horse, Prince, and I moved in a slow pace with a wind so strong that I could not breathe. We were covered with snow and became lost in the last hard snow of the season.

I saw only an endless sea of white, and my face stung from the icy flakes of snow. How long we were out in this storm, I did not know. My senses began to dull as the snow kept coming in giant waves of white. The wind was biting, and it excited my horse to try harder to get to a safe place. As we plodded along, the horse and I became weaker and weaker. I tried to smile, but my lips were frozen stiff. I was thinking of the fun we used to have in the snow. I became very sleepy, but I was aware of Prince falling to the snowy ground with me along with him. I sunk into the cold, soft snow. My teeth no longer chattered as I slipped into a dream-like state. As my senses further dulled, I lay there in a trance, dreaming of the scents of home-fires, warm food, and a spicy mug of cider. I fell into an unconscious state with my much-loved Prince beside me.

—From the Journal of Lucy Brice

Back at the Homestead

Lance Painter pulled the barn door closed behind him and faced the fury of the storm coming in from the north. Pulling the collar of his duster up around his neck, and pushing the brim of his hat down over his face, he braced himself for the gusts of wind that almost forced him to the ground.

Lance had only taken a few steps as he headed back to the ranch house when he heard the loud barking of his dog, Clancy. He yelled, "Be quiet, Clancy, come here!" The hound dog pranced toward him, his ears erect, and his wiry coat covered with snow.

Since the time when Clancy was left on the plains and Lance had found the lost puppy, the two began a certain kinship. Clancy kept up his constant barking, and Lance's patience snapped. He was cold, tired, and hungry. He did not want this excited dog keeping him from the warmth of his home. Lance struggled through the freezing drifts, but old Clancy kept it up. The house was now only a short distance away.

Finally, it seemed that the dog cried off and went away. As Lance braced himself against the door of his home and pushed inward, Clancy came beside him. The dog was chafing at the bit and seemed to be holding some object between his teeth as he raced back and forth at Lance's feet. He jumped up on Lance, and at the same time, the dog shook a red and yellow neck scarf in his teeth. Lance grabbed it, and as Clancy raced around him, he understood.

Without waiting one more second, he followed Clancy into the great white void. He stumbled across the wind-driven snow and stopped where Clancy led him. On the ground was what appeared to be a human form. He bent over and felt a pulse on a young girl's wrist; she was still breathing. He scooped her up into his arms. As he turned to head back to the ranch, his trusty dog's ears perked up once more. Clancy saw the girl's horse pawing at the snow. He then guided Prince back to the barn, as Lance, carrying the girl, slowly but surely made it to the ranch house.

Kicking open the door and placing the girl on the rug, Lance pulled the frozen coat off and discovered Lucy Brice, the daughter of a cowpoke who worked on his ranch. Although Lucy was quiet and pale in color, Lance knew that Clancy had saved the young girl's life that day.

Answer Key: face, Lucy, Brice, fence, Prince, pace, icy, excited, place, trance, scents, spicy, cider, unconscious, Lance, faced, braced, forced, Clancy, pranced, since, certain, patience, distance, raced, placing

Activity: Joke: Gracie

To play: Ask your child to tell you the joke. Then have her explain to you the different versions of *c* in the joke.

> Gracie, who was 4, was drinking from her juice box. All of a sudden she began to hiccup. It wouldn't stop. She said to her mom, "Please don't give me this juice again. It makes my teeth cough."

Answer Key: Gracie (soft *c*), juice (soft *c*), hiccup (hard *c*), cough (hard *c*)

Activity: Poem: Baby's Dance

To play: Read the poem and let your child pick out all the *c* words and write them down.

Baby's Dance

Dance, little baby, dance up high,

Never mind baby, mother is by;

Crow and caper, caper and crow,

There little baby, there you go:

Up to the ceiling, down to the ground,

Backwards and forwards, round and round.

Then dance, little baby, and mother shall sing,

With the merry gay coral, ding, ding, a-ding, ding.

—Ann Taylor (1800s)

Answer Key: dance, crow, caper, ceiling, coral

Gauging the Sounds of g

After dealing with the variations of the *s* and *c* sounds, you may be feeling like a phonics genius — or maybe you feel a little gaga. Either way, that's great because it's time for a genial discussion of the letter *g!*

Like the letter *c,* the letter *g* can make two different sounds: the *hard g* (as in *gum*) and the *soft g,* which sounds like a *j* (as in *age*). Guidelines governing the sound of *g* aren't as rigid as those for *c,* as you discover in the upcoming sections. But I give you some genuinely good clues to help you recognize when to say the hard *g* and when to say the soft *g.*

Hard g sound before a, o, and u

Make a flashcard with this statement:

> A hard *g* says *g* before the letters *a, o,* and *u.* For example, *game, gong,* and *gull.*

The hard *g* is spoken because the letter *g* precedes the letter *a, o,* or *u.* Most kids know the hard *g* in *gum, got, game, gut* — words that come early in their reading experience. Some of the early words they learn, like *give* and *get,* don't follow this guideline. However, because it applies to so many *g* words, the guideline helps.

Sometimes *g* is hard before the letters *i* and *e*.

Have your child read this list of words. Emphasize to her that these words start with the hard *g* sound and have her notice which vowels follow the letter *g* in these words.

gale	gave	God	gull
gallop	gaze	gong	gulp
game	goad	gosh	gush
gap	goal	gown	gust
gash	goat	gulch	gut

Have your child read the following sentences for practice:

See the goat graze on the hillside.

Grandmother began to brace herself for a big gust of wind.

The sea gull swooped down to get the fish.

Listening for soft g at the beginning of a word

Make a flashcard with this statement:

> At the beginning of a word, the letters *ge*, *gi*, and *gy* **may** make the soft *g* sound **or** the hard *g* sound. Example include the words *get* and *gem*, and *gills* and *gin*.

You see that very few words that begin with *gy* have a hard *g*. That means that the letter *g* sounds like *j* in nearly all the *gy* words that you encounter.

Have your child read this list of words. It's a sampling of words that have the *j* sound at the beginning. Make sure that she pronounces the *j* sound rather than the hard *g*. Point out to her that these words start with the letters *ge*, *gi*, or *gy*.

gem	germ	gin	gym
Gene	gibe	gist	gyp
gent			

Have your child read each sentence to herself and then say it out loud with expression, naturally speaking the words in the sentence:

Nancy and Gene went to the gym.

Gina sneezed and she said, "I must have a germ."

George was a dapper gent with his hat and cane.

Saying j for ge at the end of a word

Make a flashcard with this statement:

The letters *ge* say the *j* sound when they appear at the end of a word, as in *huge*.

Have your child read the next list of words. Observe the *j* sound at the end of these one-syllable words. Make sure your child says the *j* sound and doesn't attempt to end these words with a hard *g* sound. The spelling is tricky here, so have her practice the words not only for decoding but also for spelling.

age	gorge	large	splurge
badge	huge	lodge	urge
cringe	judge	sledge	wage

Have your child read the following sentences for practice. Ask her to read them silently to herself first, and then read them out loud. The goal is for her to be able to read the way she speaks.

Let's splurge and go to the mall for a shopping trip.

All men should make a decent wage.

Madge and George made a huge snowman.

Activity: Sentence Completion: *g*

Preparation: Make a copy of or rewrite the sentences. Your child also needs a pencil.

To play: Read each of the following sentences. Choose the proper word to complete the sentence from the word bank to the right of the sentence. Write the word on the line.

1. When I was that _____, I liked to skate. (year, age, tag)

2. Wheat _____ is good for you. (angel, merge, germ)

3. There was a _____ snowstorm in the east. (hour, huge, rain)

4. The _____ is a shiny stone. (girl, gone, gem)

5. The Indian went back to the _____. (silly, lull, lodge)

6. Joyce got the _____ of the joke. (gust, gist, thing)

7. I will be the one to _____ that event. (jut, judge, pink)

8. Lance took his ball to the _____. (purple, dear, gym)

Answer Key: 1. age 2. germ 3. huge 4. gem 5. lodge 6. gist 7. judge 8. gym

Activity: Riddles

To play: Ask your child to read the riddles and note the *g* sounds. Before she reads the answer to the second question, ask her to count the ridges on a dime.

Q: When is a car not a car?

A: When it turns into a garage.

Q: How many ridges does a dime have?

A: A dime has 118 ridges around the edge.

Mixing the hard and soft g

This next list presents a mixture of words that make the hard and soft *g* sounds. Have your child read the words in this table to find out how well she understands the concepts in this chapter. If your child mispronounces a word, gently tell her the correct pronunciation.

angel	gauze	goal	nudge
bilge	gear	goblin	page
bridge	gee	goes	plunge
charge	gel	gorge	ridge
dodge	gender	gosh	serge
edge	gene	grudge	singe
fringe	gentle	gulf	smudge
fudge	German	gust	suggest
gage	gerund	gutter	tragic
gall	giant	gypsum	trudge
gang	giblet	hedge	twinge
gape	gill	hinge	wedge
garden	ginger	magic	
garment	girth	merge	

Ask your child to read the following sentences for practice:

The fringe was on the edge of the garment.

We could trudge over the bridge to the glen.

The worker had a smudge of paint on the gutter.

The final list in this chapter presents multisyllable words with soft *g* sounds. These words are beyond the comprehension of a young child, but they can be fun for older children to decode. Explain to your child that the word ending *ology* means "the study of." Remind your child that she is studying *phonology,* "the study of sound."

archeological	etiological	mythological	psychologist
astrological	etymologist	mythology	seismology
biological	geological	neurological	technological
biologist	geologist	paleontology	theology
cardiologist	ideological	pathological	zoologist
cosmetologist	meteorological	phonology	zoology
ecologist	meteorology	physiological	
entomologist	musicologist	psychological	

Chapter 13

Tapping into Unusual Spellings

Some people like to say that English isn't a phonetic language. More accurately, English isn't a *completely* phonetic language. Because about 85 percent of the language generally sounds the way it's spelled, you can say that the English language is about 85 percent phonetic.

This chapter delves into the 15 percent of the English language that isn't phonetic. I look at vowel combinations to help your child become a better speller and reader. This chapter takes you through the troublesome *ie* (as in *field*), *ea* (as in *great*), *ou* (as in *cough*), *ew* (as in *blew*), and the *ei* (as in *eight*) vowel digraphs. You discover how to pronounce these sounds and pick up a few tricks to help you remember how to spell them.

Introducing Vowel Digraphs

A *digraph* is a two-letter combination that produces a single sound. Digraphs can be two vowels walking (as in *cried*) or they can be exhibited as consonant digraphs. For example, *ch* (as in *chat*), *th* (as in *thud*), and *sh* (as in *ship*) are digraphs. Chapter 5 explores consonant digraphs, and in this chapter, I talk about vowel digraphs.

A *vowel digraph* is a two-vowel combination that makes a single sound. For example, vowel digraphs appear in the words *eight, bread, tried,* and *cue*.

Vowel digraphs are two vowels that represent one sound, be it a long sound, as in *pain, bean, pie,* or *cue,* or a short sound, as in *thread,* or another sound, as in *book, oil, toy,* or *clown.*

Third sounds and diphthongs are also digraphs. Look for instances through-out the book where I discuss the sounds of *au, aw, oo, oi, oy, ou, ow* (as in *cow*), and *ew*.

Exploring the Vowel Digraph ie

When the letters *ie* appear together, you can pronounce this digraph in a couple different ways. Like other vowel digraphs, the vowel digraph *ie* has two forms:

- ✔ Say the long sound of *i*, as in *lie, died,* and *pie*.
- ✔ Say the long sound of *e*, as in *field, piece,* and *chief.*

In this instance, the learner needs to memorize the spellings. The lists and reading examples in the pages that follow will help your child do that.

The letters *ie* make the long *e* sound more than they make the long *i* sound. Here are some words to help you remember the two sounds: *piece of pie.*

Looking at ie and the long sound of i

The following list shows the vowel digraph *ie,* which says the long sound of *i.* This sound occurs in nouns, adjectives, and verbs. Have your child read the words to give him a sense of what the digraph *ie* is.

cried	flies	pies	tries
cries	fried	pried	tie
die	fries	pries	ties
died	lie	rye	vie
dried	lied	skies	vied
dries	pie	tried	

Have your child read these sentences silently first and then say them out loud.

The child cries for his mother.

The baker fries pies on Sunday.

Cindy cried when the dried flowers were lost.

Examining ie and the long sound of e

This next list shows the vowel digraph *ie,* which says the long sound of *e.* Have your child read the words in this list after he reads the digraph words in the previous list. Make sure your child clearly understands the difference between these *ie* digraphs. The only way to know the difference between the digraphs is to memorize them.

belief	fiend	priest	thieves
believe	grief	relief	wield
brief	grieves	shield	yield
chief	niece	shriek	
field	piece	thief	

Ask your child to read these sentences silently first, and then say them out loud for practice.

This field yields just a hundred ears of corn.

I believe my niece had three pieces of mince pie.

She cried with grief at the thief.

When your child is ready to learn vowel digraphs, his reading is quite advanced. He should be able to grasp these words easily. This spelling has to be memorized.

To help your child master the *ie* vowel digraphs, construct sentences using words from the first two lists in this chapter. Making a phrase or sentence with a word or words from both lists is easy. For example, *a piece of pie* contains both types of *ie* sounds. Encourage your child to invent his own *ie* vowel digraph phrases or sentences by using words from both lists.

Activity: An Unfortunate Miss

To play: Read this limerick and ask your child to point out where the vowel digraph *ie* appears. After you read it, ask your child to read it as well.

There was a young lady who tried

A diet of apples and died.

The unfortunate miss

Really perished of this:

Too much cider inside her inside.

—Anonymous

Activity: The Boy Who Cried Wolf

To play: Ask your child to read this story and pick out the words with the *ie* digraph and the long *e* sound. It contains many words with the *ie* digraphs, so it's excellent practice.

> Once upon a time the chief of the clan had many sheep. He tried to take care of them by himself, but it was too much for him. Therefore, he hired a boy to shepherd them in a nearby field. "Watch the sheep carefully," he said to the boy. "Do not let the wolf get any of them."
>
> Some men were working not far from the field. They told the boy that if a wolf did appear and try to catch the sheep he should call out loudly, "Wolf! Wolf!" They said that they would come and help.
>
> The boy watched the sheep every day and tried to shield them from harm, but no wolf came to take them. It was a great relief for him.
>
> One day, he was so bored that he wanted to play a trick. He cried, "Wolf! Wolf!" The men came running. The boy laughed and said, "There is no wolf. I was tricking you."
>
> "Good grief!" the men cried. They pointed their fingers at the boy and said, "Do not do that again! You hear?"
>
> After a few days, the boy did it again. Only two men came. "Where is the wolf?" they said. The boy said again that he was just playing with the men. The men shrieked, "You must yield to us and stop now!"
>
> However, one day the wolf really came. He grabbed the little lambs in his teeth and ran away as fast as he could. The boy was in shock, but he did cry out. "Wolf! Wolf!" he shouted. No one came. Off went the wolf with lamb dinner in his mouth. The boy never tried to play a joke on the men after that.

Answer Key: chief, field, shield, relief, grief, shrieked, yield

Activity: Tongue Twister: Caesar

To play: Read this tongue twister to your child and ask him to pick out the variety of long *e* sounds. Let him try to say the tongue twister.

He believed Caesar could see people seizing the seas.

Answer Key: he, believed, Caesar, see, people, seizing, seas

Looking Farther Into the oo's

In Chapter 8, you study the third sounds of *o* and *u* in two-syllable words. You discover that the third sound of *o* says ōō (as in *move*) and the third sound of *u* says ŏŏ (as in *bush*). These two sounds — ōō and ŏŏ — are the sounds that the *oo* digraph (also called the third sounds of *o* and *u*) make. When *oo* appears in words, the letters make either the ōō sound, as in *zoo*, or the ŏŏ sound, as in *book*.

Ask your child to read the words in this list. Have him notice the third sound of *u*, the ŏŏ sound (as in *book*) in these words. Refer to the vowel chart on the cheat sheet at the front of this book. As soon as you finish with this table, move forward to the next one so that your child can contrast the two sounds that the letters *oo* make in words.

bankbook	driftwood	looker	outlook
booker	dogwood	manhood	redwood
checkbook	footer	matchbook	workbook
cooker	hardwood	notebook	

Here's a good way to remember the *oo* sounds: say *moon book*.

Have your child read these sentences silently first and then say them out loud:

Sue and Jim had a picnic by the bubbling brook and the dogwood tree.

Tony and Alex left their workbooks on the bus.

Liz placed a beef roast in the slow cooker.

The vowel digraph ōō says the sound you hear in *zoo*. The next list presents words that contain this sound. You and your child may want to write a short story with some of the interesting words in this list — doing so would make an excellent vocabulary lesson.

baboon	buffoon	looped	schooner
balloon	classroom	monsoon	spittoon
bathroom	cooler	mushroom	teaspoon
bedroom	crooner	pontoon	typhoon
boomer	doubloon	raccoon	
booster	harpoon	roofer	
booted	lampoon	rooter	

Have your child read these sentences silently first and then read them out loud:

The Spanish doubloon is an old coin.

Get the baby a booster chair.

The hot air balloon rose up in the air.

Activity: Poetry and Jokes: *oo*

Preparation: You need paper and pencil.

To play: Ask your child to read the following poem, limerick, and joke, and point out the o͞o sounds.

Hey! Diddle, Diddle

Hey! Diddle, diddle,

The cat and the fiddle,

The cow jumped over the moon;

The little dog laughed

To see such sport,

And the dish ran away with the spoon.

—Mother Goose

Answer Key: moon, spoon

Limerick

A tutor who tooted the flute,

Tried to teach two young tooters to toot

Said the two to the tutor

Is it harder to toot or

To tutor two tooters to toot?

Answer Key: tutor, who, tooted, flute, to, two, tooters, toot

Joke

Q: What kind of lights did Noah use on the ark?

A: Flood lights.

Answer Key: flood

Moving Up with Some Great ea Digraphs

It's hard to believe that the digraph *ea* makes so many different sounds. Consider these words that look somewhat alike (because they include the letters *ea*) but sound very different from each other: *eat*, *steak*, *learn*, and *heart*.

A good way to remember the sounds of *ea* is to say, "Eat more bread than steak."

The *ea* pattern words aren't hard to read or to comprehend. Most of the *ea* words you encounter in this chapter are very familiar words — the kind you read or hear every day. The problem is the spelling! Again, you usually just have to memorize the spelling of these *ea* words. You can practice the spellings in groups of words with like sounds.

Just a little tidbit before you tackle the *ea* vowel digraphs: *Dreamt* is the only English word that ends in the letters *mt*.

The following list is full of *ea* digraphs that make the ēa sound. As I mention earlier in this chapter, this digraph follows the guideline that the first vowel, *e,* is long and the second vowel, *a,* is silent. Ask your child to read the words in the list, write down some of the words, and use some of the words in sentences. Make sure he understands that the letters *ea* in these words make the long *e* sound.

beach	clean	heat	queasy
bead	dear	lease	read
beam	dream	least	ream
beast	east	peace	scream
beat	eat	plea	sea
cheat	gleam	plead	tear

For practice, have your child read these sentences silently first and then say them out loud:

The little old man had a gleam in his eye.

The child said, "Mom, I feel queasy this morning."

The printer works with one ream of paper at a time.

Table 13-1 lists the other *ea* digraphs. This table clearly shows you and your child the complicated array of sounds that can come from the two little vowels *ea* when they appear in words. Ask your child to read the words in Table 13-1 and write them in sentences.

Table 13-1		ea Digraphs	
The ĕa Sound	*The eā Sound*	*The ur Sound*	*The är Sound*
bread	break	early	hearken
dead	great	earn	heart
dread	steak	earnest	heartbeat
heavy		earth	hearten
lead		heard	heartfelt
read		learn	hearth
steady		pearl	heartless
tear		search	heartsick
wealth		yearn	hearty

Have your child read these sentences silently first, and then say them out loud.

> Caitlin heard the steady beat of her heart.

> Each of us learns to hear the least beat.

> We went in search of a pearl on the beach.

Activity: Story: *ea*

To play: Read this story to your child and ask him to pick out the *ea* sounds. Let him try to read the story as well.

> An earnest little lad was in a relative's wedding.

> As he was coming down the aisle, he would take two steps, stop, and turn to the crowd.

> While facing the crowd, he would put his hands up like claws and roar.

> So it went, step, step, roar, step, step, roar, all the way down the aisle.

> As you can imagine, the crowd was near tears from laughing so heartily by the time he reached the pulpit.

> When asked what he was doing, the child sniffed and said, "I was being the Ring Bear."

Answer Key: earnest, near, tears, heartily, Bear

Activity: Poem with a Riddle

To play: Read this riddle and point out the *ea* words. Ask your child to read it after you for reinforcement of *ea*.

> There is one that has a head without an eye,

> And there's one that has an eye without a head

> You may find the answer if you try:

> And when all is said,

> Half the answer hangs upon a thread.

> —Christina Rosetti

Answer Key: head, thread (The answer to the riddle is *a needle.*)

Activity: Zephyr

To play: Read the poem and point to the words *heifer* and *deafer.* Ask your child to read the poem after you for reinforcement of the spelling.

> **Zephyr**
>
> A farmer once called his cow Zephyr,
>
> She seemed such a lovable heifer.
>
> When the farmer drew near,
>
> She kicked on his ear.
>
> And now he is very much deafer.

Cueing You to another View of u

Continuing your adventures in unusual spellings, you now come to the long *u* sound. This sound is heard in words with such different spellings as *sue, feud, few, suit,* and *fuse.* Spelling the long *u* sound in words is the kind of thing that drives English language students crazy. Never let anyone tell you that the English language is easy to spell. But, that's what makes phonics cool, because it allows the child to be able to spell so many words!

The long *u* also comes into play in one-syllable words that end in *e,* such as *cube.* In these words (I call them magic *e* words because the *e* at the end is silent), the *u* makes the *ū* sound (Chapter 7 looks in detail at making long vowels in words with the silent, magic *e*).

And that's still not the end of it. After the letters *j* (*jute*), *r* (*rule*), and *l* (*Lewis*), and the initial blend *ch* (*chew*), the letter *u* makes the third sound of *o* (ōō). These pages look into the whys and wherefores of decoding the long sound of *u*.

Exploring the long sound of u

Table 13-2 lists words that have the long sound of *u.* As your child reads the words in this table, make sure that he enunciates the long *u* sound clearly. If you follow the guideline that, in a syllable with two vowels the first vowel is usually long and the second is usually silent, these words will be much easier to pronounce. In ordinary speech, however, most people replace the long sound of *u* with the third sound of *o* (ōō). This is particularly true when the letter *u* follows *d* (as in *due*), *t* (as in *tube*), or *s* (as in *suit*).

Ask your child to read the words in Table 13-2 and apply the long sound of *u* to each word. Point out how the silent, magic *e* words make the same *u* sound as the words with the *ue, ui, ew,* and *eu* vowel digraphs. After he masters the words, dictate the words to him in an oral spelling quiz.

Table 13-2		Long Sound of u
Digraphs	*Digraphs*	*Magic E Words*
cue	deuce	cube
due	dew	cure
dues	feud	cute
hue	few	fume
sue	hew	fuse
suit	mew	mule

For practice, have your child read these sentences silently first and then say them out loud:

> The deuce of hearts trumped the ace of clubs.
>
> The library book is due on Thursday.
>
> I wish there were a cure for the common cold.

Exceptions to the long u

After the letters *l, r,* and *j,* and the initial blend *ch,* the letter *u* doesn't make the long *u* sound (ū); it makes the third sound of *o* (ōō). Listen to the letter *u* combinations in these words to see what I mean: *blue, rude, Judy,* and *chew.*

Learning how to handle the letter *u* when it comes after *l, r, j,* and *ch* can be tiresome. The following list makes it a little easier by giving your child some practice.

Ask your child to read the words in this list. Then ask him to spell some of the words. Make sure he understands that the words in this list are pronounced a little differently from the long *u* words in Table 13-2.

blew	crude	jubilee	rue
blue	drew	Jude	rude
brute	flew	Judy	rule
chew	flue	Jupiter	threw
clue	flute	jute	true
crew	glue	plume	

For practice, ask your child to read these sentences silently first and then say them out loud:

The news of the feud drew a large crowd.

Judy drew a crude mule for the crew.

The clue to the crime was found in the blue suit.

Activity: Limerick

To play: Ask your child to read the limerick and point out the long *u* words.

An oyster from Kalamazoo

Confessed he was feeling quite blue

"For," he said "as a rule,

When the weather turns cool

I most always get put in the stew."

Answer Key: Kalamazoo, blue, rule, cool, stew

Weighing In On ei

When it comes to spelling, the first thing that most people learn is "*i* before *e* except after *c*." And then they quickly learn that this has a number of exceptions. And then they get discouraged.

This little ditty shows just how complicated spelling *ei* and *ie* words can be:

It's *i* before *e*, except after *c*,

Or when it sounds like *ā*, as in *neighbor* and *weigh*,

Or when it sounds like *ēar*, as in the word *weird*,

Unless it sounds like *ēek*, as in desert *sheik*!

You can find *ei* digraphs in many familiar words, most of which have strange and challenging spellings. This section discusses the vowel digraph *ei*.

The following list is filled with words containing the *ei* digraph. These words are sometimes spelled incorrectly even by seasoned spellers. (By the way, two of the words in this list, *seizure* and *leisure*, make the *zh* sound. This sound is explored in Chapter 17.)

Read the words in the list with your child. You can use this list as a reference when exploring grammar and composition.

ceiling	either	perceive	sleigh
conceit	feign	receipt	their
conceive	freight	receive	veil
deceit	heir	receiver	vein
deceive	leisure	rein	weigh
eight	neighbor	seize	weird
eighth	neighborly	seizure	weir
eighty	neither	skein	weight

For practice, have your child read these sentences silently first, and then say them out loud for practice:

Neither baby weighs eight pounds.

Their job is to seize the key.

They will either stay or obey.

Activity: Picking Out *ei* Digraphs

Preparation: You need paper and pencil.

To play: Read the joke with your child and have him pick out the *ei* digraphs. He can write them on a separate piece of paper.

Q: Why was 6 (six) afraid of 7 (seven)?

A: Because 789 (seven eight nine).

Answer Key: eight

Dealing with the Troublesome Letters *ou*

The hardest digraph of all to master is the *ou* combination, which is also a diphthong. The *ou* combination is two vowels coming together to make a completely new sound (as in *out, pout,* and *shout*). (Diphthongs, when two vowels come together in one syllable and make one *double* vowel sound, are explained in Chapter 9.) The letters *ou* represent no fewer than seven different sounds:

- ✔ The /ou/ sound, as in *out* and *about*.
- ✔ The ō sound, as in *soul* and *though*.
- ✔ The ŏ sound, as in *cough* and *ought*.
- ✔ The ŭ sound, as in *trouble* and *country*.
- ✔ The third sound of o, as in *soup* and *group*.
- ✔ The third sound of u, as in *could* and *your*.
- ✔ The ur sound, as in *courage* and *nourish*.

This section looks into these troublesome *ou* words. Knowing the meanings of these words and using a tape recorder to reinforce the sounds is of great help with the *ou* words. Make a tape or CD of the words so your child can hear the sounds for reinforcement.

By the way, young readers usually find these three *ou* words word the most confusing: *though, thought,* and *through*.

Table 13-3 presents all six variations of the *ou* diphthong. Ask your child to take crack at reading the words in this table. This table also makes a nice reference.

Table 13-3			The Six Sounds of ou		
ō	ŏ	ŭ	ōō	ŏŏ	*our = ur*
course	bought	country	group	could	courage
court	brought	couple	soup	should	courteous
dough	cough	double	through	would	courtesy
four	fought	famous	tour	your	flourish
mourn	ought	southern	tourist	yours	journal
pour	sought	touch	wound		journey
soul	thought	trouble	you		nourish
though	trough	young	youth		scourge

Have your child read these sentences silently first and then say them out loud.

> The young couple could be brought to court.
>
> He fought for their country in his youth.
>
> The four tourists were in double trouble.

Activity: Filling in the Blanks: *ou*

Preparation: You need paper and pencil.

To play: Read the sentences and choose a troublesome *ou* word from the three words in parentheses to correctly complete each one. You may copy these sentences or rewrite the exercise for your child.

1. The child had a _____ today. (clout, cough, sick)

2. I like the _____ states. (upset, sauce, southern)

3. Daniel Boone began his _____. (journey, cape, ounce)

4. The music was _____. (soup, soulful, sandy)

5. Mark and Dan took a _____ on car repair. (clown, coaster, course)

Answer Key: 1. cough 2. southern 3. journey 4. soulful 5. course

Looking at helpful vowel sound comparisons

The table in this sidebar is a reference table designed to improve your child's spelling and decoding skills. Notice some spelling patterns in this table:

- Columns 1 and 2 show a basic recap of the vowel digraph *ow* (blow) as seen in Chapter 7, and the diphthong *ow* (now) as seen in Chapter 9.

- In columns 3 and 4, when *ge* (cage) is preceded by a vowel, you hear the long vowel sound; when the vowel is followed by *dge* (ledge), you hear the short vowel sound.

- Columns 5 and 6 also follow a spelling pattern. This is the sixth syllable type in the English language, the consonant *le* syllable. When there is one consonant before *le* (as in *rifle*), the preceding vowel is long; when there are two consonants preceding the letters *le* (as in *brittle*), the vowel is short (the word *triple* is one of very few exceptions to this guideline).

Give your child extra help with the table. Just being able to read these words is sufficient. If you care to, select some of the vowel patterns in the table and develop them with your child.

Vowel Sound Comparisons

Digraph	Diphthong	Long	Short	Long	Short
shown	brow	raged	edge	able	fumble
follow	frown	cage	nudge	trifle	sprinkle
shadow	prow	page	pledge	noble	mantle
flow	browse	stage	budge	cable	uncle
mow	powder	huge	sledge	rifle	struggle
bow	bow	sage	drudge	fable	sniffle
sow	sow	caged	ledge	maple	brittle
row	row	oblige	lodge	stable	trample

Activity: Tongue Twister: *ough*

To play: This is an old tongue twister that contains nine ways you can pronounce the combination *ough*. If your child can read it, have him say it out loud. I wouldn't begin to ask him to write down the words. He'll probably be worn out!

A rough-coated, dough-faced, thoughtful ploughman strode through the streets of Scarborough; after falling into a slough, he coughed and hiccoughed.

Grouping the Difficult y

The letter *y* is a consonant, but you use it more often as a vowel. One challenge facing your child as he learns to read is being able to determine which vowel sound the letter *y* makes in words.

Read the words in Table 13-4 with your child, keeping in mind that the letter *y* creates all kinds of difficulties where reading is concerned. You can treat Table 13-4 as a reference table and return here when you child needs help decoding *y* words.

Table 13-4		Finalizing the Y	
Y as a Consonant	*Y Makes the ī Sound*	*Y Makes the ǐ Sound*	*Y Makes the ē Sound*
yams	apply	cynic	cozy
yanked	cycle	cyst	gravy
yarn	dye	gym	guppy
yawn	hybrid	gyp	hefty
year	lyre	gypsum	noisy
yeast	reply	lyric	pouty
yelped	supply	myth	salty
yoke	try	oxygen	sandy
yule	type	system	tawny

Have your child read these sentences silently first and then say them out loud for practice.

William gave a noisy yelp in the gym.

Our supply of yarn can be yanked from Junior.

This year they played a lyric on the lyre.

Exploring Some Miscellaneous Homophones

Because (if you're reading the chapters in order) you're exploring different kinds of spellings and groupings of words, this is a good time to take a brief detour and look at some words that sound the same, but are spelled differently. A *homophone* is a word that's pronounced the same as another word but has a different spelling and meaning. For example, *carat, caret,* and *carrot* are homophones. Following is an assorted group of homophones that you can ask your child to read and memorize, place in a sentence, and spell out. These homophones underscore some of the vowel digraphs and diphthongs presented in this chapter:

blew, blue	four, fore	steak, stake	veil, vale
brewed, brood	mourn, morn	there, their, they're	wear, ware, where
chews, choose	pour, pore		
dew, due, do	read, red	threw, through	weight, wait
eight, ate	sleigh, slay		

Activity: Fill in the Blanks: Homophones

To play: Read the sentences and choose the correct word from the homophones in parentheses to correctly complete the sentences. You may copy these sentences or rewrite the exercise for your child.

1. Mom and I want you to go, _____. (to/too/two)

2. If the _____ breaks, the cradle will fall. (bough, bow)

3. Jack and Alex _____ a hundred books last year. (read, red)

4. Join us today as we _____ for the bus. (weight, wait)

5. We're going out for a _____ tonight. (steak, stake)

6. John and James tied _____ horses to a wood rail. (ate, eight)

Answer Key: 1. too 2. bough 3. read 4. wait 5. steak 6. eight

Chapter 14

Digging Deeper into Prefixes and Suffixes

In This Chapter

▶ Understanding prefixes, suffixes, and word roots

▶ Discovering prefixes and how they modify words' meaning

▶ Exploring how suffixes change the meaning of words

T his chapter explores the use of *roots* or *root words* as units of meaning. You can call it a *word root*, a *root word*, or you can use the expression *base word*. Prefixes and suffixes (or, collectively, *affixes*) are placed before and after a root word to create a new word. Prefixes tend to change the meaning of words. Suffixes tend to make a word a different part of speech, change the meaning, and change the tense, among other things. A child who understands what root words are and how they can be altered by prefixes and suffixes can greatly improve her aptitude for reading and spelling. She can increase her vocabulary by leaps and bounds. The goal of this chapter is for your child to instantly recognize root words, prefixes, and suffixes while reading.

In this chapter, you jump headlong into prefixes and suffixes. The lessons start simply with an exploration of simple prefixes and suffixes, and then you go on to the advanced variety. Some of the words I present in this chapter may be too advanced for your child. Not to worry! The idea here is for your child to get a solid grasp of what prefixes and suffixes are. She can increase her vocabulary and spelling skills mightily in this chapter by mastering prefixes and suffixes.

Understanding Roots

To understand what prefixes and suffixes are, you need to know what a root is. The *root* is the main part of the word that contains the basic meaning, and you can add affixes to it to create related words. It's also the form of the word after *removing* any or all prefixes and suffixes from the word. Prefixes and suffixes change the meaning of the root to which they're attached. Generally speaking, prefixes don't usually change the spelling of the root word; however, the spelling of a root word can change when a suffix is added, as in the word *inspiration*. Here are some simple definitions:

- A **root word** is a word to which you can add affixes to create related words (such as *hemi-sphere* or *co-author*)

- A **suffix** is a word part that you can add to the end of a root word (such as *dark-ness*)

- A **prefix** is a word part that you can add to the beginning of a root word to create a new meaning (such as *re-gain* or *in-complete*)

A brief history of English

The English language has many fathers and mothers, but its primary parents are German and Latin. And because the Greek language is part of Latin's heritage, English has inherited many Greek words and root words by way of Latin.

Although the Latin-speaking Romans conquered England in 55 B.C. under Julius Caesar and remained in England for the next 450 years, the native population didn't adopt Latin. They spoke a Celtic language similar to modern-day Welsh. That changed in the fifth century, however, when Germanic tribes — the Angles, Saxons, and Jutes — arrived in England. These settlers brought German to the island and established the German basis of the English language. If you've ever wondered why some words and expressions are similar in German and English (*guten morgen* and *good morning,* for example), look to the Angles, Saxons, and Jutes for the answer. Over the centuries, the German dialects they brought to England from the European continent coalesced into a language now called Old English.

In 1066, French-speaking Normans conquered England, and for the next 300 years England had two languages, French and Old English. The ruling-class Normans spoke French and their underlings spoke Old English, but over time the languages merged to form the English language. Because French draws heavily from Latin, Latin roots found their way into this new English language through its French heritage.

Over the centuries, English has been enriched by words from many languages. Wherever the English established colonies, they borrowed words from native speakers. For example, *shampoo* came from India, *ketchup* from China, and *moccasin* from the Iroquois. Immigration to the United States also added many words to English, as the immigrants contributed their words to the English language. For example, Yiddish gave English-speakers *chutzpah,* Yoruba gave *goober,* and Tagalog gave *boondocks.* The foundation of English, however, is in German and Latin.

The roots of many words in the English language originate in a parent language of English, such as Greek, Latin, or German. You can find the Latin word *trudere,* for example, in several English words. *Trudere* in Latin means "to thrust." From this word comes the English words *intrude* (to thrust in without invitation), *extrude* (to thrust something out), and *protrude* (to stick out). When you add the prefixes *in, ex,* and *pro* in front of the root *trude,* you get different words with slightly different meanings.

Suffixes appear at the end of word roots; sometimes they change the spelling as well as the meaning of the root. Take the word *credible,* for example. The Latin root word of incredible is *credo,* and the base word *creed* is shortened by one *e* when you add the suffix *ible* to get *credible.*

Discovering word roots can be easy, using some basic prefixes. Remember that they come before the root words and, in this exercise, your child can play with relative ease.

Activity: Prefix Elimination

Preparation: Make a copy of or rewrite the words. Your child also needs a pencil.

To play: Ask your child to read these words, cross out the prefix, and write the word root on the line.

Example: ~~en~~joy: <u>joy</u>

    1. return: _____

    2. unfit: _____

    3. defrost: _____

    4. replay: _____

    5. inside: _____

    6. mistake: _____

    7. perform: _____

    8. rename: _____

    9. complain: _____

  10. precede: _____

Answer Key: 1. turn 2. fit 3. frost 4. play 5. side 6. take 7. form 8. name 9. plain 10. cede

Activity: Creating Sentences with Prefix and Suffix Words

Preparation: You need the following phrases. Your child needs a pencil and a piece of paper if you want her to write out the sentences.

To play: Ask your child to use the following phrases in declarative and interrogative sentences. Your child can do this exercise orally or write the sentences on a piece of paper.

Example: to enjoy . . . My goal is to enjoy the game.

> the westward wind
>
> after the dispute
>
> on the pavement
>
> to promote sales
>
> in the darkness
>
> in the suburb
>
> to invite your friend
>
> an unknown object
>
> with deep respect
>
> his prepaid ticket

Profiling Prefixes and Suffixes

The spelling of prefixes and suffixes usually follows normal phonics patterns. And if you and your child looked at the simple suffixes *ing, ed,* and *er* in Chapter 11, you have some understanding of suffixes. Pronouncing words with prefixes and suffixes is usually just a matter of recognizing the word root and knowing which syllable to stress.

The following sections offer advice and exercises for exploring roots, prefixes, and suffixes.

Changing roots by adding prefixes

The following list demonstrates how words can change meanings when you add prefixes to them. This list presents simple, two-syllable words in which the first syllable is the prefix. Ask your child to read the words in the list. Ask her the meaning of the word root and what she thinks each prefix means. Later in this chapter, you encounter these simple prefixes again, along with more advanced prefixes.

adjoin	enjoy	perform
adjunct	enroll	person
adjust	exit	prepaid
combat	expel	prepare
comfort	expect	preside
conquest	impart	propel
conscript	imply	protect
consent	impress	provide
define	inroad	rejoin
defrost	inside	retrace
delight	intake	return
disburse	misstep	unfit
display	mistake	unknown
distrust	mistrust	undo
enable	perchance	

Have your child read the following sentences for practice. Ask her to read them silently to herself first, and then read them out loud with expression to you, naturally speaking the words in the sentence. The goal is for her to be able to read the way she speaks.

It is a mistake to consult or invite him.

Perhaps he will admit the entire mistake.

They prefer to retrace their steps.

Activity: Prefix and Root Arithmetic

Preparation: Make a copy of or rewrite the word parts. Your child also needs a pencil.

To play: Reading from left to right, add the prefix to the root to construct the whole word.

Prefix	+	Root	= Word
un	+	kind	= _____
be	+	tray	= _____
un	+	wise	= _____
pre	+	fix	= _____
re	+	shape	= _____
sub	+	tract	= _____
sub	+	mit	= _____
ex	+	port	= _____
im	+	port	= _____
re	+	port	= _____
de	+	port	= _____
ad	+	verb	= _____
ad	+	here	= _____
con	+	duct	= _____
dis	+	arm	= _____
dis	+	own	= _____
dis	+	cord	= _____
in	+	dent	= _____

It's absolutely amazing how prefixes change the meaning of words, especially the prefixes *re* (back again), *un* (express the contrary), *a* (away from), and *de* (out of). Table 14-1 shows you what several different prefixes mean and how you can attach them to different roots. Most of the words in this table won't be familiar to your child. That's okay, because they'll give her excellent practice in decoding and spelling.

Table 14-1		Advanced Prefixes
Prefix	**Definition**	**Examples**
ab	away	absorb, absolve, abhor, abduct
ad	to	addict, adhere, adverb, adjunct
be	totally	betray, behead, becalm, bequest
com	with	compute, compete, compact, combat

Prefix	Definition	Examples
con	with	contrast, consign, concise, congeal
de	from	defeat, deflate, detract, default
dis	opposite	disarm, dishonor, disown, discord
en	in	enact, enclose, encircle, entangle
ex	out of	exhume, extract, export, exhale
in	in	innate, indent, inspire, inborn
in	not	invalid, insane, inhuman, inactive
mis	bad	misguide, miscount, mislead, mistrial
per	through	perfect, permit, persuade, perspire
pre	before	precede, prefix, prewar, prepare
pro	before	proceed, prolong, proclaim, produce
re	again	reshape, rewrap, rejoin, reelect
sub	under	subtract, submit, submerge, subdue
un	not	unwise, undo, unfazed, unlaced

Have your child read the following sentences for practice:

> My son, Jim, lives in constant disorder.
>
> I can persuade him to go to the circus.
>
> The gravy started to congeal.

Activity: Creating Sentences

Preparation: You need the following phrases. Your child needs a pencil and a piece of paper if you want her to write out the sentences.

To play: Ask your child to use the following phrases in declarative and interrogative sentences. Your child can do this exercise orally or write the sentences on a paper.

> to rewrap the gift
>
> in contrast with
>
> to prepare a meal

to promote the book

prolong the lesson

mislead the girls

preceding the event

preview the show

with deep regret

submit the bid

Activity: Filling in the Blanks: Advanced prefixes

Preparation: Make a copy of or rewrite the sentences. Your child also needs a pencil.

To play: Read the following sentences. Choose the correct word from the three words in parentheses and write it in the blank.

Example: The Titanic began to <u>submerge</u> into the sea. (submerge, rose, exit)

1. That was an _____ feat. (into, incredible, implore)

2. His clock worked in _____. (precision, protect, upon)

3. Tim was in _____ shape. (retrace, remarkable, into)

4. This is a great _____ book. (rejoin, enlist, reference)

5. Zack, can you please _____? (concentrate, perhaps, audit)

6. Oh, we had a _____ day! (mistake, perfect, must)

7. I want to _____ the truth. (entire, enroll, proclaim)

8. He is such an _____ child. (agreeable, admit, enroll)

9. The Romans _____ Gaul. (unknown, invaded, entire)

10. It was an _____ volcano. (inactive, perform, prevent)

Answer Key: 1. incredible 2. precision 3. remarkable 4. reference 5. concentrate 6. perfect 7. proclaim 8. agreeable 9. invaded 10. inactive

Changing roots by adding suffixes

A *suffix* is an addition to the end of a word root that modifies the word's meaning. A suffix can also serve a grammatical function. It can indicate what part of speech — a noun, verb, adjective, or adverb — a word belongs to. This section looks into suffixes and helps your child understand what they are and how they change words' meanings.

This next list presents your child with words that contain simple, one-syllable suffixes. By examining the words in the table, she can find out how adding a few letters to the end of a word root changes the word's meaning. Ask her to read the list carefully and tell you the meaning of the word roots and the suffixes. She may require some help from you. At this point, you want your child to identify suffixes. Later in this chapter, you look more closely at advanced suffixes.

action	foolish	nearly	statement
boyish	formal	nervous	station
breakable	forward	notion	strongest
capable	guidance	nuisance	suitable
careful	harmless	pavement	treatment
central	highest	plainness	upward
cheerful	joyful	pleasant	useless
cloudless	joyous	remnant	weekly
darkness	lengthwise	sadness	westward
dental	likewise	selfish	
distance	loudly	sidewise	
famous	merchant	smoothest	

Ask your child to read these sentences for practice, naturally speaking the words in each sentence.

Their careful statement is famous.

To be selfish is to be foolish.

They fell on the pavement in the darkness.

Activity: Root Word Arithmetic

Preparation: Make a copy of or rewrite the word parts. Your child also needs a pencil.

To play: Reading from left to right, add the suffix to the root word to construct a whole word.

Root	+	Suffix	= Word
love	+	ly	= _____
rock	+	er	= _____
clang	+	ing	= _____
poor	+	ly	= _____
mirth	+	ful	= _____
self	+	ish	= _____
play	+	ful	= _____
use	+	less	= _____
like	+	wise	= _____
pave	+	ment	= _____
smooth	+	est	= _____
near	+	ly	= _____
dark	+	ly	= _____
plain	+	ness	= _____
calm	+	ly	= _____
form	+	al	= _____
friend	+	ly	= _____
like	+	ly	= _____
time	+	ly	= _____

Activity: Filling in the Blanks: Suffixes

Preparation: Make a copy of or rewrite the sentences. Your child also needs a pencil.

To play: Read the sentences. Find the incomplete word that's italicized in the sentence and choose a suffix for this word from the two choices in parentheses. Write the correctly spelled word in the space provided.

Example: Please be *care* at the park. (ful, ish) <u>careful</u>

   1. Don't act *help*! Pick it up. (less, est) _____

   2. Sally sat *quiet* reading. (ish, ly) _____

   3. Jack's shirt was *color*. (est, ful) _____

4. My brother Steve has a *friend* dog. (ly, ing) _____

5. Mom was *clean* the dishes. (ful, ing) _____

6. Grandma told me my dress was *love*. (est, ly) _____

7. My dog *fetch* the ball for me. (ed, ly) _____

8. The actor was *say* his lines. (er, ing) _____

9. My house is *large* than yours. (ful, er) _____

10. She is a *joy* child. (ful, est) _____

Answer Key: 1. helpless 2. quietly 3. colorful 4. friendly 5. cleaning 6. lovely 7. fetched 8. saying 9. larger 10. joyful

Activity: Joke: Suffixes

To play: Read and explain this joke to your child. Show the joke to her and have her pick out the words with suffixes.

> The teacher was giving her class of 7-year-olds a natural history lesson. "Worker ants," she told them, "can carry pieces of food five times their own weight. What do you conclude from that?"

> One child was ready with the answer: "They don't have a union."

Answer Key: teacher, giving, natural, worker, conclude, union

Activity: The Grateful Swan

Preparation: Make a copy of the following story. Your child needs a pencil or crayon.

To play: Ask your child to read the story and circle the suffix words.

> One day a poor peddler was returning to his home after a hard day's work. He was very tired, and his pack was heavy.

> Suddenly he heard something go flippety-flop. It sounded like a bird with large wings. He looked up in the air, but could see nothing. He looked north and south, east and west, but not a bird was in sight.

> His pack seemed to grow heavier and heavier, and by the time he reached his little home he was so tired that he could scarcely walk.

> As his wife came to help him loosen the straps that held the pack on his back, she cried, "Oh, John, where did you get this beautiful swan?"

But the man answered, "What swan?"

"Why, sitting right on top of your pack is the loveliest swan I have ever seen," said the good woman.

"That is what I heard go flippety-flop," said John, "and no wonder my pack felt very heavy today."

"Her wings are like lilies, and her beak is like a rose," said the wife, "but dear me, the poor thing has a broken leg."

"I have some bandages in my pack," said John. "I will get some of them, and we will fix the leg in no time. But what shall we use for splints?"

"Oh, I know just the thing," said the wife. And she ran to the shelf and got her fan and broke it into splints.

The good man and his wife bound up the broken leg very carefully, and then they gave the swan part of their supper.

The swan's leg kept getting better, 'til before long it was as well and strong as ever.

Still the swan stayed on with the peddler and his wife, and they were very happy together all summer. But when the grass grew brown and the leaves fell from the trees, John said, "Wife, the birds are all going south for the winter. Before long our swan will leave us and we may never see her again."

And one day after this the swan lifted her snowy wings and sailed away toward the south.

The peddler and his wife stood with tears in their eyes, and watched her 'til all they could see was a tiny speck.

The winter was long and they were very lonesome for the swan. Finally, the snow was all gone, the leaves were coming out on the branches, and the good wife started making her garden.

One day she saw in the distance a speck as white as snow. Nearer, and nearer it came, right into her garden.

"Oh John," she cried, "here is our swan. Far from the south she has come, but what is that shining in her mouth?"

"A diamond, as sure as I live," cried John.

The swan came nearer and walked up to the woman and dropped the lovely sparkling diamond into her apron.

And ever after that the swan flew away with the other birds in the fall, but each spring came back to spend the summer with the peddler and his wife. And every time that she came back she brought the good woman some wonderful gift from the south.

—Alice Cary

Answer Key: peddler, returning, tired, suddenly, flippety, sounded, looked, nothing, looked, seemed, heavier, reached, scarcely, loosen, cried, beautiful, answered, sitting, loveliest, lilies, bandages, broken, carefully, supper, getting, stayed, going, lifted, snowy, sailed, toward, watched, lonesome, finally, coming, started, making, distance, nearer, shining, walked, dropped, lovely, sparkling, wonderful

Activity: Poem: Two Little Kittens

Preparation: You need the following poem. Your child needs a pencil and piece of paper.

To play: Ask your child to read the poem and write down the words with suffixes.

Two Little Kittens

Two little kittens, one stormy night,

Began to quarrel, and then to fight;

One had a mouse, the other had none,

And that's the way the quarrel begun.

"I'll have that mouse," said the biggest cat;

"You'll have that mouse? We'll see about that!"

"I will have that mouse," said the eldest son;

"You shan't have the mouse," said the little one.

I told you before 'twas a stormy night

When these two little kittens began to fight;

The old woman seized her sweeping broom,

And swept the two kittens right out of the room.

The ground was covered with frost and snow,

And the two little kittens had nowhere to go;

So they laid them down on the mat at the door,

While the old woman finished sweeping the floor.

Then they crept in, as quiet as mice,

All wet with the snow, and cold as ice,

For they found it was better, that stormy night,

To lie down and sleep than to quarrel and fight.

—Anonymous

Some trivial trivia

Only four words in the English language end in the suffix *ous* with a *d* preceding it. Those words are *tremendous, horrendous, stupendous,* and *hazardous.* In these words, the *d* sound had to be added to the *ous* suffix for pronunciation purposes.

Here's another tidbit for you: Only two words in the English language are spelled with all five vowels in alphabetical order. Those words are *abstemious* and *facetious.*

Answer Key: stormy, begun, biggest, eldest, seized, sweeping, covered, finished, better

Affixes fore and aft

The words in this list have both a prefix and a suffix. They look difficult, but have your child give them a try. Have her start with the prefix, slide through the word root, and then tackle the suffix. Your child may have some difficulty, so be patient and be ready to help your child read these words.

absorbent	disheartened	perfectibility
advantageous	enlightenment	premeditated
bereavement	extemporaneous	reemphasize
computerization	idiosyncrasy	transparently
consequently	impossibility	unchangeableness
deliberateness	misappropriate	uncivilized
disagreeable	misinterpretation	unenthusiastically

Ask your child to read these sentences for practice:

Mr. Jones is a disagreeable person.

The paper plates are absorbent.

It is an impossibility for Patrick and David to attend.

Part IV
Tackling the Trickier Side of Phonics

The 5th Wave   By Rich Tennant

©RICHTENNANT

"I'll say this—a piping bag full of frosting and a sheet cake go a long way toward getting your kids to practice sounds."

In this part . . .

In these chapters, I introduce you and your child to some advanced phonics lessons. Here, you discover the schwa — what it means and what it does to spelling and pronunciation. You and your child also encounter the silent elements in words like *lamb, sign,* or *hymn.* Finally, I present the complexities of *x* and *zh* and their many sounds. It's tricky stuff, but well worth mastering for sharp reading skills.

Chapter 15

Schwinging with Schwa: Finding the Quick *uh* Sound

....

....

*I*t's there, even though it really isn't meant to be. It's lurking in multisyllable words, bridging consonants, and making vowels disappear. What is this mischievous critter? It's called the *schwa,* and it makes a quick *uh* sound.

You hear the schwa in the first syllable of *cadet* and the second syllable of *bridal.* Instead of making the short or long *a* sound, you say the *a* quickly so that it sounds like *uh,* or the short *u* sound. If you pronounce each syllable in a multisyllable word formally and distinctly, people may think you're putting on airs. Or they may think you're a little wacky. The schwa, or *uh* sound, prevents you from sliding sounds together too quickly.

Interestingly, Americans, the British, Canadians, and Aussies — English speakers all — have all been known to place the accent schwa on a different syllable in the same exact word.

This chapter introduces your child to the mischievous schwa sound. It explores how to pronounce the schwa sound in different words, how to recognize where a schwa sound appears, and how to read the schwa symbol in a dictionary. This chapter gives your child plenty of practice with the schwa concept.

Introducing Your Child to the Schwa

You see the schwa symbol in dictionaries as an upside-down *e*, like this: ə. When you see the schwa symbol, you know not to use the short or long vowel sound — you just say *uh*. The idea may sound crazy, but the schwa can take the place of every single vowel — *a, e, i, o,* and *u*. Just listen to the schwas in these words: *local, ago, sudden, robin, bottom,* and *circus.* Although the vowel is different, the sound is the same — a schwa.

 The schwa symbol looks like an upside-down and backward *e*, which creates a problem when you write the symbol on a piece of paper and you're sitting across the table from your child. Your child may think that you're writing the letter *e* rather than the schwa. To prevent this problem from occurring, make sure you're sitting next to your child instead of across from him when you write the schwa.

Introduce your child to the schwa by following these steps:

1. **Write the schwa symbol and say, "This is a schwa."**

2. **Ask your child to say the word "schwa."**

3. **Ask him to write the symbol on his own sheet of paper.**

4. **Ask your child to repeat a word with a schwa in it (like *bottom*).**

5. **Tell him to spell the word on paper, or write it down for him as he says it.**

6. **Ask him to say *cadet* (or whatever schwa word you chose) slowly, and catch him in the middle of the *uh*.**

   Explain to him why he's making the schwa sound rather than the short or long vowel sound. Tell him that the schwa keeps him from running the sounds in the word together.

The origin of the schwa

The word *schwa* is taken from the Hebrew word *sewa*, meaning *nought.* It was used to indicate the schwa vowel sound as well as the complete absence of a vowel sound. The schwa basically meant "there is no vowel sound." It has evolved to mean that the unstressed syllable has the sound of a quick *uh*, or short *u*.

Schwa's rise to phonetic fame

In the past, dictionaries typically assigned eight different sounds to *a*, and almost as many to the other vowels. To illustrate how complicated these vowel assignments were, you may remember the movie *My Fair Lady* (if you haven't seen it, shame on you). In one scene, Professor Higgins appears with hundreds of symbols surrounding him that indicate the hundreds of sounds that the five vowels make. Today, the schwa replaces a lot of these sounds and symbols. Despite how it shows up in the dictionary, the schwa sounds slightly different everywhere you go, and in some regions of the United States, words even get an extra schwa. In the southern United States, for example, *power* is pronounced *powuh*.

As you get into the more difficult words in this book, take these steps to help your child remember his spellings:

- ✔ Exaggerate vowels the first time you say a word. For example, in the word *important*, exaggerate the short sound of *a* in the third syllable the first time you say it.

- ✔ The second time you say the word, use the correct unaccented *a* so that your child hears the schwa.

Exploring the Schwa-Syllable Connection

Fortunately for you and your child, the English language has rigid guidelines as to when a schwa shows up in a word. One-syllable words? Never. You find the schwa only in multisyllable words.

Here are the facts about where the schwa shows up:

- ✔ Schwas appear only in multisyllable words.
- ✔ Schwas never appear on the accented syllable.
- ✔ Schwas rarely appear in place of a long vowel sound.
- ✔ Almost every multisyllable word contains at least one schwa.
- ✔ Whenever you can cross out a vowel without changing the pronunciation, that vowel is probably a schwa.

Try this exercise to help your child understand what a schwa is and how the schwa symbol appears in dictionaries:

1. **Flip open your dictionary, show your child where the schwa appears in words, and ask him to look up a few one-syllable words in the dictionary.**

Point out that none of these words has a schwa. Tell him that the schwa doesn't appear because only words with two or more syllables have a schwa.

2. **Have him look up a few two-syllable words that use the schwa (check out Table 15-1, later in this chapter, for a list of some of these words).**

Point out that the schwa never appears in syllables that have the accent mark on them. (In your travels through the dictionary, your child may find more than one schwa in a single multisyllable word. Don't worry about it for now. By the time your child reaches the advanced reading stage, he will understand what the schwa is and how it affects pronunciation. I see no advantage in overstating the presence of schwas at this time.)

Some children have a hard time understanding the difference between the schwa sound and the short *u*. To make the distinction clear, write down the word *rumpus*. Say the word slowly as you point to the letters, but put the accent on both syllables and let your child hear you say the short *u* sound in both syllables. Then say the word correctly, letting him hear the schwa at the tail end of the word.

Getting Acquainted with Schwa Words

Table 15-1 lists some common words that include the schwa sound. Read the words in the table with your child, sounding out the vowels and encouraging him to read, recite, and remember. Your child can get a good start seeing and hearing the schwa by reading the words in this table. Make sure your child hears the quick *uh* sound in the words.

Table 15-1		Beginning Schwa Words			
The A Is the Schwa (Beginning of the Word)	*The A Is the Schwa (End of the Word)*	*The E Is the Schwa*	*The I Is the Schwa*	*The O Is the Schwa*	*The U Is the Schwa*
along	bridal	bitten	muffin	beckon	rumpus
away	local	stiffen	cabin	Boston	circus
ago	floral	sudden	bobbin	bottom	locust
alike	normal	towel	robin	cannon	crocus

The A Is the Schwa (Beginning of the Word)	The A Is the Schwa (End of the Word)	The E Is the Schwa	The I Is the Schwa	The O Is the Schwa	The U Is the Schwa
amuse	mortal	kennel	victim	kingdom	humus
awake	caress	camel	pencil	lemon	lawful
ajar	cadet	burden	pupil	carbon	sinful
alone	canal	vessel	stupid	fathom	willful

Have your child read these sentences for practice. The goal is for him to be able to read as he would speak, so you want him to read each sentence to himself and then say it out loud with expression, naturally speaking the schwa sound where it appears.

The pupil's pencil is in his pocket.

He is alone in the bottom of the vessel.

They went away to the cabin near Boston.

Activity: Flipping and Flashing Schwa Cards

Preparation: Make a set of diacritical mark flashcards that include the schwa symbol (upside-down and backward *e*) and the words in Table 15-1.

To play: Use the flashcards in the following script:

1. Say, "Here's a flashcard with the schwa symbol."

2. Show the learner the flashcard.

3. Say, "This upside-down *e* is a symbol for a schwa. The schwa means a quick *uh* sound. It's close to a short *u*, as in *up*. But the tone of this sound is short and unstressed — a short-short *u*."

4. Hold the schwa card, and ask your child to repeat: "*Uh,* the schwa says *uh.*"

5. Show the flashcards with the words from Table 15-1 to the learner.

   As you page through the flashcards, ask your child, "Which letter in this word makes the schwa sound?"

To reinforce the schwa sound, add words like *rumpus* and *circus* to the diacritical mark cards. Make sure your child recognizes the schwa and how it sounds in the words.

Activity: Underlining and Highlighting Schwas

Preparation: Make a copy of this exercise or rewrite it on a piece of lined paper.

To play: Have your child read the words. Have him write each word and put a space between its syllables. Then have him underline or highlight the schwa syllable.

Example: pupil, pu'pəl

1. level
2. alarm
3. nickel
4. seven
5. pencil
6. lemon
7. focus
8. private
9. bridal
10. Boston

Answer Key: 1. lev'əl 2. ə larm' 3. nick'əl 4. sev'ən 5. pen'cəl 6. lem'ən 7. fo'cəs 8. pri'vəte 9. brid'əl 10. Bos'tən

Activity: Spotting the Schwa

Preparation: You need lined paper and a pen or pencil.

To play: Copy or rewrite this lesson on a piece of lined paper. Let your child read the sentences, and then underline and write the schwa symbol over the correct part of the word. Schwas may appear more than once in each sentence.

Example: The rabbit hopped at random. (Both underlined letters are schwas.)

1. Along the bottom of the vessel a crack appeared.
2. Madam Larkin asked for a ripe banana.
3. The student's easel was the focus of the problem.
4. His random shot at the victim caused acute pain.

5. The cadet is annoyed and vocal about his budget.

6. There was no reason for the playful rumpus.

7. The merchant was adept in his use of stencils.

8. They could not fathom her sudden and willful tantrum.

Answer Key: 1. ə long', bot'təm, ves'səl, əp peared' 2. Mad'əm, Lark'ən, bə nan'ə 3. stu'dənt, ea'səl, fo'cəs, prob'ləm 4. ran'dəm, vic'təm, e cute' 5. cə det', ən noyed', vo'cəl, budg'ət 6. rea'sən, play'fəl, rum'pəs 7. mer'chənt, ə dept', sten'cəls 8. fath'əm, sud'dən, will'fəl, tan'trəm

Activity: Seeking Schwas in Poetry

Preparation: You need this poem and a pencil.

To play: Have your child read the following poem and circle the schwa sylla-bles. Or read the poem to him, and tell him to shout "schwa" at the appropri-ate times.

> **My Snowball Pal**
>
> I made myself a snowball
>
> As perfect as it could be.
>
> I wanted to keep it as a pet
>
> And allowed it to sleep with me.
>
> I made it purple pajamas
>
> And a cushion for its head.
>
> Then last night it ran away
>
> But first it wet the bed!

Answer Key: per' fəct, want' əd, pur' pəl, pə jam' əs, cush' ən, ə way'

Delving into Some Harder Schwa Words

You've been warned: The words in Table 15-2 are more difficult than those in Table 15-1. Remember that no matter which of the five vowels (*a, e, i, o,* or *u*) is in a word, the schwa sound is always pronounced like the *u* in *circus.* Get the feel of the accented syllable by tapping softly. If you want to, you can ask your child to make up sentences with some of these words.

Table 15-2		Intermediate Schwa Words			
The A Is the Schwa (Beginning of the Word)	*The A Is the Schwa (End of the Word)*	*The E Is the Schwa*	*The I Is the Schwa*	*The O Is the Schwa*	*The U Is the Schwa*
aloud	merchant	channel	solid	freedom	beautiful
abrupt	feudal	parcel	pulpit	crimson	cherub
adept	oral	student	rabbit	reason	focus
acute	formal	budget	cousin	squalor	lettuce
annoy	vocal	locket	habit	carrot	playful
alarm	portal	moisten	morbid	caldron	locus
achieve	banal	kernel	lucid	random	fretful
atomic	portal	easel	rapid	apron	wampum
affirmed	fiscal	comet	victim	wisdom	zestful

Activity: Reading "Mr. Schwing's Schwa"

To play: Reading stories like "Mr. Schwing's Schwa" provides fun, facts, and fluency. Reinforce your child's schwa-finding abilities by having your child read the following story, and then take the following steps:

1. **Make a copy of this story or write it on a separate piece of lined paper.**

2. **Number the paper from 1–40.**

3. **Have your child highlight or underline as many schwa sounds as he can find in three minutes.**

4. **Ask him to write each word that he finds on the paper, using the schwa for the unstressed syllable.**

   Example: sud´ dən

Mr. Schwing's Schwa

Mr. Schwing lived in a village far, far away. Every day he would amuse himself by reading the local paper. One day, he was sitting alone in his kitchen reading the paper in his denim suit while eating a muffin when an article caught his eye.

There was going to be a big contest at the carnival this year! The contest was for all of the local artists in the village. All of the contestants would have to paint a picture of a schwa. The winner would receive a one-night stay at the mayor's cabin and a golden parrot statue!

Mr. Schwing had been a pupil a few years ago at the Cadet Art School. He thought this contest would be a fun challenge, so he got to work right away on the picture of his inverted *e*.

He got out his easel, carbon pencils, and all of his paints. His paintbrush caressed the canvas, and it wasn't long before he had a masterpiece. The schwa was so colorful it looked like it belonged in a floral shop.

On the day of the carnival, people were rushing here and there to get their paintings ready to be judged in the big contest. When the judging began, Mr. Schwing felt his body begin to stiffen. He was so nervous!

When the judges came to his painting, a sudden look of amazement came over their faces. The judges huddled together, and then one of them walked up to the podium and declared Mr. Schwing the winner of the Schwa Painting Contest! Mr. Schwing got a sudden rush of excitement! The judge asked him to come receive his prizes. Mr. Schwing walked away that day the happiest man in the village.

Mr. Schwing hung his special schwa painting in his house where he could look at it proudly every day. He never would have fathomed that he could have made such a beautiful work of art.

—Angela M. Eddingfield

Answer Key: village, away, every, amuse, local, alone, kitchen, denim, muffin, article, carnival, local, village, contestants, cabin, golden, parrot, pupil, Cadet, challenge, away, inverted, easel, carbon, pencils, caressed, canvas, floral, carnival, people, stiffen, nervous, sudden, excitement, amazement, huddled, podium, sudden, happiest, village, special, fathomed, beautiful

Activity: Schwas for Two

To play: This activity is great for two kids together. Have one child read the following story to the other child, who should clap every time he hears a schwa. Have the kids take turns reading and clapping. Or you can read the story to one child and have him clap at the schwas.

Abraham Lincoln in the Early Years

In a small, poor cabin in the wilds of Kentucky a little boy was born. He was named after his grandfather, Abraham Lincoln. Abe knew very little about his first home, because his father moved the family to a new farm when he was five.

For a smart boy like Abe, the new place was the beginning of many great adventures. The woods were full of birds and wild animals. Scenic ravines with running water cut through the land. The water was so clear you could see the pebbles at the bottom. The largest stream was called Knob Creek.

In those days when a boy was five, he was old enough to work and help his mother and father. Young Abe hauled wood, picked berries, and helped with the planting. Those were just a few of his many jobs.

Life on the farm was not all work though. There was some fun and adventure. Abe and his sister, Sarah, had schoolmates that they visited when school was not in session.

One Sunday, Abe and some friends were out looking for partridges. They were walking along Knob Creek. It was spring and the water was very high. Abe tried to walk a log and fell in the water. Abe's playmate, Austin, seized a stick, ran to Abe and extended it over the water. Abe grabbed the stick and Austin saved his life. Neither had ever learned to swim.

Most of the education of a pioneer was to learn the lessons of nature. They followed the tracks of animals, listened to birdcalls, and probably ran from many real or imaginary bears.

Even though Abe and his sister did not have a lot of formal schooling, Tom and Nancy Lincoln wanted their children to know more than they did. The parents would sit on the doorstep and tell the children all the stories they knew. There would be stories from the Bible, of their own lives, and of the lives of all their ancestors. The Lincolns had a simple life of adventure and hardship, but a very interesting one.

Answer Key: cabin, Kentucky, Abraham, Lincoln, family, adventures, animals, Scenic, ravines, bottom, adventure, Sarah, visited, along, extended, Austin, Austin, education, pioneer, lessons, animals, listened, probably, imaginary, formal, Lincoln, wanted, children, parents, children, Lincolns, adventure

Activity: Rapid Reading

To play: Each of the following words ends with a schwa. Have your child read these words quickly to reinforce the general guideline that an *a* at the end of a word is usually a schwa. See how quickly your child can read the words.

alleluia	gala	polka
alpha	Georgia	pupa
aqua	gorilla	quota
arena	Honda	saga
asthma	larva	salsa
aura	lava	Santa
beta	llama	soda
boa	mama	sofa
camera	mesa	Tampa
cha-cha	mica	toga
cheetah	nausea	tuba
cobra	Noah	tuna
Coca-cola	okra	tundra
comma	opera	ultra
data	panda	vanilla
delta	papa	villa
diva	parka	visa
Donna	pasta	vista
era	pizza	zebra
extra		

Chapter 16

Explaining English Exceptions

*A*ll rules have exceptions, which is why you've probably heard the expression, "The exception that proves the rule."

This exceptional chapter is about exceptions — it's about spelling patterns and letter combinations that defy the guidelines and patterns laid down in the previous chapters of this book. Approximately 85 percent of English words are phonetic; this chapter looks at the other 15 percent.

This chapter deals with silent consonants as in the word *hymn* and *gnome.* You see and learn words that contain unusual pronunciations, such as *marry* and *very,* and vowels appearing together that make their sounds separately like *trio* and *giant.* I look at words that don't follow the guidelines, such as *bolt* and *ton.* And this chapter enlightens you about French and Greek words that Americans use, which makes you feel like a scholar.

Many of these words are "outlaws" and need to be memorized. But don't despair — most of them are at least partially phonetic. And look at it this way: The fact that these words don't follow standard guidelines makes them stick in your child's mind, which makes them easier to remember. I also use jokes, stories, and poetry that I hope will edify and hone your child's love for literature and laughter.

Dealing with Silent Letters

A *silent letter* is just what it sounds like: a letter that appears in a word even though you can't hear the sound of the letter when you say the word. When you write the word, however, the silent letter calls for the correct spelling, and that's where learning how to decode and spell words with silent letters gets dicey. Sorry folks, but no definite guidelines apply in regard to silent letters. All you can do is remember how to recognize silent letter patterns and, in some cases, memorize them. The following pages explain how to do that.

A different kind of consonant digraph

Two consonants joined together that make a single sound are called a *consonant digraph,* as you find out in Chapter 5. Consonant digraphs include the letter combinations *ch, th, ng,* and *nk.*

When a silent letter appears as one of the letters in a consonant digraph, it's still considered a consonant digraph. In this different kind of consonant digraph, one of the letters is silent, and the other one makes its normal sound — the normal sound your child has already learned. Silent letter consonant digraphs are simple to read but a royal pain to spell.

The five most common silent consonant digraphs are:

- ✔ *wr* (as in *write*)
- ✔ *kn* (as in *know*)
- ✔ *gn* (as in *gnaw*)
- ✔ *mb* (as in *dumb*)
- ✔ *mn* (as in *hymn*)

Table 16-1 lists some silent-letter consonant digraphs in these five groups. Ask your child to read the words in the table. Point out to your child that each digraph makes a sound that she already knows.

Table 16-1		Silent-Letter Consonant Digraphs		
The wr Digraph	*The kn Digraph*	*The gn Digraph*	*The mb Digraph*	*The mn Digraph*
wrap	knee	assign	bomb	autumn
wreck	knelt	consign	climb	column
wren	knew	design	comb	condemn
wrench	knife	gnarl	crumb	contemn
wring	knit	gnash	dumb	damned
wrist	knob	gnat	lamb	hymn
write	knock	gnaw	limb	limn
wrong	knot	gnome	numb	solemn

Have your child read these sentences for practice. Have her read each sentence to herself and then say it out loud.

They knew they could climb out on the limb.

He wrenched his knee in the wreck.

He would know to write the sign on the column.

Activity: Filling in the Blanks: Silent-Letter Consonant Digraphs

To play: Read the words in the provided word bank and then read the sentences, correctly completing each one with word chosen from the word bank. You may copy these sentences or rewrite the exercise for your child.

Word Bank: solemn, hymn, wrong, autumn, lamb, knock, sign, gnome, knob, wrench, knot, kneel, wrist, knife, gnat, bomb, comb, gnash, numb, wrote, crumb, condemn

1. There was a _____ on the drawer.

2. I sprained my _____ at the gym.

3. _____ on the door and they will let you in.

4. The tot put the tiny cookie _____ in his mouth.

5. The _____ needs to be sharpened.

6. The _____ leaves are falling.

7. Mary had a little _____.

8. The _____ book fell on the floor.

9. I saw a little flying _____ around the fruit.

10. David needs to run a _____ through his hair.

Answer Key: 1. knob 2. wrist 3. Knock 4. crumb 5. knife 6. autumn 7. lamb 8. hymn 9. gnat 10. comb

Activity: Anecdote: Moms Aren't Always Right

To play: Read this story to your child and ask her whether she understands the story. After you discuss it with her, ask her to read the story.

Moms Aren't Always Right

A little girl in first grade was doing very well, especially in spelling.

One day she came home with new words to study for an upcoming test and she asked her mother to help.

They came to the word "knit" and her mother asked her to spell it. She said, "n-i-t." Her mother said, "No, try again." She said, very slowly, "n-i-t."

Her mother said, "Now, honey, I know you know how to spell this word. Try again." Very aggravated and very slowly, as if her mother was just not getting the whole picture, she spelled, "n-i-t!"

Finally, her mother told her that the correct spelling was k-n-i-t. The little girl looked at her mother, put her hands on her hips and said, "Mom! The _k_ is silent!"

Activity: Poems: Silent Letter Consonant Digraphs

To play: Have your child read the following poems. Notice the silent letter in the words _autumn_ and _lambs_.

Autumn Fires

In the other gardens

And all up the vale,

From the autumn bonfires

See the smoke trail!

Pleasant summer over

And all the summer flowers,

The red fire blazes,

The gray smoke towers.

Sing a song of seasons!

Something bright in all!

Flowers in the summer,

Fires in the fall!

—Robert Louis Stevenson

Picture Books in Winter

Window robins, winter rooks,

And the picture storybooks.

Water now is turned to stone

Nurse and I can walk upon;

Still we find the flowing brooks

In the picture storybooks.

All the pretty things put by,

Wait upon the children's eye,

Lambs and shepherds, trees and crooks,

In the picture storybooks.

We may see how all things are

Seas and cities, near and far,

And the flying fairies' looks,

In the picture storybooks.

How am I to sing your praise,

Happy chimney corner days,

Sitting safe in nursery nooks,

Reading picture storybooks?

—Robert Louis Stevenson

Activity: Joke: Knock, knock!

To play: Ask your child to read this joke for *kn* reinforcement.

Knock! Knock!

Who's there?

Police.

Police who?

Police stop telling these awful knock knock jokes!

Looking at some complex silent-letter digraphs

Table 16-2 presents some complex silent-letter digraphs. You and your child are probably familiar with most, if not all, of the complex words in this table. Ask your child to read the words in the columns. She can spell some of the words orally or write them down on a piece of paper as you dictate them. Your child will get the most from studying this table by noticing and memorizing the silent-letter digraphs.

Table 16-2		Complex Silent-Letter Digraphs		
Silent l	*Silent h*	*Silent u*	*Silent e*	*Silent t*
folk	hour	guess	ample	often
calf	school	guy	simple	listen
half	honest	guard	sample	fasten
halves	ghost	guest	little	soften
calm	John	guide	puzzle	whistle
palm	Thomas	guilt	tremble	castle
alms	ghastly	built	twinkle	bristle
chalk	heir	buy	sizzle	hustle
walk	honor	buoy	scramble	nestle

Have your child read these sentences for practice, first to herself and then out loud.

Thomas had a great voice for folk songs.

John can guide the guest to the lodge.

Listen to him whistle to the guard.

Activity: Poem: Old Man on the Border

To play: Reading poetry increases your child's ability to read smoothly and with expression. Have your child read this poem and find one word in the poem that has a silent letter.

There Was an Old Man on the Border

There was an old man on the border,

Who lived in the utmost disorder;

He danced with the cat, and made tea in his hat,

Which vexed all the folks on the border.

—Edward Lear

Answer Key: folks

Activity: Joke: Ice Cream

To play: Ask your child to read this knock knock joke and pick out the two words with a silent letter.

Knock! Knock!

Who's there?

Ice cream.

Ice cream who?

Ice cream every time I see a ghost!

Answer Key: knock, ghost

Discovering Exceptions to Standard Murmur Diphthongs

Chapter 9 explains that murmur diphthongs make the *er* sound and are typically spelled with these letter combinations: *ur, ir,* and *er*. These *r*-controlled murmur diphthongs are simple to read but can be difficult to spell. Some words look like murmur diphthongs, but it would be a great mistake to read or pronounce them that way. The vowel-consonant combinations in the words in the upcoming list may appear to be murmur diphthongs that make the *er* sound but, in fact, they don't make that sound. These words are exceptions. In these diphthongs, you hear the vowel sound and the consonant sound separately.

Almost all murmur diphthong exception words make a short-vowel sound. In this list, for example, you can hear the short vowels in *carry, berry, mirror,* and *sorry.* Only two exceptions occur: *Florida* and *forest* have both sounds (the *or* diphthong and the short *o*), depending upon what part of the country you live in. Also, the pronunciation of some of these exceptions have mutated in the last century.

Ask your child to read the words in this list carefully. Point out the funny spellings and caution your child against thinking that these words sound like murmur diphthongs.

berry	forage	Jerry	orange
Carol	forest	Larry	perish
carrot	Harry	marrow	sorrow
carry	horrid	marry	sorry
cherry	irregular	merit	stirrup
cirrus	irresolute	merry	syrup
derrick	irrigate	mirror	tarry
ferry	irritant	morrow	torrid
Florida	irritate	narrow	very

Have your child read these sentences — to herself and then out loud — for practice:

Harry and Carol will marry tomorrow.

Florida has torrid and rainy weather.

Jerry and Larry took a ferry out to the oil derrick.

Activity: Filling in the Blanks: Murmur Diphthongs

Preparation: You need paper and pencil.

To play: Read the sentences. Have your child choose the correct word from the word bank to complete each sentence. Write the word on the line provided.

Word Bank: cherry, ferry, forage, irritate, merit, mirror, narrow, perish, stirrup, syrup

1. The bear began to _____ in the forest for an orange.

2. The cowboy fixed the broken _____.

3. I love maple _____ on my pancakes.

4. The boy scout earned a _____ badge.

5. The hiker climbed past the _____ gorge.

6. George Washington chopped down the _____ tree.

7. Mary Sue caught a _____ to cross the Potomac River.

8. The _____ tells all.

9. Percy said, "_____ the thought."

10. Terry can _____ his teachers.

Answer Key: 1. forage 2. stirrup 3. syrup 4. merit 5. narrow 6. cherry 7. ferry 8. mirror 9. Perish 10. irritate

When Joined Vowels Aren't Digraphs

Two vowels that appear one after the other don't necessarily make a vowel digraph. When vowels appear together in some words, they may actually form two separate syllables. For example, the vowels in the words *trial, doer,* and *lion* form the dividing point between one syllable and the next. The vowel combinations in these words clearly aren't digraphs because the vowels don't run together to form a continuous sound. In these words, each vowel makes its own sound.

This next list is full of words in which two vowels that aren't digraphs appear in succession. Many of the words in this list are borrowed from other languages. The odd spelling was retained when the words came into common use. Reading and decoding these words is harder for nonnative speakers than it is for native English speakers.

Have your child read the words in this list, paying special attention to where syllables break in these words.

area	heroic	Ohio	ruin
aviator	Iowa	orient	science
bias	Joey	patriot	studio
boa	liable	period	Suez
client	liar	piano	theater
dial	lion	piety	theory
diary	manual	plier	trial
diet	Maria	poet	trio
doer	medium	quiet	truant
dual	neon	radio	variety
fiery	Noah	react	violet
fluent	Noel	real	violin
fluid	nucleus	reliant	
giant	oasis	rodeo	

Have your child read these sentences for practice. Have her read each sentence to herself and then say it aloud.

The Suez Canal is far away from the Ohio River.

Joey and Noah took their violins to the theater.

Maria placed her piano manual on the sofa.

Exceptions to Long-Vowel Guidelines

In Chapter 8, I tell you that if a word or syllable has only one vowel, expect it to be a short sound. If a word or syllable has two vowels, count on the first vowel being long and the second one being silent. Americans adopted this approach from "olde" England. As you look at the word *olde,* you can see that the magic *e* is silent — because it adheres to the long-vowel guideline.

Every word in Table 16-3 has a long-vowel sound. These words are exceptions to the long-vowel guideline; no second vowel or magic *e* is present in these words, yet they still make the long-vowel sound. Perhaps those "olde" ancestors took the silent *e* off these words.

Column by column, have your child read the words in Table 16-3. Make sure she pronounces the long-vowel sounds in these words. After she's finished, have her spell the words. Because many of these words are in the same *word family,* you can quiz her in a rhyming fashion after she writes the first word in the pattern on a separate piece of paper. After she writes the words down, she can read them back to you.

Table 16-3			Exceptions Using Long Vowels		
Words with old	**Words with olt**	**Words with oll**	**Words with ost**	**Words with ind**	**Words with ild**
cold	bolt	boll	ghost	blind	child
colds	bolts	roll	ghostly	find	mild
fold	colt	roller	host	grind	milder
gold	dolt	rolls	hostess	hind	mildest
hold	jolt	scroll	most	kind	mildly
scold	molt	stroll	post	mind	wild
sold	molts	toll	poster	rind	wilder
told	volt	tolling	posting	wind	wildest

Have your child read these sentences for practice. Have her read each sentence to herself and then say it aloud.

> I got hold of most of the bolt of cloth.
>
> She is a most kind hostess.
>
> I told you that she is a wild child.

Activity: Joke: Melanie

To play: Ask your child to read the following joke. After you both laugh, ask her to pick out the words that are exceptions to the long-vowel guideline.

> One day, a sweet little child named Melanie, who was five years old, went to visit her kind grandmother.
>
> As they sat at the table having tea and rolls, Melanie asked Grandma how old she was. Granny replied that she was so old that she didn't remember anymore.

Melanie said, "If you don't remember, Grandma, you must look in the back of your undies. Mine say five to six."

Answer Key: child, kind, rolls, old

Words in Which Every o Is a Short u

Take a close look at the words in the next list. In each word, the *o* makes the short sound of *u* (examples include *mother, won,* and *above*). Mysterious, no? Some of the words in the list are common words that your child learned a long time ago. Some, however, like *slovenly* and *covetous,* are brand new. It doesn't hurt anyone to learn words that they won't use often in everyday speech. Ask your child to read the words and to be aware of the short *u* sound in each word.

above	covetous	lover	shove
become	done	Monday	slovenly
brother	dove	money	smother
color	dozen	monk	some
come	govern	monkey	son
comely	governor	month	stomach
comfort	honey	mother	ton
company	hover	none	tongue
compass	London	nothing	undone
cover	lovable	of	won
covering	love	other	wonder
covet	lovely	oven	wondrous

Have your child read these sentences for practice. Have her read each sentence to herself and then say it aloud.

He is a month late in coming to London.

None of my brothers had money to spare.

Some other company could come for the month.

Activity: Completing the Sentence with the Mysterious *u* Sound

To play: Read the sentences. Choose the word from the word list that correctly completes each sentence. Write the word you choose on the line provided.

Example: Greg and Liz are such <u>lovable</u> children. (passing, lovable, noun)

1. Mother placed the _____ around me for warmth. (camera, comforter, cast)

2. The monkey began to _____ his fellow monkey from the branch. (shove, table, hair)

3. Grandma loved to _____ me with hugs and kisses. (sweep, knit, smother)

4. _____ of us is above the law. (Monkey, Loving, None)

5. On the front _____ a picture appeared. (tree, back, cover)

6. Joyce lost at least one _____ every season. (glove, sky, ocean)

7. The aircraft began to _____ over our city. (laugh, hover, ghost)

8. On Monday we took the train to _____. (rough, London, fright)

9. In one _____ I will have enough money. (thigh, done, month)

10. If you keep spending, you will have _____ left. (who, nothing, been)

Answer Key: 1. comforter 2. shove 3. smother 4. none 5. cover 6. glove 7. hover 8. London 9. month 10. nothing

Arresting the Outlaw Words

The words in the next list follow no guidelines. I call them "outlaw words" because they aren't subject to strict phonics guidelines. At least half of the words in the list will be familiar to your child from early reading, but you have to introduce these words to your child as sight words. Most of the words are partially phonetic, and yet some are real outlaw words with pretty wild spelling. I think the *i* and *y* are interesting. You sound out the vowel *i* as the consonant *y* in *onion,* and the consonant *y* as a vowel in *bury*.

Ask your child to read the words in the list and take a spelling quiz, which you can dictate to her. For the quiz, start with the words that she reads well to reinforce the lesson and what she already knows. Then slowly start pushing the harder words in the spelling quiz.

again	flood	once	two
answer	friend	one	very
any	genius	onion	view
are	give	pretty	want
beauty	gone	said	was
been	have	says	wash
blood	heard	sew	watch
bury	height	shoe	were
busy	his	should	what
child	iron	some	where
color	island	sugar	who
come	juice	sure	woman
could	junior	their	women
does	laugh	there	work
done	learn	through	world
don't	lose	toward	would
eye	love	truth	you
find	many	twelve	your

Have your child read these sentences for practice. Have her read each sentence to herself and then say it aloud.

What a beauty the busy child was!

What genius was working there on the island?

What color and fabric would the women find?

When I teach the "outlaw words," I build a jail for them. Every time my students come across one of these words, I have them dramatically throw its word card in jail.

Activity: Story: Sacágawea

To play: Ask your child to read this time-honored story about a great Native American. After she finishes, have her pick out the words that are exceptions — the "outlaw words" — and write them on a piece of paper.

Sacágawea

Sacágawea (sa-cá-ga-we-a), a child of the Shoshones, who lived west of the Bitter Root Mountains in what is now Idaho, was born more than two hundred years ago. She was a strong beautiful Indian girl, loved by all the people of her tribe for her quick understanding and gentle, willing kindness. She was the most fleet of foot among the children of the village who raced along the shores of the rolling Snake River and none surpassed her in courage and endurance on the long treks through the narrow mountain gorges or trackless forests to the water. No one, not even the wise medicine men, ever dreamed that this heroic daughter of the wild Shoshones was to have a great part in giving to America a domain vast and rich beyond the desires of covetous kings. She was carried off to the land of the Dakotas by a warring band of Indians, sold as a slave, and later married to a Frenchman who was part Indian. Although well treated by her adopted tribe, she longed to see her people beyond the Bitter Root Mountains.

In a period after 1804, the Lewis and Clark expedition, in sore need of a guide and interpreter, reached the Minnetaree tribes and camped with them for the winter. The leaders had undertaken the daring and hazardous tasks of blazing a trail through an unexplored, mountainous wilderness that was beset with hostile Indians. They sought a guide who knew the way to the Bitter Root Mountains and the land beyond to the Pacific. They sought one who would help them make friends with the various tribes, for their errand was a peaceful one.

Sacágawea, with her newborn child wrapped in a buffalo robe and strapped to her back, accompanied the expedition safely. They went on a journey covering many miles to the land of her own people and to the great empire beyond.

This story has been written by many and continues to capture the ideals and imagination of people of all ages. The grateful people of several states remember Sacágawea's great service. People named a lofty peak in the mountains after her. It overlooks the home of her childhood. In Portland, Oregon, there is a statue showing the young Indian woman with her baby son on her back as she steps forward pointing the way west.

Answer Key: beautiful, Indian, kindness, rolling, narrow, forests, heroic, wild, covetous, carried, sold, married, period, guide, sought, errand, child, wrapped, covering, told, son

Activity: Joke: Poodle Snobbery

To play: Read this joke to your child, spelling out of the names of the dogs. It's probably beyond her knowledge, but she'll laugh when you explain it.

> **Poodle Snobbery**
>
> Two well-groomed French poodles were prancing about their estate and looked down the driveway to see a bedraggled little mutt standing there. Having superb manners and being kind, they went to the gate. One said, "Hi! My name is FiFi, F-i-F-i." The other poodle said, "Hello! My name is MiMi, M-i-M-i." The sorry looking little dog of questionable lineage answered in a well-bred accent, "Hello, my name is Phydeaux, P-h-y-d-e-a-u-x."

Discovering Special Consonant Digraphs

A digraph is a pair of letters that represents a single speech sound. I discuss digraphs in detail in Chapter 5, but this section deals with two special consonant digraphs: *ph* and *gh*. Learning these digraphs requires study on your child's part. These digraphs are downright odd to anyone who isn't accustomed to seeing them in the course of reading. Check out this list for more information:

✔ The consonant digraph *ph* is a basic consonant digraph in the strictest sense of the word. The two letters make a new sound, *f*.

✔ The consonant digraph *gh* makes several different sounds, including the following:

- When *gh* starts a word, it always makes the sound of a *g* (as in *ghost*).

- When *gh* is followed by a *t* (as in *thought*), it's always silent.

- The *gh* can also be silent when it isn't followed by a *t* (as in *though*).

- The *gh* can make the sound of *f* (as in *cough*).

Table 16-4 lists common *ph* and *gh* words that are hard to spell. Memorizing these words is the best way to learn how to spell them correctly. After your child catches on to the look and sound of *ph* or *gh* within these words, spelling them is a cinch. In order to make these words easier to apply in reading and spelling, mark this page with a bookmark or sticky note, and use Table 16-4 as a reference.

Teach your child about the sound of *f* for *ph* and the sound of *g* for *gh*. Explain that *ph* and *gh* are consonant digraphs just like *sh, ch, th, wh, ng,* and *nk* (refer to Chapter 5). Also, ask her to notice the difference between the different sounds of *gh*. Then she's ready to read the words in Table 16-4 and copy some of the more recognizable words on a piece of paper.

Table 16-4	Special Consonant Digraphs		
The ph Makes the f Sound	*The gh Makes the f Sound*	*The gh Makes the g Sound*	*The gh is Silent*
alphabet	cough	aghast	bright
elephant	enough	Ghana	fright
orphan	laugh	ghastly	high
paragraph	laughing	Ghent	light
Philip	laughter	gherkin	might
phone	rough	ghetto	sigh
phonics	roughly	ghost	slight
phrase	tough	ghostly	straight
prophet	trough	ghoul	thigh

Ask your child to read these sentences for practice. Have her read each sentence to herself and then say it aloud.

The light by the phone was high and bright.

Phillip can jump mighty high in fright.

It was enough to laugh at the tough elephant.

Activity: Poem: Daylight and Moonlight

To play: Ask your child to read this poem and choose four exceptional *ph* or *gh* words from the lesson.

Daylight and Moonlight

In broad daylight, and at noon,

Yesterday I saw the moon

Sailing high, but faint and white,

As a schoolboy's paper kite.

In broad daylight, yesterday,

I read a poet's mystic lay;

And it seemed to me at most

As a phantom, or a ghost.

But at length the feverish day

Like a passion died away,

And the night, serene and still,

Fell on village, vale, and hill.

Then the moon, in all her pride,

Like a spirit glorified,

Filled and overflowed the night

With revelations of her light.

—Henry Wadsworth Longfellow

Answer Key: light, high, ghost, night

Activity: Poem: Rocket Explorer

To play: After your child reads this poem, ask her to explain the meaning.

A Rocket Explorer

A rocket explorer named Wright

Once traveled much faster than light

He set out one day

In a relative way

And returned on the previous night.

—Edward Lear

Activity: Poem: To a Skull

To play: Read this poem and save it for Halloween.

To a Skull

Ghastly, ghoulish, grinning skull,

Toothless, eyeless, hollow, dull,

Why your smirk and empty smile

As the hours away you wile?

— Joshua Henry Jones, Jr.

Activity: Poem: Beauty

To play: Read this poem and laugh.

A Beauty

As a beauty I'm not a great star,

There are others more handsome by far,

But my face, I don't mind it,

Because I'm behind it.

'Tis the folks in the front that I jar.

— 13th Century Limerick

Exploring Words with the French and Greek ch Sounds

Just when you become accustomed to looking at the *ch* as a consonant digraph with the sound *ch* (as in *inch*), along comes the French *ch* and Greek *ch* sounds. Rather than making the *ch* sound you know and love, the French *ch* is pronounced like *sh*. The French *ch* does make for some beautiful words. Say these words and relish how good they sound: *chalet, chagrin, chiffon,* and *chemise*. The Greek *ch* makes the *k* sound (as in *echo*). These pages introduce your child to the French *ch* and Greek *ch* sounds. They show her how to pronounce these sounds when they appear in English words adopted from French and Greek.

Table 16-5 lists words with the typical *ch* sound that you're used to, as well as the French *ch* and Greek *ch* sound. In the table, I arrange the words so that you can see the patterns and sounds of these words. Ask your child to carefully read the columns, and ask her to study the likenesses and differences between these sounds.

Table 16-5	The French and Greek *ch* Sounds	
The ch (Traditional) Sound	*The sh (French) Sound*	*The k (Greek) Sound*
chatter	chagrin	ache
check	chaperon	character
chubby	charade	chemist
crutch	chauffeur	Christmas
inch	Chevrolet	chrome
merchant	chevron	echo
scratch	Chicago	mechanic
sketch	chute	scheme
stretch	parachute	stomach

Recognizing French word origins

Many English words were acquired from the French and the Greek — words such as *chamois* and *scheme*. After the Norman invasion of England, the English language acquired about 10,000 French words, and around 75 percent of them are still in use today. Many of those words, in turn, originated from Greek.

English derives more than a third of its words directly or indirectly from French. Lexicographers estimate that English speakers who have never studied French already know 15,000 French words.

Ask your child to read each of the following sentences to herself and then say them all aloud.

My stomach aches from eating the cheese.

The chauffeur drove the Chevrolet to Chicago.

The chemist gave the children the picture.

Examining Six sh-Sound Spelling Patterns

So many *sh* sounds, so many different letters. Table 16-6 is a desperate attempt to classify words with *sh* sounds to make it easier for your child to spell these words. By classifying *sh*-sounding words this way, I hope to enable your child to recognize these words when she reads them. Many Americans say these words incorrectly at times. For example, have you heard the word *chic* or *crochet* said in different ways? Have your child carefully read the words in Table 16-6. See whether she can pick up on the six *sh*-sound spelling patterns.

Table 16-6		Six sh-sound Spelling Patterns			
tion Makes the shun Sound	*sion Makes the shun Sound*	*ci Makes the sh Sound*	*ti Makes the sh Sound*	*su Makes the sh Sound*	*ch Makes the sh Sound*
attention	compassion	facial	initial	assure	chalet
condition	confession	glacier	partial	censure	charlotte
nation	extension	precious	patient	erasure	chamois
observation	fission	racial	martial	fissure	chateau
position	mansion	spacious	impatient	insure	chef
protection	mission	special	impartial	pressure	chic
quotation	pension	spatial	patience	reassure	chiffon
station	session	specious	facetious	sugar	crochet
vacation	tension	official		sure	machine

Have your child read these sentences for practice:

The protection of the nation was assured.

Charlotte lost her precious position.

The special patient was under tension.

Table 16-6 is a cousin to Table 16-5. It really helps to study these tables together. Ask your child to observe the differences in spelling between the words in the tables. They all contain the same sound, *sh*.

Activity: Story: Elephant

To play: Ask your child to read this story. Some words may be difficult, but she can ask for help in sounding them out. Within this story are several non-phonetic words for her to decode.

The Elephant

What creature gains the most attention at the circus? The central act that people come to glimpse is — what? The elephants! I think people come because they want to see how big these pachyderms are, and how they can be so calm and gentle.

There are two main classes of elephants, Asian and African. The Africans get taller, though not as fat as the Asians. Their height can be 11 feet for the Africans. But the best place to examine is the elephant's head. The African's head is round, like a dome, and it has big floppy ears. The Asian elephant's ears are much smaller, and it has two bumps on top of its head. The African elephant's tusks are longer. They can grow to be over 12 feet long.

All elephants have tusks, except some of the female Asians. Tusks are actually their teeth. Tusks grow close to 2 inches each year all through their lives. Sometimes the tusks will get broken off when they fight with other elephants, or evil hunters will cut them off with a large knife. By nature, a new one grows right back, though. Sometimes the owners of tamed elephants will keep their tusks trimmed and spruced up, or have them carved off to keep them safe.

Did you ever wonder why elephants seem to walk in silence? It is because they sort of walk on tiptoe. Under the heel is a large pad, and it protects the foot like a gym shoe. (Imagine that! Built-in gym shoes!)

The skin, or hide, of an elephant is both thick and rough. Even though it is so thick, he can feel pain. He can even tell if a tiny insect lands on it. Maybe that's why they can be tamed and guided around the tent area. If they are smacked, or poked, it probably hurts pretty badly.

On that whole huge body, the touchiest organ is the nose, better known as the trunk. The Asian elephant has a finger on the end of its trunk for grabbing things. The African elephant has two fingers. The trunk has several functions. It can smell, of course. But it can also grab things and make frightful noises. With its trunk, an elephant can chirp, squeal, whistle, trumpet, thump on the ground, and rumble. It can rumble in so low a voice that only other elephants can hear it. These rumbles can be used to talk with other elephants that are far away.

You will often see an elephant using its trunk to carry or drag large cargo. An elephant can use its trunk to lift food, water, or other things high into its mouth. What it cannot do is use its trunk like a straw for drinking. Remember, it is a nose.

If you give the elephant access to a water trough, he will drink 50 to 100 gallons of water a day. They crave fresh grass, and of course they continue to love peanuts. Could you even consider feeding them tobacco, stale donuts, or even paper? Some people do and they eat it. Elephants are the biggest creatures on earth and very interesting as well.

—Joanne Engel

Answer Key: creature, attention, pachyderm, calm, Asian, height, head, fight, knife, nature, walk, shoe, rough, guided, area, function, frightful, rumble, talk, carry, high trough, love, some

Activity: Joke: Phonograph Records

To play: Read the joke to your child. You'll probably have to give her a little herb and history lesson, but the punch line is worth it. After that, you can have her pick out five words that she learned from the lessons in this chapter.

One day a friend and I got out the old phonograph records and were listening to one of my golden Simon and Garfunkel albums. We were having a good time reminiscing and laughing over the good old days.

My grandchild came into the room and wondered what all the fun was about. We motioned for her to sit down on the sofa and listen. When one particular song was finished, she asked me, "Well, did he?" I said, "Did he what?" She replied, "Did Parsley save Rosemary in time?"

Answer Key: old, phonograph, golden, laughing, motioned

Rounding Up the ch Sounds

This list presents an assortment of the *ch* words that I introduce earlier in this chapter. Mixing all the sounds together like this may be quite a challenge for your child. Ask her to go up and down the columns, reading the words. After she reads the words in the list, engage her in conversation about the meaning of the words. You'll have a field day with this exercise. Choose the words you want to develop for meaning and spelling. She can write the words on a piece of paper.

chalice	chassis	checkmate	cherub
chance	chatelaine	cheer	cheval
change	chattel	chef	Chevrolet
chaperone	chauffeur	chemise	chivalry
character	chauvinist	chemist	church
charade	cheat	cherish	chute
chase	check	cherry	

Have your child read these sentences — to herself and then out loud — for practice.

The class needed a chaperone for the skating party.

The chauffeur drove the Rolls Royce around the estate.

Chivalry is not dead.

Activity: Story: Fulton's Fabulous Folly

Preparation: You need paper and pencil.

To play: Ask your child to read this story and pick out the words that are exceptions. Ask her to write them down on a piece of paper.

Fulton's Fabulous Folly

Robert Fulton was a pretty good artist. His self-portrait hangs in a museum in Kansas City, Missouri. That's rather chic, but I guess you could just call it a sideline. His real passion was machines, especially floating machines.

Fulton fashioned a fascinating submarine in 1800, before we even had motorized ships. It was called the Nautilus, and he tried to sell it to the French government, and then the British government. But neither of them saw the potential of such a ship.

Next, Robert decided that the world needed to travel with more acceleration over water, even when there wasn't enough wind to push the sailing ships along very fast. He had watched the steam engine being used for such things as pumping water in mines and for running machines. In his mind, he envisioned a steam engine as propulsion for a boat.

He used all of his powers of persuasion to convince our nation's ambassador to France, Robert Livingston, that it could be done. Livingston's contribution was money, and they became partners. Imagine Livingston's elation when Fulton fashioned a paddleboat with a steam engine called the Clermont. Even though people initially called it "Fulton's Folly," their attention was captured by this vessel when it went from New York City to Albany, a trip of 150 miles, in just 32 hours. It took only 30 hours for the return navigation.

Soon steamboats were a common way to travel and to ship products from one part of the country to another. Eventually, steamships were used for ocean navigation, also. Robert Fulton was surely a man of special vision.

—Joanne Engel

Answer Key: persuasion, museum, chic, passions, machines, fashion, envisioned, propulsion, nation, initially, ocean, vision

Chapter 17

Zeroing In on x and zh

This chapter throws you a couple of oddballs: the *x* and *zh* sounds. Words with these sounds have eccentric spellings. Unfortunately your child has no recourse but to memorize words that make the *x* and *zh* sounds. Your child has to learn these words by sight.

The beauty of it is that there aren't a lot of *x* and *zh* words, so your child doesn't have to take on a bunch of new information. And your child will find many fun activities in this chapter to help him master *x* and *zh*.

Differentiating the x Sounds

The letter *x* makes no sound of its own. The letter *x*, you could say, is like one of those people who's always borrowing items from the neighbors — in other words, *x* borrows its sounds from other letters. Your child already knows that *x*, with its keyword *box*, makes the *ks* sound when it appears at the end of a word. The other two *x* sounds also borrow from other letters. The *x* can also make the *gz* sound (as in *exact*) and the *z* sound (as in *Xavier*).

Until your child gets used to seeing *x* in its three conventions, he has to rely on *x* words as sight words. This section of the chapter introduces your child to the different sounds of *x* and gives him practice in recognizing which *x* sound to make when he encounters *x* words in his reading.

Looking at some x guidelines

Guidelines for the sound of the letter *x* are as follows:

- ✔ At the end of a word, *x* makes the *ks* sound (as in *fox*).
- ✔ At the end of the syllable *ex,* the letter *x* may make the *gz* or *ks* sound (as in *exam* and *exile*).
- ✔ At the beginning of a word, *x* makes the *z* sound (as in *xylophone*).

Of course, these guidelines have plenty of exceptions. For example, some people say the *ks* sound in the word exit. This isn't a regional preference as much as it is a personal preference. The dictionary considers *ks* second on the pronunciation preference.

Here's the lone exception to the three *x* guidelines: the word *x-ray*. Smart children will tell you that *x* also makes the sound *x* in the word *x-ray*. You can tell these smart children that this *x* is the algebraic *x*, the "unknown" ray as it was called when first discovered.

X at the beginning, middle, and end of words

Table 17-1 presents examples of the three sounds of *x*. Ask your child to read each column from top to bottom and to be aware of how the *x* sound differs in each column. The words in the third column are seldom used, so you may need to help your child with these scientific words.

Table 17-1	The Three Sounds of X	
The ks Sound	*The gz Sound*	*The z Sound*
lax	exit	Xavier
mix	exam	xenon
hex	exist	xanthin
tax	exult	xylem
rex	exact	xyloid
fix	exalt	xylene

The ks Sound	The gz Sound	The z Sound
fox	example	xylophone
wax	exhaust	xylitol
box	exhibit	xylonite

Have your child practice these sentences. Have him read each sentence to himself and then say it out loud.

> The exhibit was an example of types of fuels.
>
> Rex will exit the stadium.
>
> The tax exam will take place on the campus of Xavier University.

Activity: Filling in the Blanks: X

Preparation: You need paper and pencil.

To play: Read the following sentences and choose a word from the word bank to correctly complete each one. (You may copy these sentences or rewrite this exercise for your child.) Ask him to write the words on a separate piece of paper and identify the *x* at the beginning, middle, or end of each word by circling it.

Example: The child took the <u>exam</u>.

Word Bank: exhaust, fox, tax, xylitol, exhibit, wax, Xenon, exist, exact, xylophone

1. Rhett and Annie prepared their annual _____ form.
2. The science _____ was held in the gym.
3. Stephanie and David have the _____ change.
4. The _____ pipe fell off the car.
5. James Richard can play the _____ quite well.
6. _____ is a gaseous substance.
7. The boys simply _____ to tease girls.
8. Isn't _____ in chewing gum?
9. The _____ was watching the hen house.
10. Jeff and Nicky wanted to _____ their sports car.

Answer Key: 1. tax 2. exhibit 3. exact 4. exhaust 5. xylophone 6. Xenon 7. exist 8. xylitol 9. fox 10. wax

Activity: Help For the _x_ Sound

To play: Have your child read the following sentences and tell you which sound of _x_ he hears: the _ks_, _gz_, or _z_ sound.

1. Listen to _x_ in _ax_.

2. Listen to _x_ in _exact_.

3. Listen to _x_ in _xylophone_.

4. Listen to _x_ in _xylene_.

5. Listen to _x_ in _example_.

Answer Key: 1. ks 2. gz 3. z 4. z 5. gz

zh: A Consonant Sound with No Distinct Spelling

The _zh_ sound has so many spellings that the words have to be taught as sight words. You may be surprised by how many words make the _zh_ sound. You can hear it in such unrelated words as _fusion, usual, azure,_ and _loge._ The young reader must be able to hear the difference between the voiced _zh_ sound and the consonant digraph, the voiceless _sh._ You can hear the difference between these sound in the words _glazier_ and _glacier._

This section helps your child get acquainted with the _zh_ sound and the new sight words that he must learn to master _zh._ Here you can find a helpful, heaping portion of exercises to help your child master _zh_ spellings.

Table 17-2 lists _zh_ words and organizes them according to the different ways in which the sound is spelled in words. Some of these words are difficult. Take it slowly so that your child can learn these words without getting frustrated.

Table 17-2		The zh Sound	
si = zh	*su = zh*	*zi, zu = zh*	*ge = zh*
Asia	pleasure	glazier	garage
fusion	usual	glaziery	barrage
decision	usury	azure	loge
provision	measure	seizure	rouge

Have your child practice these sentences. Have him read each sentence to himself and then say it out loud.

> It would by my pleasure to visit Asia.
>
> Jim spends most of his leisure time in the garage.
>
> Watch the beautiful azure sky.

For the corresponding sound on the CD, listen to Track 40 for the *zh* sound.

Activity: Filling in the Blanks: zh

Preparation: You need paper and pencil.

To play: Ask the young reader to smoothly read the following sentences. Fill in the blank in each sentence by printing the correct word from the word bank.

Word Bank: exposure, unusual, television, explosion, glazier, rouge, Asia, seizure, fusion, vision

1. They have camels in _____.
2. I saw you on _____ last night.
3. There was an unlawful _____ of cargo.
4. This is an _____ turn of events.
5. Martin Luther King had a _____.
6. A _____ works with tile.
7. The atomic theory deals with _____.
8. The climber had severe _____ to the cold.
9. John said that he heard an _____ at the mine.
10. The doll maker applied the _____ to the dolls cheeks.

Answer Key: 1. Asia 2. television 3. seizure 4. unusual 5. vision 6. glazier 7. fusion 8. exposure 9. explosion 10. rouge

Activity: Imperatives

Preparation: You need paper and pencil.

To play: Use the following phrases in imperative sentences (commands). Do this as a verbal exercise and then ask your child to say these imperative sentences and write them on a separate piece of paper. If you need to, you can dictate the sentences to him.

1. Watch the azure

2. Demand the glazier

3. Prevent that collision by

4. Use the precious

5. Insure the machine for

6. Treasure the Grecian

7. Assure him of

8. Be an efficient

Activity: zh Poems

To play: Ask your child to read the following poems. Two words in these poems exhibit the lesson of the simple *z* and the *zh* sounds in this chapter. After he finishes, ask him to find the one *zh* word and point out the *z* sounds he hears.

The Eagle

He clasps the crag with crooked hands;

Close to the sun in lonely lands,

Ringed with the azure world, he stands.

The wrinkled sea beneath him crawls;

He watches from his mountain walls,

And like a thunderbolt he falls.

—Alfred, Lord Tennyson

Zante

I'll never step ashore and feel your beach

the way I felt it as a barefoot child,

or see you waver in the windy reach

of goddess-bearing azure sea.

You were the island

Venus made with her first smile,

Zante, the moment she was born.

No song embraced your leafy sky,

not even his who sang the fatal storm

and how Ulysses, his misfortunes past

and beautiful with fame, sailed home at last.

—Ugo Foscolo

Answer Key: azure, Zante

Activity: Story: Unlucky Ladder

To play: Ask your child to read the story and find all the words that have the *x* and *zh* sounds.

The Unlucky Ladder

It all started on a cool morning in late September. The air was just beginning to feel crisp, and the Halloween exhibits were making their first appearances on the front lawns of the suburban homes. Janet Lately was on her way to school when she passed beneath a wooden stepladder. Mr. Gregly was painting Halloween colors on his WELCOME sign that hung above his candy-store window.

Just before she walked beneath it, Mr. Gregly called down, "Hey, Janet. Unlucky to walk under a ladder you know. You might want to walk around. Don't want to get mixed up in anything. Don't want to put a hex on you."

But Janet ignored Mr. Gregly's advice and zipped right through. Had she known then what she knew now, she would have heeded that warning.

As she reached the next corner, she saw her best friend, John. John and Janet were once next-door neighbors. John had to move, though, because his father said that he was tired of looking at the Bracket's unsightly lawn and unpainted garage. Janet waved to him excitedly. She wanted to tell him all about the new family that had moved into his old house.

John gave her a queer, perplexed look and kept right on walking. "John!" she yelled and chased after him. She caught up with him right outside the local music store. She could hear one of the customers inside trying out the xylophone that had been displayed in the window all summer. "Hey," she said panting as she clapped her hand on his shoulder, "Wait up."

John gave her that same bewildered look again. "Who are you?" he asked, as he continued to walk.

"What's the matter with you?" Janet replied. She picked up her pace to stay with him as he walked. He totally ignored her for the rest of the trip to school. He didn't even say goodbye as they headed toward their homerooms.

Janet arrived at her classroom just as the first bell rang. The other children ran to their seats and sat quietly. The teacher blocked Janet's way as she tried to enter the room.

"Well hello, little girl. Can I help you with something?"

"Okay," Janet explained, with tears in the corner of her eyes. "I've had just about enough of this. You know darn well that my name is Janet Lately, and that I'm a student in this class. My seat is right over there!" Janet pointed to her usual corner of the room.

Her desk! It was gone. Janet fled from the room and ran to her locker. She had left her student ID in her science book. Once she showed them an ID, that would be proof enough. They would have to stop their silly games. Janet dialed her combination and yanked on the handle. It stayed tightly locked. She dialed it again and pulled. Nothing.

Janet didn't know what to do. She started for the exit door of the school when she caught sight of Mrs. Kelly from the third grade. If Mrs. Kelly didn't remember her, then no one would. Mrs. Kelly, between math and spelling lessons, had tutored Janet to help her pass the exam on the Constitution of the United States of America.

Mrs. Kelly saw the trouble in Janet's eyes and promptly asked her, "What's wrong little girl. Are you lost?"

That was enough for Janet. She ran from the school building, ignoring the hall monitor's threat of suspension if she tried to leave without a pass. As she headed home, a frightening thought occurred to her. What if her own mom and dad didn't recognize her? What if her identity had been completely erased?

As she turned a corner, she spotted Mr. Gregly's freshly painted orange and black sign swaying in the gentle breeze. It suddenly struck her that

Mr. Gregly was the last person who had spoken her name that morning . . . right before she had gone under his ladder. She ran into his candy shop and up to the counter.

"What can I do for you, Missy?"

Even Mr. Gregly didn't remember her. Janet quickly devised a plan. "Um . . . sir? I was playing with my toy airplane and it landed on your roof. I'm in a fix. Do you think you could get it for me?" Mr. Gregly, whether he remembered Janet or not, was the nicest man in the city. He would think nothing of climbing up on a roof for one of the neighborhood children.

"No problem, Missy. I've already got the ladder out. I was just using it this morning to paint my sign up for Halloween." He grabbed the large wooden stepladder and headed for the exit.

As soon as he had set the ladder up and was stretching his head high enough to see the rooftop, Janet walked backwards beneath the ladder.

"I don't see anything up here," she heard Mr. Gregly say. He looked down and spotted her. "Oh, hello, Janet. Hey, watch out. You know, it's bad luck to walk under a ladder."

"Yes sir." Janet said, and quickly walked around the ladder.

—Eric and Ronnie Engel

Answer Key: exhibits, mixed, hex, garage, excitedly, perplexed, xylophone, explained, usual, exit, exam, fix

Part V
The Part of Tens

The 5th Wave   By Rich Tennant

"It's a multisensory approach to phonics. We say the letter, trace its shape with our finger, and then eat the flashcard."

In this part . . .

I bet you love to hear about the top ten songs of the year, the top ten movies, the top ten golf pros, or *something* that's the top ten in some way. How about the ten worst dressed women at the Oscars? Even when I go to the doctor, he asks me to rate my pain from one to ten.

Ten is the magic number for lists of all kinds, and the chapters in this part are no exception. Here you find out about additional resources to help you with phonics. I also give you some fun yet challenging activities to help you and your child further refine your phonics expertise. And, yes, these things are in top ten lists of my own, presented here for your consideration and enjoyment.

Also included here are four appendixes. Appendix A, B, and C include important information that you can use for reference. For those of you who want to perfect the sounding of the letters, Appendix D completes this part with a description of and directions for the CD that accompanies this book.

Have fun!

Chapter 18

Ten Challenging Activities for Reinforcement

*T*his chapter presents some activities that your child can do at home to help her learn how to read with the phonics method. Most of the activities I present here are homemade — you can create these games on your own with materials in your household; some of the games I suggest must be purchased. All these games are meant to make learning fun and enjoyable.

When you're too tired or busy for intensive one-on-one teaching, you can rely on the games in this chapter. Children can do most these activities on their own without your supervision. The activities in this chapter are presented from the easiest to the most difficult.

Word Scramble

The Word Scramble gives a child experience in editing and proofing her work. It also sharpens her phonics skills in spelling and reading. The Word Scramble can be difficult for a beginning writer, but it's as an excellent skill-boosting activity.

Activity: Word Scramble

Preparation: To do this exercise, you need a piece of paper and a pencil, and a drawing of an animal or clown with a tummy prominent enough that you can print each vowel on it. Next to the drawing, write scrambled words such as *pna, tpa, tas, cta,* and *naf,* and draw a circle around each scrambled word. You can try scrambling these words: *man, pan, cat, gap, bat, tap, pad, jab, can, sat, and, hat, map, lap, fan, tax, yam, van, had,* and *ham.*

To play: Have your child:

1. **Decode each scrambled word, one by one.**
2. **Read the word to herself.**
3. **Write down each word on the piece of paper.**

Draw a clown or animal for each vowel and its accompanying set of scrambled words. After your child masters the short vowels, you can draw clowns or animals for long-vowel word families.

Froggy Phonics Learning Game

You can purchase the Froggy Phonics Learning Game at a school store. Depending on what parts of the game you're interested in, the game costs $35 or less. It's great for building reading skills and can have one or more participants. As the children play the game, they discover that the same phonics skills they learn in this book are presented in a game form. Players spin a phonics skills spinner and try to be the first to find a matching word on their lily pads. The first player to put down four froggies wins. The game board is double-sided, with each side addressing different phonics levels. It covers most of a basics phonics course. Go to www.highsmith.com and enter *Froggy Phonics* in the search field. (The game is made by Edupress Educational Products.)

"Sounds Great!" Phonics Song

The kids love "Sounds Great!" and it's super for warming up the sounds of the consonants, the short vowels, and the long-vowel sounds! At Saturday School, I play the audiocassette song as the kids come into the room. They sit down at the table and we sing the alphabet, making the consonant sounds and the short sounds of the vowels; as time progresses we do the long sounds.

"Sounds Great!" is a unique, multisensory, letter-sound program for young children (ages 3-7), designed by 15 educators from the Oak Hills School District in Cincinnati, Ohio. The program consists of 34 characters and verses set to music; the student book and tape represent the core program. Go to www.soundsgreat.cc to get an overview of "Sounds Great!" online.

Take

Take is a sound-matching card game that teaches the essentials of sounding out letters and words. Players don't need to know loads of sounds to begin playing the game. The game is excellent for reinforcing short-vowel sounds.

Activity: Take

Preparation: Start by making 2 sets of 52 playing cards, 1 with short-vowel words and 1 with long-vowel words (see Chapters 4 and 7 for lists of short-vowel and long-vowel words). You need 104 note tags or index cards that are about the size of playing cards, scissors, and a fine-tipped pen. Using the pen, draw a line dividing each card in two.

To continue with the preparation, on each card, write the same short-vowel (or long-vowel) word twice, once at each end of the card so that the word can be read by players sitting on opposite sides of a table. For example, you can write the word *pig* at one end of the card, pivot the card around, and write the word *pig* on the other end. After you make 52 short-vowel playing cards and 52 long-vowel playing cards, you're ready to start the game.

To play: Have the players (two or four can play) sit opposite one another at a table. You can play with one or both sets of playing cards. The object of the game is for each player to gather as many pairs as she can. Follow these instructions:

1. **Shuffle the cards thoroughly.**
2. **Place the stack of cards facedown in the center of the table.**
3. **From the top of the deck, draw three cards and lay them face-up in the center of the table.**
4. **In turn, have each player take one card from the top of the deck and place it face-up in front of her.**
5. **The player reads the word on the card, says its vowel sound, and compares it to the three face-up cards on the table:**

- If the word on the card has the same vowel sound as a face-up card, the player has a match. The player says something like, "*Pig* takes *jig* because of the *i* sound." The player can then pick up the matching face-up card in the middle of the table (*jig*), put it together with the card she drew from the deck (*pig*), and set the cards aside as a pair.

   When one of the three face-up cards in the center is taken, the player draws another card from the deck to replace it. This card is placed face-up beside the other two cards in the middle of the table so that there are always three face-up cards, and the next player takes her turn.

- If the word on the card doesn't match any vowel sound on the three face-up cards in the middle of the table, there isn't a match. The player places the card she drew from the deck on the discard pile and the next player takes her turn.

When all the cards in the deck have been turned up and matched or put into the discard pile, the discard pile then becomes the new deck, and players draw from it. Play continues as long as matching cards are available. Then each player counts her tricks, and the player with the most tricks wins.

Mix and Match

Mix and Match is a homespun game that's fun for your child to play. The purpose of this game is to promote skill in decoding and reading words.

Activity: Mix and Match

Preparation: Find and cut out small pictures, 1 to 2 square inches, that illustrate simple one-syllable words. For example, cut out a picture of a box, ship, girl, boy, hen, cow, dog, cat, car, ball, frog, and duck. You get the idea. Then glue these pictures onto cardstock or index cards.

Next, cut longer pieces of cardstock — 2-x-8 inches. On each of these pieces of cardstock, write down a word for one of the pictures you cut out, and then write a short, simple sentence using the word. For example, if you cut out the picture of a frog, write down the word *frog* along with a sentence that includes the word *frog*.

To play:

1. **Place the picture cards face-up in a pile and position the sentence cards in rows and columns on a table.**

2. **For each picture card, have your child try to find its matching sentence card.**

3. **When your child finds a match, have her say the word, place the picture card over the sentence card, and read the sentence.**

   For example, when your child finds the frog card, she places the picture of the frog on the card, says "frog," and reads the sentence with the word *frog* in it.

Packing My Suitcase

Packing My Suitcase is a phonics version of an old game. The purpose of the game is to promote skill in memory and language use. The game also reinforces an understanding of alphabetical order. Two or more children (along with adults) can play.

Activity: Packing My Suitcase

Preparation: Before you start playing, choose a category. For example, you can choose girls' or boys' names, animals, flowers, or food. For this game, you pretend that you're going to pack items from the category for a long journey.

To play: The first player says, "I'm packing my suitcase, going to New York, and I'm taking an aardvark (or some other *a* word from the category you choose)." The second person says, "I'm packing my suitcase, going to New York, and I'm taking an aardvark and a baboon." The third person says, "I'm packing my suitcase, going to New York, and I'm taking an aardvark, a baboon, and a camel." Each person in his turn has to name every item that came before and add an additional item to the list. Keep going until you pack items from *a* to *z*.

Here are *a* to *z* examples of animals in case you choose animals as the category: aardvark, ant, alligator, ape; bat, baboon, butterfly, bird, bunny; cat, camel, cow; deer, doe, dog; eagle, elephant, eel, emu; fish, fawn, ferret, finch, fowl; giraffe, goat, gecko; hog, hippo, hare; iguana, impala, inch worm; joey, jaguar, jellyfish, jackal; katydid, kangaroo, kinkajou, kiwi; llama, lion, lamb; monkey, mouse, mockingbird, mongoose, moose; newt, nightingale; octopus, ocelot, okapi, owl, orangutan; pig, panda, peacock; quetzal, quail; rat, rhino, raccoon, reindeer; swan, salmon, starfish, seal; turkey, tern, tiger, tuna, turtle; umbrella bird; vulture, vole; walrus, wallaby, woodpecker; xenops, xylotrechus; yellow tail (fish), yak, yellow jacket; zebra, zorilla. (A zorilla, also known as a striped polecat, is a carnivorous animal in Africa akin to a weasel or skunk.)

Before you start playing this game, research the categories and have in mind the brain stumpers that players are likely to get stuck on. In the animal category, for example, *xenops* is a brain stumper. Of course, the brain stumpers are the tiebreakers. This game is great for the car. For a greater challenge, have the children spell the words and put them in sentences.

Journaling

One way to get your child to begin writing is to have her keep a journal. Your child doesn't have to display her emotions on paper, but a child who is 6 to 8 years old is capable of writing simple, descriptive sentences, and you want to capitalize on that.

When I'm teaching a child who's slow at writing, I tell her parents to get a notebook, fancy it up with stickers, and tell her that it's her journal. She can write what she's going to do on a given day or what she's already done. She can write about anything she wants — about sports, school, or her friends. The idea is to encourage her to start writing.

Journaling works great in the summer when more time is available and more interesting things are happening. Writing in a journal is a way to document important events. It also gives parents the opportunity to see how well their children write. Correct the grammar and spelling mistakes in your child's journal on a weekly basis. I recommend writing at least three sentences per day. If your child dates her journals entries, she can get more enjoyment from them later in life.

Kinesthetic Activities

Kinesthetic learning is a teaching and learning method in which the student learns while engaging in physical activity, rather than listening to a lecture or watching a demonstration. If you determine that kinesthetic activity helps your child learn to read, here are some helpful kinesthetic learning techniques. These techniques are naturally motivating and can be used in pairs, in groups, or with adults.

- Clap or tap out letters, syllables, and words.
- Write words on a rough surface as you dictate them. This tactile exercise helps develop a "lane to the brain."
- Allow the child to talk to himself for motor feedback.

✔ Introduce letters with stencils.

✔ Use large floor or wall puzzles and large maps.

✔ Dramatize and act out using songs, rhythm, and mnemonics.

✔ Write on a gel pad or engage in "air writing."

✔ Crawl or do somersaults during breaks.

I created a pathway to my schoolroom from a long roll of wallpaper with foot-prints on it named for letters of the alphabet. When the kids come in, they walk on the footprints and call out the name of each letter. It's good practice for kids who thrive on learning by doing. You can create these wallpaper pathways with short-vowel words, also.

Tried-and-True Games

Here's a list of tried-and-true games that children have enjoyed from the old days to present times. Some of these games can be made at home and some must be purchased. Most of these games enhance decoding, reading, and spelling. The *Authors Game* is neat because it gives the children a fantastic listing of classic poems and books by famous authors, which really comes in handy when they get to high school. At any rate, if you don't know about these games, look them up on the Internet. I arrange them here in order from beginning games to advanced games:

Tic-tac-toe, LeapFrog and Fisher-Price Phonics Products, Go Fish, Old Maid, Bingo With Letters, Concentration or Memory, Authors, Hangman, Boxes Game, Scrabble Jr., Text Twist for Kids, Boggle, Pictionary, and Guesstures

Book Making

As soon as your child can string sentences together, she can make her first book. You can help her construct a book or purchase a blank one with lined pages and room for making illustrations. Making a book is an excellent activity for children because it increases their language abilities and builds confidence. Books should be made with standard-size paper that's stapled or threaded together on the left side. Have your child put her name on the book and decorate its cover.

Possibilities for personal books are:

- ✔ **A dictated story:** The parent takes down the child's words as she tells her story.

- ✔ **A picture-story book:** The child makes up a story to go along with pictures she draws.

- ✔ **A picture dictionary:** The child describes what the pictures represent.

- ✔ **A language experience book:** The parent organizes a list of phrases with participles, and the exercises center on the use of particular words. For example: Growing vegetables, describing a feast, going to the aquarium, riding in a spaceship, snorkeling at the Great Barrier Reef, galloping on a horse, whale watching, or changing the oil in a car. The experiences can be fictional or nonfictional.

Chapter 19

Ten (Well, Not Just Ten) Recommended Supplemental Resources

*T*his chapter offers Web sites and other sources that can help you help your child learn how to read. These resources are highly reliable and have a long track record of success with helping kids to read better. Here you can find many sources for lessons, exercises, and other activities that make learning to read fun for your child. Some of the sources I include are for education centers that can help your child if he's struggling to learn sounds and words.

Brookes Publishing Company

Brookes is a highly respected resource for textbooks, activity books, curricula, and other materials specializing in communication and language, inclusive and special education, learning disabilities, and more. Many of the materials are aimed toward teaching kids phonics, and the Sample Form Downloads are very useful. You can visit the Web site at www.brookes publishing.com.

Educators Publishing Service

I've used materials from Educators Publishing Service (EPS) for 23 years. The company has published more than 800 titles, such as Merrill Linguistic Readers and the Mac and Tab Phonetic Storybook Readers. EPS also works with some of the industry's top reading experts. Its books and products, such as *Primary Phonics* and *Touchphonics,* and *Right into Reading,* are great tools that you can use to teach phonics, vocabulary, and reading comprehension. Make sure you check out the *Spectrum* phonics workbooks, which are perhaps the best on the market for older kids.

The EPS Web site contains detailed information on the company's products and free teaching resources. EPS continually updates and adds fantastic material to its catalog. For more information, visit the Web site at www.eps books.com.

Homeschool World

For more than 20 years, *Practical Homeschooling Magazine* publisher Mary Pride has helped hundreds of thousands of families home-school with confidence. Even if you don't home-school, the resources on *Practical Homeschooling Magazine*'s official Web site are useful. The site also contains information on *Mary Pride's Complete Guide to Getting Started in Homeschooling,* which has great tips that you can apply toward teaching phonics at home. Visit www.home-school.com.

Huntington Learning Center

The Huntington Learning Center is the oldest and most respected supplemental education provider in the nation. Since 1977, it has helped tens of thousands of students improve their reading, math, and study skills and sparked their desire to learn. The center's staff members consult privately with parents to offer testing and diagnosing the child. Then they recommend a personalized program of instruction.

The center's educational materials include a strong emphasis on phonics. After going through these exercises in the language arts, children show significant improvement in their reading skills. The learning centers exist all over the country, and if your child needs extra help, I highly recommend them. For more information, visit www.huntingtonlearning.com.

Intelli-Tunes

Intelli-Tunes' audio CDs are great for phonics students because their contents are aligned with national learning standards, basic skills and concepts, and teaching themes. The CDs are fun, fast paced, and provide you with song-based ideas, activities, games, and strategies to enrich your child's learning experience. Authors Ron and Nancy Brown, who provide national and international workshops and professional development seminars, produce the CDs. Visit their Web site at www.intelli-tunes.com.

Ladybug Phonetic Readers

Ladybug Readers is the best buy for your buck. This six-book set of phonics readers ($15) follows the sequence of sounds in *Phonics For Dummies*. Author Jean Bischel continues to write phonetic stories as her hobby, so stay tuned for the next batch of phonics storybooks. Her first series is Ladybug Phonetic Readers, which you can order directly from her. With her son, Mark, who is an illustrator, she has written *Whales and Snails and Heavenly Tales,* which is published by Neumann Press. Obtain more information by e-mailing her at Phonics_jkb@yahoo.com, or you can reach her by phone at 510-868-5468.

Langsford Learning Center

Langsford Learning Center is a private educational center dedicated to developing lifelong, independent learners. The center focuses on reading, spelling, comprehension, visual motor skills, and math. Highly trained teams implement individual action plans in an atmosphere of enthusiasm and encouragement.

Langsford Learning Center helps children and adults at all levels of learning. Two of the phonics programs it offers are Lindamood Phoneme Sequencing and Seeing Stars, which are scientifically based programs designed for people who struggle with phonetic sounds and reading. Langsford also teaches research-based programs in language comprehension and fluency. See the center's Web site at www.weteachreading.com.

The Moore Foundation

The Moore Foundation assists parents who want to home-school their children. The foundation provides individualized curriculum, educational materials, and unit studies for home-schooling, along with aid in learning disabilities, and gifted education. You can search the foundation's Web site for adventures in learning. The bookstore contains valuable resources to help families nurture and instruct their children: www.moorefoundation.com.

Scottish Rite Learning Centers

Scottish Rite Learning Centers, founded in 1994 to help children with dyslexia, can be found all over the USA. These centers are concerned *only* with teaching reading and spelling, and children are eligible regardless of economic status, race, religion, or Masonic affiliation. Many people have found them very useful in helping their children learn to read, and they're an excellent resource. To learn more and find the center closest to you, visit www.childrenslearningcenters.org.

Starfall

The Starfall learn-to-read Web site is offered free as a public service. Starfall free resources include worksheets, group exercises, and puzzles, and it also offers writing journals and books at a very low cost. Your beginning reader can use the books and games to explore and interact with words and the sounds that make up those words. Starfall is primarily designed for first graders, but you can also use the Web site with prekindergarten, kindergarten, and second-grade students. Your child can have a lot of fun on this Web site. All he has to do is click on the screen, watch, and listen! Visit www.starfall.com.

More Wonderful Web Sites!

Here's a list of my favorite links to phonics-related Web sites. I've been collecting them for about a year. Some of them offer reading instruction and English grammar lessons. Some are just for kids to play on or for moms and dads to download printable lessons. I tried to stick with Web sites that offer free material. Enjoy!

- ✔ **CanTeach** (`www.CanTeach.ca`): Offers lesson plans in different categories.

- ✔ **Internet4Classrooms** (`www.internet4classrooms.com`): Provides phonetic animation and audio resources.

- ✔ **The Amazing Flash Card Machine** (`www.flashcardmachine.com`): Making your own flashcards.

- ✔ **Phonicsworld** (`www.phonicsworld.com`): Making available free phonics printables.

- ✔ **Poetry4Kids** (`www.poetry4kids.com`): Offers poetry — good and silly — with lessons.

- ✔ **Skillswise** (`www.bbc.co.uk/skillswise`): Offers an incredible amount of phonetic material. Unbeatable, interactive, and educational.

- ✔ **Eva Easton** (`www.evaeaston.com`): Provides tons of free phonics materials.

- ✔ **Succeed to Read** (`www.succeedtoread.com`): Helping parents and children to make books.

- ✔ **Learning Abilities Books** (`www.learningbooks.net`): Making available lesson plans and stories.

- ✔ **SchoolExpress** (`www.schoolexpress.com`): Providing free phonics printables.

Appendix A

Phonics Guidelines and Definitions

This appendix offers phonics guidelines and definitions that you can use as a reference. You can find consonant guidelines, vowel guidelines, syllabication guidelines, and a mini-glossary.

Some people shy away from guidelines and definitions, but they often come in handy. Give it a chance and you may find this reference downright indispensable.

Consonant Guidelines

Check out the following consonant guidelines for phonics:

✔ **Guidelines for the sound of the letter *c*:**

- Hard *c*: The letter *c* says *k* before *a, o,* and *u* (as in *cap*).

- Soft *c*: The letter *c* says *s* before *e, i,* and *y* (as in *cent*).

- Before a consonant: The letter *c* says *k* (as in *crack*).

✔ **Guidelines for the sound of the letter *g*:**

- Hard *g*: The letter *g* says *g* before *a, o,* and *u* (as in *gum*).

- Soft *g*: The letters *ge* say *j* at the end of a word (as in *page*).

- At the beginning of a word: The letters *ge, gi,* and *gy* may be a hard or a soft *g* (as in *get* or *gem*); usually soft.

✔ **Guidelines for the sound of the letter *s*:**

- At the end of a word: The letters *se* often have the sound of *z* (as in *hose*).

- After voiced consonants: The letter *s* says *z* (as in *dogs*).

✔ **Guidelines for the sound of the letter *x*:**

- At the end of a word: The letter *x* says *ks* (as in *fox*).

- At the end of the syllable: The letters *ex* and *x* may say *gz* or *ks* (as in *exam* or *expel*).

- At the beginning of a word: The letter *x* says *z* (as in *xylophone*).

Vowel Guidelines

Learning vowel guidelines helps children so much. If they learn them and take them to heart, they can instantly recognize the words to which the different guidelines apply. Here are the vowel guidelines, divided into basic vowel guidelines and vowel guidelines that apply to word endings.

Five basic vowel guidelines

These five basic vowel guidelines will never lead you astray:

1. When a word or syllable has only one vowel, and the vowel comes between two consonants, the vowel is usually short. (Example: *not*)

2. When a word or syllable has only one vowel, and the vowel comes at the beginning, the vowel is usually short. (Example: *on*)

3. When a word or syllable has two vowels, the first vowel is often long and the second is silent. (Example: *note* and *oak*) Please note that there are a lot of exceptions here, as in *book*, *zoo*, *couch*, *toy*, *boil*, *fruit*, and *bread*.

4. When a word or syllable has only one vowel, and the vowel comes at the end, the vowel is usually long. (Example: *no*)

5. When *a* is followed by *u, w, r, ll,* or *lt* in the same syllable, it often has the third sound of *a*. (Example: *salt*)

Additional vowel guidelines for word endings

These additional vowel guidelines pertain to word endings:

1. When *y* comes at the end of a word that has two or more syllables, *y* has the sound of a long *e* if the *y* syllable is unaccented. (Example: *puppy*)

2. When *y* comes at the end of a word that has two or more syllables, *y* has the sound of a long *i* if the *y* syllable is accented. (Example: *reply*)

3. When words end with the suffix *ing, ed,* or *er,* the first vowel is usually short if it comes before two consonants. (Example: *getting*)

4. When words end with the suffix *ing, ed,* or *er,* the first vowel is usually long if it comes before a single consonant. (Example: *riding*)

Guidelines for Syllabication

Syllabication refers to how words are divided into syllables. After your child is well on her way to mastering basic phonics, she can begin focusing on simple syllables. And she can turn to these pages for a summary of syllabication guidelines.

✔ A word containing one vowel sound is never divided into syllables.

- fat, fact, fame, curl

✔ A compound word is divided between the two words that make the compound.

- up-set, in-to, sun-beam, bath-room

✔ If a word has a prefix, it's divided between the prefix and the root.

- mis-take, un-loose, ex-cel, ad-mit

✔ If a word has a suffix, it's divided between the root and the suffix.

- plant-ed, end-ed, sing-ing, high-ness

Exception: The suffix *ed* doesn't add a syllable to a word if the word ends in the consonant sound *t* or *d.*

- mixed, helped, smelled, lacked, cashed

✔ If one consonant is between two vowels, the word is usually divided after the consonant if the first vowel sound is short. It's called a closed syllable.

- rob-in, com-ics, grav-el, pol-ish

✔ If one consonant is between two vowels, the word is usually divided after the first vowel if the vowel sound is long. It's called an open syllable.

- la-bor, mu-sic, pho-to, Po-lish

✔ If two or more consonants come between two vowels, the word is usually divided between the first two consonants.

  • let-ter, cof-fee, splen-did, hun-gry

Exceptions: Blends and strong digraphs aren't separated. The strong consonant digraphs are *sh, ch, ck, wh,* and *th.*

  • se-cret, gath-er, punch-es, pro-gram

✔ If a vowel is sounded alone in a word, it makes a syllable by itself.

  • a-go, o-bey, mon-u-ment, pi-a-no, vi-o-let

✔ If two vowels are together in a word but are sounded separately, the word is divided between the two vowels.

  • di-et, fu-el, ra-di-o, cre-ate

✔ If a word ends in *le* preceded by a consonant, the word is usually divided before the consonant.

  • tum-ble, twin-kle, tin-gle, ri-fle

Exception: The strong digraph *ck* is never divided.

  • tack-le, trick-le, knuck-le

Phonics Terminology

Here's a reference source for all things phonic! It classifies the different kinds of consonants and vowels.

Consonants

Consonants fall into three categories: single consonants, consonant digraphs, and blends.

✔ **Single consonants:** All the letters of the alphabet except *a, e, i, o,* and *u.*

✔ **Consonant digraphs:** A single consonant sound made by two letters:

  • Basic digraphs: *ch, sh, wh, ~~th~~, th, ng, nk, zh*

  • Other digraphs: *ck, ph, gh, wr, kn, gn, mn, mb*

✔ **Blends:** *br, cr, dr, fr, gr, pr, tr, scr, str, bl, cl, fl, gl, pl, sc, sk, sm, sn, sp, st, sw, tw*

Vowels

Vowels fall into three categories: single vowels, vowel digraphs, and diphthongs.

- **Single vowels:** *a, e, i, o, u,* and sometimes *y* and *w* (as in *by* and *low*)
- **Vowel digraphs:** A single vowel sound made by two vowels. Vowel digraphs fall into these categories:
  - Regular digraphs: The first vowel is always long, and the second vowel is silent: *ai, ay, ea, ee, ei, ie, ao, oe, oo, ou, ow, ue, ui (ui = ōō).*
  - Irregular digraphs: These digraphs have three categories:

    The first vowel is heard but doesn't make the long sound:

    haul (a³), head (ĕ), too (o³), lawn (a³), cough (ŏ), soup (o³)

    The second vowel is heard:

    steak (ā), shield (ē), rough (ŭ), could (u³)

    Neither vowel is heard:

    veil (ä), true (o³), earn (ur), they (ā), flew (o³), took (u³)

- **Diphthongs**: A gliding vowel sound made by two vowels. Diphthongs fall into these categories:
  - Plain: ou, ow, oi, oy
  - Murmur: ar, or, er, ir, ur

Take note of the following regarding diphthongs:

- The third sound of *a* is *ä*.
- The third sound of *o* is the same as Webster's two *o*'s (ōō) and Thorndike's two dot *ü*.
- The third sound of *u* is the same as Webster's two *o*'s (ŏŏ) and Thorndike's one dot *ü*.

A Mini-Glossary

Following is a mini-glossary of phonics terms. Memorize these terms and you're well on your way to becoming a master of phonics:

Blend: Two or three consonants are spoken together, with each keeping its own sound.

Consonant digraph: Two consonants that together make one consonant sound.

Diphthong: Two vowels joined in one syllable that make a double sound. There are plain and murmur diphthongs.

Irregular vowel digraph: Any of the basic vowel sounds other than the long sound of the first vowel.

Phonics: The system of representing word sounds with letters.

Regular vowel digraph: The first vowel is long and the second is silent.

Schwa: The unstressed vowel sound that's pronounced like short *u*.

Syllable: A word or part of a word that contains one vowel sound.

Vowel: The letters *a, e, i, o, u*, and sometimes *y* and *w*.

Vowel digraph: Two vowels that together make one vowel sound.

Appendix B

Recommended Books for Your Kid's Library

*O*ne of my goals in writing this book is to set your child on a lifelong journey of reading enjoyment. To that end, this appendix presents the names of carefully selected books, authors, and series that will not only help develop your child's reading skills, but also help nourish her love of reading. Now that she can read on her own, you want to direct her to the kind of reading that educates and elevates the mind.

One easy way to start building a book collection for your child is to begin with authors. Wonderful authors can be found in most reading categories. That stands to reason. These authors have passed the test of time. They have talent that has lasted for more than one season:

- ✔ Louisa May Alcott
- ✔ Beverly Cleary
- ✔ Doreen Cronin
- ✔ Kevin Henkes
- ✔ George McDonald
- ✔ E. Nesbitt
- ✔ H.A. Rey
- ✔ Kate Seredy
- ✔ E.B. White
- ✔ Laura Ingalls Wilder

Following is an alphabetical list, by title, of books, series, and other written works that I recommend for children. Naturally, any list of this kind is incomplete. These resources will keep your child reading for many exciting years. You can find many of these books in multiple formats with several editions by numerous publishers. I list the titles, authors, and publishers of the versions that are easy to find, but if you have trouble finding exactly what I list, keep looking. Check your local bookstore, or www.amazon.com, or www.abebooks.com to find the latest and greatest information on these and other books.

1000 Facts on Sharks by Miles Kelly, Ltd (Barnes & Noble Books)

26 Fairmount Avenue series by Tomie de Paola (Putnam Juvenile Series)

Abraham Lincoln by Ingri and Edgar Parin D'Aulaire (Beautiful Feet Books)

Aesop's Fables (Running Press Book Publishers)

The Amazing Life of Benjamin Franklin by James Cross Giblin (Scholastic)

Annie Oakley by Jean Flynn (Enslow Publishers)

Bear Snores On by Karma Wilson (Scholastic)

Bethlehem series (Bethlehem Books)

Bill Nye the Science Guy series by Bill Nye (Scholastic)

Bob Books by Bobby Lynn Maslen and John R. Maslen (Scholastic)

Bobbsey Twins series by Laura Lee Hope (Grosset & Dunlap)

Boxes for Kate by Candace Fleming (Didax)

The Boy Who Saved Baseball by John H. Ritter (Puffin)

Brooklyn Bridge by Lynn Curlee (Atheneum)

Bunnicula series by James Howe (Aladdin)

Cam Jansen series by David A. Adler (Puffin)

Charlie and the Chocolate Factory by Roald Dahl (Puffin Books)

Charlotte's Web by E.B. White (Scholastic)

Children's Book of Virtues by William J. Bennett and Michael Hague (Simon & Schuster)

A Child's Garden of Verses by Robert Louis Stevenson (Simon & Schuster Children's Publishing)

The Chronicles of Narnia: The Lion, the Witch, and the Wardrobe by C.S. Lewis (Harper Trophy)

The Circus: And Other Essays and Fugitive Pieces by Joyce Kilmer (Kennikat Press)

Cloudy with a Chance of Meatballs by Judi Barrett (Scholastic)

Continental Press Phonics Readers (EPS)

The Cricket on Times Square by George Selden (Bantam Doubleday Dell)

D'Aulaire's Book of Greek Myths by Ingri D'Aulaire and Edgar Parin D'Aulaire (Delacorte Books for Young Readers)

EPS Merrill Linguistic Readers (EPS)

EPS Phonetic Storybooks (EPS)

Eric Carle series (Philomel)

The Everything Kids' Science Experiments Book by Tom Robinson (Adams Media Corporation)

Eyewitness Science: Time and Space by John Gribbin (Dorling Kindersley Publishing)

Falling Up: Poems and Drawings by Shel Silverstein (The Book Press)

Famous Inventors series (Hammond Corp.)

Flotsam by David Wiesner (Clarion Books)

Forces of Nature: The Awesome Power of Volcanoes, Earthquakes, and Tornados by Catherine O'Neill Grace (National Geographic Children's Books)

Gander Phonics Books (Gander)

Goblin Market and Other Poems by Christina Rossetti

Hank the Cowdog series by John R. Erickson (Puffin)

Hank Zipzer by Henry Winkler and Lin Oliver (Grosset & Dunlap)

Hans Christian Andersen Fairy Tales (Smithmark)

Heidi by Johanna Spyri (Puffin)

Henry and Mudge series by Cynthia Rylant (Atheneum/Richard Jackson Books)

Henry Wadsworth Longfellow: A Bibliography of the First Editions in Book Form. Compiled Largely from the Collection Formed by the Late Jacob Chester Chamberlain (Haskel House)

The Hobbit by J.R.R. Tolkien (Ballantine)

How I Became a Pirate by Melinda Long (Harcourt Children's Books)

It Looked Like Spilt Milk by Charles G. Shaw (HarperTrophy)

The Jolly Postman by Allan Ahlberg (LB Kids)

Kids Pick The Funniest Poems by Bruce Lansky (Meadowbrook)

Ladybug Readers (Neumann Press)

LeapFrog Phonics Products (LeapFrog)

Lewis and Clark by Andrew Santella (Franklin Watts)

Liberty by Lynn Curlee (Aladdin)

Magic School Bus series (Scholastic)

Make Way for Ducklings by Robert McCloskey (Puffin)

The Midshipman Quinn by Showel Styles (Bethlehem Books)

Nate the Great series by Marjorie Weinman Sharmat (Delacorte Books for Young Readers)

On the Night You Were Born by Nancy Tillman (Feiwel & Friends)

Owen & Mzee: The True Story of a Remarkable Friendship by Isabella and Craig Hatoff (Scholastic)

Owls in the Family by Farley Mowat (Bantam Books)

Paths of the Gospel series (Pauline)

Pegeen by Hilda van Stockum (Frederick Muller Ltd, London)

Pocahontas by Lucia Raatma (Compass Point Books)

Poems by Jack Prelutsky (Scholastic)

Poetry for Young People: Robert Frost, edited by Gary D. Schmidt and Henri Sorensen (Sterling)

The Prince and the Pauper by Mark Twain (Signet Classics)

Profiles of the Presidents series (Hammond World Atlas Corp)

Rikki-Tikki-Tavi by Rudyard Kipling (Harper Trophy)

Robin Hood of Sherwood Forest by Ann McGovern (Scholastic)

Scholastic Junior Classics series (www.just-for-kids.com)

See and Explore Library series (Dorling Kindersley Publishing)

The Singing Tree by Kate Seredy (Scholastic)

Snow Treasure by Marie McSwigan (Scholastic)

Songs of the Water Boatman: and Other Pond Poems by Joyce Sidman (Houghton Mifflin)

SRA Readers (1970s vintage) (Amazon.com)

Starfall Educational Products by the Starfall Team (Starfall Publication)

Stars and Planets by David H. Levy (Barnes & Noble Books)

Stealing Home by Robert Burleigh (Simon & Schuster/Paula Wiseman Books)

Stellaluna by Janell Cannon (Scholastic)

Summersaults by Douglas Florian (Greenwillow)

The Swiss Family Robinson by Johann D. Wyss (Yearling)

Texas Zeke and the Longhorn by David Davis (Pelican)

The Ugly Duckling by Hans Christian Andersen (Smithmark)

The Usborne Introduction to Archaeology by Abigail Wheatley and Struan Reid (Usborne Books)

The *Value Tale* series (Value Communications)

Whales, Snails and Other Tales (Neumann Press)

What is the World Made Of? by Kathleen Weidner Zoehfeld (HarperCollins)

Wishbone Classics series (www.Amazon.com)

With You All The Way by Max Lucado (Scholastic)

Young Thomas Edison by Michael Dooling (Holiday House)

Appendix C

Keyword Cards You Can Use

● ●

*I*n Chapters 2 and 3, I tell you about flashcards and keyword cards that you and your child can use to help reinforce what you learn about letters, sounds, and words. In this appendix, I provide you with examples of keyword cards that you can photocopy and attach to index cards for your own use. The cards represented here include consonant sounds and one vowel (a), which I cover in detail in Chapter 3. But you can create your own cards, using any keywords you want, by using these as a starting point. Be creative and have fun!

A a

apple

B b

bed

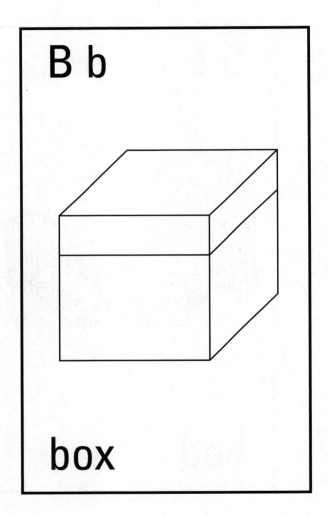

B b

box

C c

cat

C c

clock

D d

duck

F f

fish

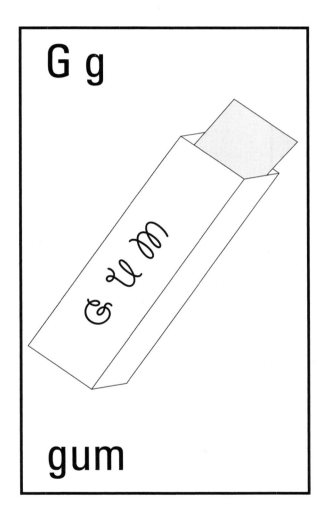

G g

gum

H h

hat

J j

jet

K k

kid

L l

lamp

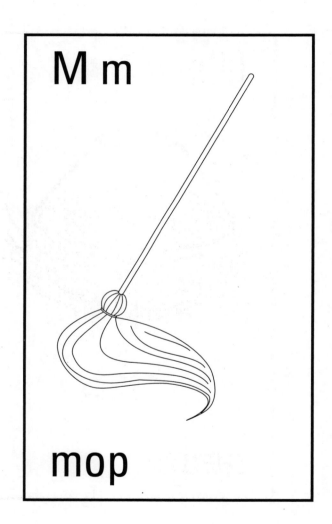

M m

mop

N n

nest

P p

pup

Q q

quack

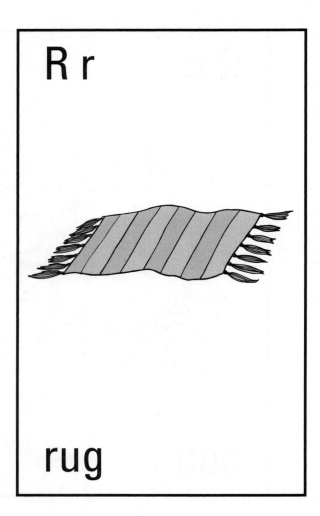

R r

rug

S s

sun

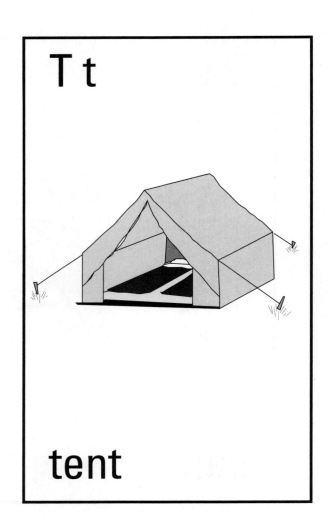

T t

tent

V v

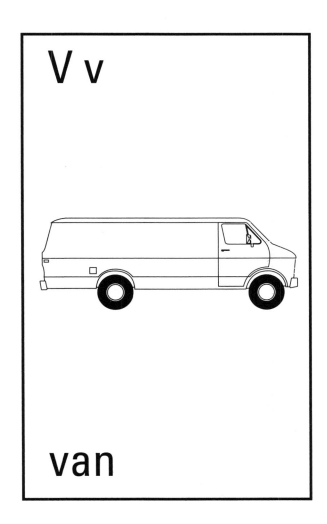

van

W w

web

Y y

yak

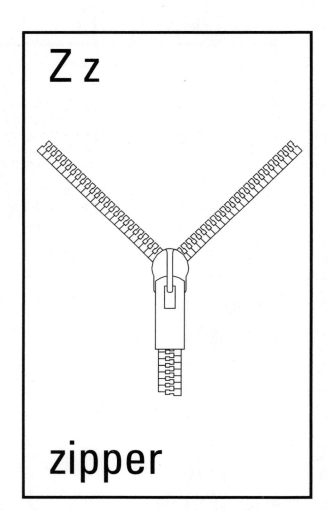

Z z

zipper

Appendix D
On the CD

. . . .

*F*ollowing is a list of the tracks that appear on this book's audio CD, which you can find tucked into a sleeve inside the back cover. Please note that the CD is audio-only, and you can put it in your CD player or (with the right software) play it on your computer any time you please. It will help your child with some of the pronunciations covered in *Phonics For Dummies*.

For each word in the track list, first the *grapheme (/sound/)* is given, which is the written representation of the sound. Following each grapheme is a word containing the sound.

Track 1: Introduction

Track 2: /m/ as in *mop* (Chapter 3)

Track 3: /s/ as in *sun* (Chapter 3)

Track 4: /t/ as in *tent* (Chapter 3)

Track 5: /a/ as in *apple* (Chapter 3)

Track 6: /d/ as in *duck* (Chapter 3)

Track 7: /g/ as in *gum* (Chapter 3)

Track 8: /f/ as in *fish* (Chapter 3)

Track 9: /h/ as in *hat* (Chapter 3)

Track 10: /p/ as in *pup* (Chapter 3)

Track 11: /r/ as in *rug* (Chapter 3)

Track 12: /n/ as in *nest* (Chapter 3)

Track 13: /b/ as in *bed* (Chapter 3)

Track 14: /j/ as in *jet* (Chapter 3)

Track 15: /v/ as in *van* (Chapter 3)

Track 16: /k/ as in *kid* (Chapter 3)

Track 17: /w/ as in *web* (Chapter 3)

Track 18: /y/ as in *yak* (Chapter 3)

Track 19: /z/ as in *zipper* (Chapter 3)

Track 20: /l/ as in *lamp* (Chapter 3)

Track 21: /i/ as in *fish* (Chapter 4)

Track 22: /u/ as in *duck* (Chapter 4)

Track 23: /o/ as in *ostrich* (Chapter 4)

Track 24: /e/ as in *elephant* (Chapter 4)

Track 25: /sh/ as in *ship* (Chapter 5)

Track 26: /ch/ as in *chess* (Chapter 5)

Track 27: /hw/ as in *wheel* (Chapter 5)

Track 28: /th/ as in *thumb* (Chapter 5)

Track 29: /t̶h̶/ as in *this* (Chapter 5)

Track 30: /ā/ as in *ate* (Chapter 7)

Track 31: /ē/ as in *eat* (Chapter 7)

Track 32: /ī/ as in *ice* (Chapter 7)

Track 33: /ō/ as in *old* (Chapter 7)

Track 34: /ū/ as in *use* (Chapter 7)

Track 35: /ä/ as in *father* (Chapter 8)

Track 36: /ōō/ as in *soon* (Chapter 8)

Track 37: /ŏŏ/ as in *look* (Chapter 8)

Track 38: /ou/ as in *mouse* (Chapter 9)

Track 39: /oi/ as in *toy* (Chapter 9)

Track 40: /zh/ as in *measure* (Chapter 17)

Track 41: Exit

Index

....

• *Symbols* •

• *A* •

• K •

• L •

• M •

• Q •

q, 55–56, 58

• R •

r
  a followed by, 123, 124
  blending table for, 53
  on the CD, 54
  ea digraph with, 209–212
  er suffix, 181–183
  initial blends, 87, 88
  in murmur diphthongs, 140, 145–152, 256–257
  or diphthong versus ore, 149
  ou digraph before, 216, 217
  overview, 53, 54
  in regional dialects, 124
  review for, 58
  u as third sound of o after, 213
  vowels in r-controlled words, 118, 124
  wr digraph, 250, 251
r-controlled diphthongs. See murmur diphthongs
readers or storybooks, 18, 19, 297
reading. See also reading sentences
  age-appropriate material for, 13
  in basic lesson plan, 15
  long-vowel words with suffixes, 184
  oral, tips for smooth and fluent, 48
  pattern recognition needed for, 76
  short-vowel words with suffixes, 182, 183
  starting place for, 10, 11, 41
  teaching grammar with, 52
reading lips for diphthongs, 140
reading sentences. See also activities
  with c (hard and soft), 191–194
  with c, k, ck, and l, 61
  with ck, 91
  with compound words, 107, 109
  with consonant digraphs, 81
  with cvc pattern, 77
  with d and g, 51
  with ea digraph, 210, 211
  with ed words, 178
  with end blends, 86
  with f and h, 52

with French and Greek ch sounds, 270, 273
with g (hard and soft), 199, 200, 202
with gh digraph, 266
with ie digraph, 204, 205
with initial blends, 88
with long u, 213, 214
with long vowels ending words, 121
with long vowels in r-controlled words, 118
with long vowels with w and y, 120
with long-vowel words with suffixes, 184
with m, s, t, and short a, 44, 45
with murmur diphthongs, 146, 257
with n and b, 55
with oi/oy diphthongs, 144
with oo digraph, 207, 208
with or diphthong, 149
with ou/ow diphthongs, 142
with ow diphthong versus digraph, 142, 143
with p and r, 53
with plurals using es, 103, 104
with plurals using s, 100, 190
with prefixes, 225, 227, 234
review, 58
with schwa, 241, 244
with short a and i difference, 66
with short e, 73
with short i, 64
with short o, 71
with short u, 67
with short-vowel words with suffixes, 182
sight words in, 100
with silent e, 113
with suffixes, 229, 234
with tch, 94
with third sound of a, 126
with third sound of a, o, and u, 136, 137
with third sound of o, 130, 131
with third sound of u, 130, 133
with v, j, w, and q, 55
with vowel digraph exceptions, 259
with vowel digraphs, 117
with words with short u sound for o, 261
with x sounds, 277
with x, y, and z, 57
with y sounds, 219
with zh sound, 279

• *W* •

BUSINESS, CAREERS & PERSONAL FINANCE

0-7645-9847-3

0-7645-2431-3

Also available:
- Business Plans Kit For Dummies
  0-7645-9794-9
- Economics For Dummies
  0-7645-5726-2
- Grant Writing For Dummies
  0-7645-8416-2
- Home Buying For Dummies
  0-7645-5331-3
- Managing For Dummies
  0-7645-1771-6
- Marketing For Dummies
  0-7645-5600-2

- Personal Finance For Dummies
  0-7645-2590-5*
- Resumes For Dummies
  0-7645-5471-9
- Selling For Dummies
  0-7645-5363-1
- Six Sigma For Dummies
  0-7645-6798-5
- Small Business Kit For Dummies
  0-7645-5984-2
- Starting an eBay Business For Dummies
  0-7645-6924-4
- Your Dream Career For Dummies
  0-7645-9795-7

HOME & BUSINESS COMPUTER BASICS

0-470-05432-8

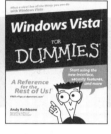

0-471-75421-8

Also available:
- Cleaning Windows Vista For Dummies
  0-471-78293-9
- Excel 2007 For Dummies
  0-470-03737-7
- Mac OS X Tiger For Dummies
  0-7645-7675-5
- MacBook For Dummies
  0-470-04859-X
- Macs For Dummies
  0-470-04849-2
- Office 2007 For Dummies
  0-470-00923-3

- Outlook 2007 For Dummies
  0-470-03830-6
- PCs For Dummies
  0-7645-8958-X
- Salesforce.com For Dummies
  0-470-04893-X
- Upgrading & Fixing Laptops For Dummies
  0-7645-8959-8
- Word 2007 For Dummies
  0-470-03658-3
- Quicken 2007 For Dummies
  0-470-04600-7

FOOD, HOME, GARDEN, HOBBIES, MUSIC & PETS

0-7645-8404-9

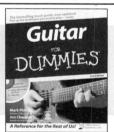

0-7645-9904-6

Also available:
- Candy Making For Dummies
  0-7645-9734-5
- Card Games For Dummies
  0-7645-9910-0
- Crocheting For Dummies
  0-7645-4151-X
- Dog Training For Dummies
  0-7645-8418-9
- Healthy Carb Cookbook For Dummies
  0-7645-8476-6
- Home Maintenance For Dummies
  0-7645-5215-5

- Horses For Dummies
  0-7645-9797-3
- Jewelry Making & Beading For Dummies
  0-7645-2571-9
- Orchids For Dummies
  0-7645-6759-4
- Puppies For Dummies
  0-7645-5255-4
- Rock Guitar For Dummies
  0-7645-5356-9
- Sewing For Dummies
  0-7645-6847-7
- Singing For Dummies
  0-7645-2475-5

INTERNET & DIGITAL MEDIA

0-470-04529-9

0-470-04894-8

Also available:
- Blogging For Dummies
  0-471-77084-1
- Digital Photography For Dummies
  0-7645-9802-3
- Digital Photography All-in-One Desk Reference For Dummies
  0-470-03743-1
- Digital SLR Cameras and Photography For Dummies
  0-7645-9803-1
- eBay Business All-in-One Desk Reference For Dummies
  0-7645-8438-3
- HDTV For Dummies
  0-470-09673-X

- Home Entertainment PCs For Dummies
  0-470-05523-5
- MySpace For Dummies
  0-470-09529-6
- Search Engine Optimization For Dummies
  0-471-97998-8
- Skype For Dummies
  0-470-04891-3
- The Internet For Dummies
  0-7645-8996-2
- Wiring Your Digital Home For Dummies
  0-471-91830-X

* Separate Canadian edition also available
† Separate U.K. edition also available

SPORTS, FITNESS, PARENTING, RELIGION & SPIRITUALITY

0-471-76871-5

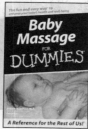

0-7645-7841-3

Also available:
- Catholicism For Dummies
  0-7645-5391-7
- Exercise Balls For Dummies
  0-7645-5623-1
- Fitness For Dummies
  0-7645-7851-0
- Football For Dummies
  0-7645-3936-1
- Judaism For Dummies
  0-7645-5299-6
- Potty Training For Dummies
  0-7645-5417-4
- Buddhism For Dummies
  0-7645-5359-3

- Pregnancy For Dummies
  0-7645-4483-7 †
- Ten Minute Tone-Ups For Dummies
  0-7645-7207-5
- NASCAR For Dummies
  0-7645-7681-X
- Religion For Dummies
  0-7645-5264-3
- Soccer For Dummies
  0-7645-5229-5
- Women in the Bible For Dummies
  0-7645-8475-8

TRAVEL

0-7645-7749-2

0-7645-6945-7

Also available:
- Alaska For Dummies
  0-7645-7746-8
- Cruise Vacations For Dummies
  0-7645-6941-4
- England For Dummies
  0-7645-4276-1
- Europe For Dummies
  0-7645-7529-5
- Germany For Dummies
  0-7645-7823-5
- Hawaii For Dummies
  0-7645-7402-7

- Italy For Dummies
  0-7645-7386-1
- Las Vegas For Dummies
  0-7645-7382-9
- London For Dummies
  0-7645-4277-X
- Paris For Dummies
  0-7645-7630-5
- RV Vacations For Dummies
  0-7645-4442-X
- Walt Disney World & Orlando
  For Dummies
  0-7645-9660-8

GRAPHICS, DESIGN & WEB DEVELOPMENT

0-7645-8815-X

0-7645-9571-7

Also available:
- 3D Game Animation For Dummies
  0-7645-8789-7
- AutoCAD 2006 For Dummies
  0-7645-8925-3
- Building a Web Site For Dummies
  0-7645-7144-3
- Creating Web Pages For Dummies
  0-470-08030-2
- Creating Web Pages All-in-One Desk
  Reference For Dummies
  0-7645-4345-8
- Dreamweaver 8 For Dummies
  0-7645-9649-7

- InDesign CS2 For Dummies
  0-7645-9572-5
- Macromedia Flash 8 For Dummies
  0-7645-9691-8
- Photoshop CS2 and Digital
  Photography For Dummies
  0-7645-9580-6
- Photoshop Elements 4 For Dummies
  0-471-77483-9
- Syndicating Web Sites with RSS Feeds
  For Dummies
  0-7645-8848-6
- Yahoo! SiteBuilder For Dummies
  0-7645-9800-7

NETWORKING, SECURITY, PROGRAMMING & DATABASES

0-7645-7728-X

0-471-74940-0

Also available:
- Access 2007 For Dummies
  0-470-04612-0
- ASP.NET 2 For Dummies
  0-7645-7907-X
- C# 2005 For Dummies
  0-7645-9704-3
- Hacking For Dummies
  0-470-05235-X
- Hacking Wireless Networks
  For Dummies
  0-7645-9730-2
- Java For Dummies
  0-470-08716-1

- Microsoft SQL Server 2005 For Dummies
  0-7645-7755-7
- Networking All-in-One Desk Reference
  For Dummies
  0-7645-9939-9
- Preventing Identity Theft For Dummies
  0-7645-7336-5
- Telecom For Dummies
  0-471-77085-X
- Visual Studio 2005 All-in-One Desk
  Reference For Dummies
  0-7645-9775-2
- XML For Dummies
  0-7645-8845-1